The Collected Ewart

By the same author

Poems and Songs
Londoners
Pleasures of the Flesh
The Deceptive Grin of the Gravel Porters
The Gavin Ewart Show
An Imaginary Love Affair
Be My Guest!
The First Eleven
No Fool Like an Old Fool
Or Where a Young Penguin Lies Screaming
All My Little Ones

The Collected Ewart 1933–1980

Poems by
Gavin Ewart

Gavin Ewart

gave a Reading at Tonbridge School
11th February 1983

Hutchinson
London Sydney Melbourne Auckland Johannesburg

Hutchinson & Co. (Publishers) Ltd

An imprint of the Hutchinson Publishing Group

3 Fitzroy Square, London W1P 6JD

Hutchinson Group (Australia) Pty Ltd
30–32 Cremorne Street, Richmond South, Victoria 3121
PO Box 151, Broadway, New South Wales 2007

Hutchinson Group (NZ) Ltd
32–34 View Road, PO Box 40–086, Glenfield, Auckland 10

Hutchinson Group (SA) (Pty) Ltd
PO Box 337, Bergvlei 2012, South Africa

First published in this collection 1980
Reprinted in paperback 1982

© in this collection Gavin Ewart 1980

Set in Bembo Roman by
D. P. Media Limited, Hitchin, Hertfordshire

Printed in Great Britain by The Anchor Press Ltd
and bound by Wm Brendon & Son Ltd,
both of Tiptree, Essex

British Library Cataloguing in Publication Data
Ewart, Gavin
   Collected poems of Gavin Ewart.
   821'.9'12   PR6055.W3

ISBN 0 09 141001 0

To Margo

Contents

Introduction

This collection is a collection – and not a selection – of my poems. This is not because I consider them all equally good but because I have aimed at completeness. I have also borne in mind the fact that a poem that has ceased to have much merit for me may have hidden admirers who would be disappointed not to find it.

The only book of my verse not included here is the latest, *All My Little Ones* (published by Anvil Press Poetry). This should be regarded as a pendant to the bulky work now before you, consisting as it does entirely of short epigrammatic pieces.

Early Poems (1933–39)

Phallus in Wonderland *

'I shall draw strange fowl from this foul nest.'
                                              WEBSTER

Grammarian:

'Prima coitio est acerrima'† (Terence);
In 1889 I first encountered woman
And copulated unsatisfactorily
Owing to ignorance.

Antichrist:

The soul rises
Persistently, like yeast;
The curate eagerly pursues
The prurient attitudes
Of the full-grown priest.

Critic:

Rudyard Kipling has
'Immortalized' Surrey;
Euripides lies entombed
In Professor Gilbert Murray.

---

 * This poem, written shortly after my seventeenth birthday and published by Geoffrey Grigson in *New Verse*, was excluded by me from my first book of verse, because of its immaturity. It shows very clearly the influences of T. S. Eliot, the Pound of *Hugh Selwyn Mauberley*, and Ronald Bottrall. Auden, in early 1933, was not yet making his presence felt.

 † *Prima coitio est acerrima* means 'The first meeting is the hardest.' I used the quotation because *coitio* (coming together) suggests coition in English. The Grammarian's little speech was inspired by the case histories in Havelock Ellis's *Studies in the Psychology of Sex*.
I discovered the volumes of this great work, hidden with their backs to the wall, in a bookcase belonging to a Naval Officer in 1932.

Cherries in brandy are
Passive to the eye and docile;
Time, Place and Genius
Re-appear as fossil.

Water, falling from the air,
Is hard earth's solvent;
The wind blowing over hardens both
And shows the way the mole went.

Ice deals in details,
Picturing hard and subtle;
It is the back-thrown ink-cloud
Obscures the deep sea cuttle.

Grammarian:

'Non cuivis homini
Contingit adire Corinthum:'★ but I have hopes
And I am writing a commentary
(With marginal notes) on Dr Marie Stopes.

Ancient:

I have driven many parasangs into the wilderness
Of human inconsistencies and fears
And have discovered no oasis
Undried by passage of years.

My borders are stocked with pelargonia
Whose distended fragrance hits the sense
Pleasingly, pleasingly.
The drowsy hum of the Romantics
Is in keeping with the reliquiae
That straw my sanctuaries
And the sundial has an old inscription
That induces reveries.

★ *Non cuivis homini contingit adire Corinthum* means 'It's not every
man who has the luck to get to Corinth.' Corinth, in the Ancient
World, was the City of Pleasure – just as Paris was for the nineteenth
century Anglo-Saxons.

Student:

While the Persians
Undoubtedly were given to
Several interesting perversions

I consider
The political customs of England
Were, in growth, far rapider.

Ancient:

When the end comes and my sensoria
Cannot pick up Wordsworth on any wave-length
The ironists will say: 'Sic transit gloria
Mundi.' I shall not have strength
To quote the appropriate Tennyson
And soon I shall be 'nearer Nature'
Than all the ornithologists and flower-enthusiasts.

Chorus:

Let him drink hellebore,
Since he will be,
As he knows, in time
An usufructuary of Ge.★

The Sapient Man:

The application of standards
Has led me to be called an 'intellectual snob'
By the hairy partisans of true Unwisdom,
Whose clash of fives gloves serves to them as swords,
While the movement of the ball is their delight
As it finds its secret corners fishlike
In its unenclosed aquarium.

Person:

My friends are pleasant.
How long they will continue so
I do not know,

★ *Ge* is the Greek for Earth. Hellebore is the herb that the Greeks believed would cure madness.

Yet if there were Hell or Heaven
I would wish them out of the fiery lake
For sentiment's sake.

Young Man:

Only three buttons on her bosom
Winked at me in the light;
Yet I thought of Herrick
Half the night.

Many theologians have donned
The triple-breasted waistcoat of The Word
Without inheriting the wit
Implied in the verb,

And have obscured, unsolved, the problem
Of Individual and Fate;
The waistcoat in fact, though ornamental,
Was lunatic and strait.

Observer:

The hair over the forehead, the straight body,
The upward eye
May show proficiency at golf or swimming
Yet betray a man to women.

All things in love continue flowing;
The pleasure-going
Lip, haste-bitten, will bleed
And men emit seed.

Public Schoolboy:

Though as lustful as a stallion
I behave like a scullion;
Kissing housemaids in linen-cupboard or pantry
Is the height of my gallantry.

Poet of the Generation:

We are swept away by a strange tide.
Did Mr Eliot at Hyde
Park Corner in 1917 boarding a bus
Foresee it? He was not born in us

But we in him.
He gave us a voice, straightened each limb,
Set us a few mental exercises
And left us to our own devices.

At first we ran up trees in distraction,
Mimicked his every action,
But now are back on earth again.
Sheltered by a gourd and sane.

Individualist:

How can a man 'live fully'
Sealed in his psychic cell
Or in a narrow playground
With entrances: Sight, Taste, Hearing, Touch, Smell?

Scientist:

. . . Evolution, you see, has no appeal –
No human interest,
So that no woman in the gallery would clap her hands,
Stamp her feet or sweat in her vest.

Poet:

Blowing my trumpery trumpet,
Looking for hounds for my horn,
Shall I revert to ancient themes
And wish that I'd never been born?

No use: for man is created
Lower than angels and higher than hedgehogs.
Nor daydreams nor comfort sustain him,
Romantic poets nor fur rugs.

*Major:**

Novels by ladies
From York to Cadiz,
Deified Appeal
From Bombay to Louisville,
Cinema and press and evening dress
Bring conversation to the Officers' Mess.

'Love Thy Neighbour As Thyself':

I cannot live in another man's skin.
I cannot grow fat when he grows fat,
Grow thin when he grows thin.

I cannot live in another man's flat.
I cannot live in a spider's web
Or the hole of a mole or a rat.

I cannot feel beyond myself,
Feel with the fly in its agony
Or the spider unlow on a shelf.

I am shut in, short-circuited;
And of this kingdom the ruler
My own brain in my own head.

Promiscuous Person:

A car's head-light seen behind trees,
Erotic light behind a blind:
Can re-create the lust of the body
In the pantheistic mind.

Psycho:†

A man puts his hand down a woman's dress,
Presses a curve;
The curve on the graph of his loneliness.

* The *Major* doesn't give a very accurate account of talk in an Officers' Mess. Eight years later I found this out for myself.

† The *Psycho* is a psychologist or psycho-analyst – not a psychopath.

15

A man without a woman is quite alone.
She at his birth
With inconstant light as a star shone.

She, as his lover, was predestined
To dance with him,
Shaking his cocktails in the West End. . . .

Ancient:
Deliver me from fornication and hockey.
Let me not see the fool leaning over my fence.
The best sweet peas are Surrey's and Kent's
And a horse cannot win without a jockey.
These are axiomatic, desires and riddles;
Eighty years of pushing the pedals
Has led me to these as my goal.
Now I cannot see the light I sought
But am blind, as a mole.

Youth:

There is an energy that works in me,
Drives me like an engine or a tin me.
This is the force that would split my coffin-boards
If its loss were not the occasion for those funereal gauds.

Sensualist:
Perfume can make me love,
Challenging like a glove,
Meeting me face to face,
When flight is disgrace.

Touching can make me lust,
Before bright senses rust,
Pushing me over the cliff
Before my lips can say 'If'.

Hearing a softened voice
Presents me with a choice:
Shall I believe what it says,
Or we go our ways?

16

Seeing can make me ache,
But not for a tooth's sake,
Ache with the whole of me,
Knowing I am not free.

Ambitionist:

I should like to see
Better become best;
I should like to see the savage
Wear both shirt and vest.

I should like to see
The Daily Press
Taking its cues
From the weekly reviews.

The Great:

We do not see the resurrectory gibbet;
We do not hear our brains dissected in the lecture room;
When our equestrian statues are dusted
We do not feel the feather-broom.

The lack of sense can bring
Certain definite compensations;
We cannot read the ironic obituaries
Tastefully written by our near relations.

Ghost of the Ancient:

Now the gardener's boy who
Makes water on my careful flower-beds
Is more than me: and yet we both complete
The nitrogen cycle. For soon I'll rot,
Manure for daffodils and tulips –
But the young continue to be young
And the old continue to be old.
If two faces differ it is only by centimetres
And one cannot show mysteries to a foetus.

If a millennium come or a triumph
I shall be under the hooves of the horses.
Although I too have lived and been
The man in the saddle is not my kin.

Characters of the First Fifteen*

Match v. Cheltenham. Won 17 - 6.

Come here!
Let me whisper the glorious news in your ear.
We're proud,
We all know the tune and we're singing aloud.

Let us praise Knight,
Handing off and showing fight,
And Stephen,
Successful where the ground is uneven,
And Balfour-Paul,
Clever at dribbling, quick on the ball,
And Hamilton's hook,
Powell like a giant in a picture book,
Crawford and Wilk-
inson, as tough as an elk,
Hastings too,
Always ready with something to do.

And as for Cable,
We don't praise him for his manners at table
But for cutting through,
For kicking right-footed and left-footed too,
And Rawlence
For passing backs when they're off their balance,
And Auret,
Attacking an arrow, defensive a turret,

---

* This poem, written in October 1933, shows the influence of
Auden's verse in *The Orators*. It was set for the *Wellingtonian*, but
never appeared because the Master, F. B. Malim, vetoed it.
Perhaps he felt that the reference to Cable's table manners was
uncomplimentary (it was not intended to be) or the unseemly
smoking of the ushers' wives disturbed him. The Wellington rugby
team of 1933 was considered by all to be the best school team in the
south of England.

And Maude,
Crossing the line, a barbarian horde,
And Charteris and Birch,
Falling and kicking as high as a church,
And finally Forster,
More energized than any poster.

Now ushers' wives
Are smoking and having the time of their lives;
Success
Hangs round the buildings like fancy dress,
A pardon
Is granted by tutor walking in garden,
Elated;
To-night our success will be celebrated.

'One Incomprehensible'*

Moles go without eyes
About their business;
The claws in the dark
Are like lovers' hands in the park.

Sensation makes men sing,
Dance like toys on a rubber string;
But itself cannot be held,
Is a reed, not a tree to be felled.

* The phrase 'one incomprehensible' is from one of St Paul's
Epistles, which was being studied in the original Greek by the
Classical Sixth in 1933.

Time may be measured by clocks,
The wind turns weathercocks;
Touch leaves no record, can dissolve or fix
And is impermanent enemy to statistics.

Touch may be cocktail-shaker to the blood
Or morbid as a sod;
Pledge it, if you must; it will
Be there in the glass for good or ill.

Poems and Songs (1939)

I

The primal stone of the sheep-walls of Yorkshire, the
    iron cross hard to the hand,
These have given me pleasure
Prior to the first seizure
Of love in my adolescence.

The snowflakes falling on the travelling train, the frosted
    lines
Straight to no purpose,
The track of the porpoise,
The plumage of pheasants.

And these I enjoyed; yet always expecting the touch of a
    woman to be like the sun's
Or a wave's eddy
On my body.
Experience dissents.

II

Birds have their feet in air;
Chestnut trees root before they flower.
My noise is twittering,
A nostalgic thing.

The black houses by railway lines
That divide and go as I travel
Cannot give me root
In their clinging soot.

Thus I am nearer the birds,
Going with, and only, the wind;
My continual fate
Is to fly but not to migrate.

III

Breathing but not believing,
Clutched by the hairy pores of skin,
I've no way out but no way in.

Pulled, now, taut
By a brace of fanning birds;
But only air that girder girds.

For here cathedrals falter,
Rise O slow
Towards the sun they do not know.

IV

No Flowers by Request

The thing finished is perfect.
Death perfects in point of fact
And I am always a fraction
Of my coming perfection.

Submerged, the submarine can see
Past waves with its exalted eye.
So, in the grave, upon my eyes
These sores may fester, memories.

But, tissue touched with right reagent,
The past might well appear a pageant
Coloured and moving in its plane
Without the third dimension, pain.

V

Audenesque for an Initiation

Don't forget the things we taught you by the broken
    water-wheel,
Don't forget the middle-classes fight much harder going
    downhill,

Don't forget that new proscriptions are being posted
    now and then,
Dr Johnson, Dr Leavis and the other Grand Old Men –

Although they've very often told us that they try to do
    their best,
Are they up to the Full Fruit Standard, would they pass
    the Spelling Test?

– Because we've got our eyes to keyholes, we know
    everything they've done,
Lecturing on minor poets. 'Literature is quite good fun.'

And if you should try to fool us, imitate them, do the
    same,
We'll refuse your dummy bullets, we've had time to take
    our aim.

We've been drinking stagnant water for some twenty
    years or more
While the politicians slowly planned a bigger reservoir.

But we've dammed a different river, the water-wheel is
    going again.
Now we've stopped designing sweaters and we've
    started in to train.

We've given up the Georgian poets, teaching dance
    bands how to croon,
Bicycling in coloured goggles underneath a pallid moon.

We've destroyed the rotting signposts, made holes in all
    the pleasure boats;
We'll pull down ancestral castles when we've time to
    swim the moats.

When we've practised we shall beat you with our Third
    or Fourth Fifteen,
In spite of Royalists on the touchline. 'Oh, well played,
    Sir!' 'Keep it clean!'

Our backs are fast as motor-cycles, all our forwards
    twenty-stone.
Each of them can score unaided, running strongly on his
    own.

Every minute scouts give signals, come reporting what
    they've seen.
'Captain Ferguson is putting.' 'Undermine the
    eighteenth green.'

Before next month we'll storm the clubhouse. Messages
    are coming through:
'Darwin, doing crossword puzzles, tries to find the
    missing clue.'

The *Times* Third Leaders are decoded, pigeon-holed for
    future use;
Tennyson has been convicted of incessant self-abuse.

We've been sending notes to Priestley, orange pips to
    J. C. Squire –
'Don't defend the trench you're holding.' 'Now the fat is
    in the fire.'

We've got control of all the railways and the perfume
    factories,
We're supercharged and have connection with the
    strongest batteries.

So if you feel like playing truant, remember that the
    game is up
Or you'll find that quite politely you've been sold a nasty
    pup.

VI

Public School

A surname in this place
Is fitting. Keeps reserved
Emotional platoons
Positioned in the eyes,
Attentive for a word.

The pupils here obey
The friend's didactic voice,
Are wakeful at a smile,
Can answer questions, lie,
Express polite surprise.

If one should raise a hand,
Ask question out of turn,
Then discipline would die,
Order be broken and
The other's eye be stern.

VII

On the Author's Photograph

Yes, apprehensive eye,
We know, averted head.
I remember what I
Have done, have said.

Sleek head, you seal,
Shy pupil, still at school,
I know the pain you feel,
The pain of the fool.

VIII

The Fourth of May*

My dear old school goes back to-day,
Fumbling for tips and 'Goodbye, old boy,'
   Shall we give it a cheer?
Let us pray for its members, past and present,
Let us remember how unpleasant
   Most of them were.

To-morrow there'll be the same old rags,
The disgusted prefects going with fags,
   The long walks in the woods,
The despondent scribbling in worn-out rears,
The long discussions in comfy chairs
   On eternal goods.

*This poem, written in the summer of 1934, was published later
that year in Esmond Romilly's anti-Public School magazine *Out of
Bounds*. As a result, Mr Malim sent me a letter saying that it would not
be a good thing for me to visit the school for at least three years.

Remember how, in capitals, WOMAN
Was thought of as tart or as superhuman,
  Remember the vague
Nimbus of undefined emotion
Round the words 'Country,' 'Duty,' 'Devotion,'
  Poppies, Earl Haig.

They took me to see the working class,
I stood there feeling unwanted, an ass,
  By the London docks.
If they haven't the reputation of sinners
Toc H gives people occasional dinners,
  As sly as a fox.

But most of us never saw the slums,
The marching we knew was done to drums
  And in uniform. . .
Remember how sex was a festering sore,
How they plastered it over more and more
  As a 'matter of form'.

Interception of notes became a game,
Their only amusement, the penalty Shame.
  They knew their cues.
'Sex is God's and you mustn't touch it,
It's a beautiful shoe whose very latchet
  You may not loose.'

So we were onanists; beds at night
Used to respond with continual slight
  Creaks of their springs.
But this was love's face in a mirror
That showed fatigue, not joy or terror,
  Eyes hollow rings.

Remember the countless Latin proses,
The poems we read, about girls and roses,
  Ethereal feelings,
Lofting shots from the sensual bunker,
Buds untouched by a worldly canker,
  Sublime as ceilings.

Remember, we prayed like anything
For Peace and the Forces of the King,
     Land, sea and air,
While sexual activity became
Hockey or Rugger, any game,
     To tough and tear.

A host of rules; but it was these,
The attitudes of the authorities,
     That made us bitter;
And now we realise that we,
Try as we may, can never be
     A boundary hitter.

Emotionally we're almost dead,
To have stunned us, hit us on the head,
     Would have been better;
Our white-hot desires were twisted
Inwards by their frightful, boasted
     'Obedience to the letter.'

What should be love in us is hate,
Habits of feeling continued late
     Are with us still.
We keep alive on a series of kicks,
Occasional women and Hollywood flicks.
     We feel rather ill.

The outside world for us was a fable,
A topic that sat at the breakfast table,
     Renowned for sin.
We were trained up a different wall
And the result is that after all
     We don't fit in.

My dear old school goes back to-day;
I shouldn't cheer it, shout 'Hooray!'
     Because you know too well
That those who smile because it's new
Will find out in a year or two
     What parsons mean by Hell.

IX

Though what I think is hardly news
Thoughts in my mind like boat-race crews
   Catch, overtake each other;
Here, clothed and warm, my mental sorrow
Turns to the child to be born to-morrow,
   To whom it will be mother,

Passive, without the body's action;
'Go down with your world' is my reflection
   And some of our opponents
Are neither lunatics nor wicked;
The simple question, Is this cricket?
   Recurs again at moments.

These doubts are sharp as arrow-heads,
Poisoned, cause fevers, crumpled beds;
   But stop. Who made them first?
Not Lohengrin nor Havelock Ellis
But little men with heavy bellies,
   The wisest and the worst.

These talkers, writers, after all,
Gilding the pill or the cannon-ball,
   Were made in factories.
Sweat and boredom, hunger, dirt
Gave her her figure, her wavering skirt,
   Her scintillating eyes.

His books were written by feeble hands,
His brain cells and his sexy glands
   Formed by hermaphrodites,
Though noise of miners underground,
Would be an unfamiliar sound,
   Spoiling his summer nights.

The little men who own it all
Sit in their offices, tidy, small,
   And on their registers
Are men who sloosh themselves with water,
Sexing about with the major's daughter,
   Young women in their furs.

What can we do? The walls all round
Go four feet deep into the ground.
   But still, we have our pens;
Let this, by writing, be our purpose:
Distract the naturalist from his porpoise,
   The farmer from his hens,

To bring to those in mental attics
More than the facts of hydrostatics,
   A creed, a living thing.
For now the gods have left the hollows,
Snow-white Venuses and Apollos,
   To crown another king.

Christ was decent; but his priests,
Resembling birds rather than beasts,
   Aren't useful any more.
The city is besieged; on boats
We send our hastily scribbled notes
   Up to the warehouse door

To be deciphered by our kind,
The men who live in the tortured mind,
   To show them their condition,
To ask their help, to make them see
That these things, said again by me,
   Are worth the repetition.

X

Song

For the island that's not on the chart,
   For the whistle that isn't a bird,
The sly beckoning-on of the heart
   To admit that all action's absurd,
For the rationalization of fear,
   For the man who's turned in and not out,
For the sudden refusal to cheer,
   All patrols look out!

For the writer believing in style,
   For the liberal wanting a pat,
For the humorous people who smile,
   For the woman who looks like a cat,
For the mortification of mind,
   For the inward betrayal, the doubt
Feeding on all it can find,
   All patrols look out!

For the bounder who isn't a cad,
   For the person who plays with ideas,
The obsession that isn't a fad
   But a fault that's continued for years,
For the lust that keeps trying to be love,
   For the tickling that isn't for trout,
For the will-forced emotional bluff,
   All patrols look out!

For the virgin, malicious and ill,
   For the schoolmaster loving exams,
For imperialists eager to kill,
   Kidnapping children in prams,
For the press-gangs, the men who are sold,
   Smart girls who go proudly about,
Dreaming of youth but are old,
   All patrols look out!

For the single, spontaneous cry
    Of the man who has seen his mistakes,
For the collapsible boat of the spy,
    Patrolling the glacier lakes,
For the tortures unseen in a house,
    For the note in the hand of the tout,
For the scuffle that isn't a mouse,
    All patrols look out!

Scatter the pamphlets we gave,
    Keep secretly spreading the Word,
There are some you could easily save,
    Converted if only they'd heard.
Be alert for the beat of the gong,
    Conquer the scowl and the pout,
These things are important and right, not wrong,
    So all patrols look out!

XI

My friend is far, his assurance and despondency,
His singing and his smallness far from me,
Not to be heard or seen. The lack I feel,
Empty and monotonous, the drowned ocean bell,

Rings through my head, who sit and think.
His thoughtless touch, his ordering a drink
Occur to me, his gestures in the sun,
As I sit here alone in a strange town.

XII

He thought of being in a single room,
Working in shirt sleeves at a public school
Feeling unhappy and desiring change,
How he was on the nerves of all his friends
Fretting in solitude all that summer.

He knew that he had passed another summer,
Looked through the window of his single room
But least of all had he accomplished change
Although affectionate to different friends,
With memories fading of his public school.

He wondered vaguely, Was the world a school?
Running by rules and quite opposed to change,
Censoring love though not averse to friends,
From which were only holidays in summer,
Packing a trunk and stepping from a room?

Must he from fears and illness keep his room,
Afraid of words like 'intimacy' and 'friends',
Life seen from windows, there be never change?
His university was only school
Hardly made bearable by friends and summer.

The time for opening windows was in summer,
In love perhaps and not at ease with friends,
Feeling their presence discipline like school.
But he alone could never leave that room
Although disturbing winds whispered of change.

Some words haunted his brain, like 'love' and 'change',
Took on new significance in the summer.
Some words turned into phrases, 'O my room,'
'Open the windows', and this was his school
Teaching him grammar and the worth of friends.

XIII

To go, to leave the classics and the buildings,
So tall and false and intricate with spires,
To run in joy from the imagined wood,
As children who have never heard of good,
To feed the flames of the forgotten fires.

This is my wish but my wish cannot be.
At times I should be dead like skull or stone
Or living with the slow life of a tree
Or half-asleep as one would think the sea
Or anything content to be alone.

Not living like this, ticking of a clock,
Afraid of friends and cataloguing wants,
Knowing so little, wanting far too much –
What else is tenderness but touch?
And what so far from me, though nearer once?

XIV

Poem before Sleep

I concentrate on the moon, so cold, so far,
Conscious of all my veins, that own me king,
Even the subcutaneous inguinal ring,
All quiet as the moon or any star,
Remembering the song they have to sing.

Beauty is hair, hair animal and fluffy,
But could not stir me from my single bed.
My darling is the moon and in my head
I forget girls as schoolboys forget toffee,
Everything that I did and that she said.

The moon is lovely, our perpetual critic,
And would not hate or pity, would not try,
Acceptance of the earth and of the sky
Has made her saintly, beautiful ascetic,
Until men fear that calm, unbiassed eye.

XV

We see in parks the children of the rich
Alive in colour, tractor on a hill;
By sudden moments our soul is made rich
Like child or hill.

So we are moved, by girl's eye or a boy's,
Quick passing figures, slow ship on the sea.
Sex has torpedoes and content its buoys
In us as sea,

Who dramatize the young man's stormy passage,
A point of honour to assure the self,
Make suffering duty, underline the passage,
Sad with our self.

XVI

We who were together shall now be apart,
Nosing our way between icebergs in this immense glacial
  world,
Different courses sailing, stamping our feet
From cold or from impatience, but with the
  remembrance of warmth
Somewhere within us and somehow remembered,
Even in this iciness never quite extinguished.
And at the mast-top the eager watcher,
Ready to shout 'Land!', draws freezing breath.

XVII

Sentimental Blues

Now triumph is in deserts
And occasional victory
For the nervous is power and glory,
Religious words to peasants,
While often the lucid rain
Falls into willing earth,
The evening a flower closing,
Remission of pain.

Swimmers in seas of gloom,
Sinking the dim fathoms,
Green and brown caverns
In the furniture of a room,

Never express what we mean,
Miserable and helpless,
Laughing and sentimental,
Describe such twilight scene.

We rescue shipwrecked words
From our seas of despair,
Terror is in the air
And the inexplicable birds,
Life on the edge of death,
Sleeping on the margin,
Eating, sleeping and talking,
Talking is waste of breath.

XVIII

Song

The famous fascist, night,
With the black taking power,
Suppresses all our light
And only our desire
Puts two and two together,
Survives the coup d'état.

Once the great writer said
A logic of the blood,
Like reading books in bed,
That will restore the good;
Each waiting for the other
Remembers the words read.

But only in the brain
Is that conversion valid
And the limbs grow insane
For the touch of something solid,
For the uninhibited lover
And sexual peace again.

XIX

Dollfuss Day, 1935

The young heads that I find attractive
Turn towards a political sermon
That promises and does not give,
Like postcard of a mountain village
That vouches for the truth of beauty
It can at best allege.

The priest assures the Chancellor's smiling
Moored to the land, balloon being Heaven.
The negligent, glancing girl who might be willing
Stares at the strangers, details of their clothing,
And inattentive to death's propaganda
Remembers loving.

But costumed boys who have not heard of love
Believe the story of a brutal death,
The priest with clasping hands, the Face above,
Less distant than the town across the sea,
While in the dark the Chancellor's photo
Gleams like a Christmas tree.

XX

The Old Ladies

The indignation that nobody hears
Keeps the old ladies calm, though it distresses,
Often descending the broad, shallow stairs
In various handsome dresses.
The hope of one is for a husband's death,
Another lives expecting her son's letters;
The favourite play of many is *Macbeth*,
And some have dreamed of fetters.

What they have been and what they still might be
Appear as fantasies or an obsession.
A husband becomes man walking as a tree,
Miraculous self-possession.
And finally commanding aspect cries
To die in unconditional obedience,
Weakness prays for power dropped from the skies,
Rejecting the old expedients.

To rule or to obey, the feudal dreams,
Defeat their ends, becoming opposite,
For each is more a habit than it seems
And both inapposite;
Sympathy and affection then are rumour
And energy frozen to a glacier,
A dancing-floor for others' black-masked Humour
With his conventional rapier.

XXI

Salzburg Festival City

The fairyland fortress, grey stone growing from rock,
Stands for my will, upon unconscious self
More ordered, smaller, but not independent,
Stone upon stone, that pine trees complicate,
Springing more pure from the thick soil of dreams.

All birds are twittering questions, why I like
One girl, dislike another; answers lie
Like unkissed beauties in that sleeping forest
Or else like struggling fish from this swift stream
Hooked they lie breathless, patient angler's pride.

This town of self has now gay visitors,
Thoughts wearing feathered hats, attractive walkers,
Strange to the ordinary dull inhabitants,
Brooding on money loss, failure and fear;
The bridge has flags of hope waving in sun.

XXII

Song

Acts of anger, not acts of love,
Keep me alive for the promised dove
And the daily expected tongues of fire,
Everything that I most admire,
The forward girl and the willingness
Stepping gaily from a summer dress.

Often drinking a cup of tea,
I think of what love means to me,
How never the glances or the kiss
Were ever anything like this,
The magic compound in the crucible,
And the poor spirit's miracle.

If my eyes were further apart
I'd call somebody 'sweetheart',
But in the leafy winter gales
It seems that my attraction fails
And never ended, never begun
Are my advances to everyone.

XXIII

Election Song, 1935

The black-tipped fox is creeping up the valley,
Winter like a steel trap closing in,
Whose winds are singing won't you come and help us,
Which side do you want to win?

Winter is cold and clothes are scanty,
Food is a rare visitor to the lip.
The working class all over the country
Must watch its step.

It's a matter that concerns the old ones
And the young who kiss and cuddle,
The shy ones and the bold ones,
It's the class-struggle.

War you say now, meaning Abyssinia,
We won't have anything to do with war,
But before you know it he'll be seein' you,
You'll hear him knocking at the door.

Bombing aeroplanes carry the simple message
To France and Russia and across the Channel
It's written in mustard-gas: 'Block Mussolini's passage,
Close the Suez Canal!'

Always the rich cars come and go,
The famous duchesses are slumming,
Bitter and beautiful falls the snow,
The crisp snow coming,

Bearing no comfort to the buried lives.
'Ugly,' they say and 'Such an uncouth accent!'
'Many of them beat their wives
And they're not pure Anglo-Saxon.'

The ships are waiting for the tide
With the usual lights at port and starboard,
Over the football fields airliners glide
And the handsome centre forward.

Ships are involved, bus, tram and tube,
Societies of anti-vivisection,
Even the Methodist Tennis Club.
It's a general election.

If you enjoy the running blood,
The boring trenches and the flashing sabre,
The young man trampled in the mud,
Then don't vote Labour.

Or if you prefer the harpsichord
The folk-dancing and the tabor
Or shut your eyes and trust in the Lord
Don't vote Labour.

We shall preserve the ancient sweetness,
And books published by Faber,
But our class-culture lacks completeness,
So vote Labour.

It's food we mean and self-respect,
Not heroism in Arabia,
And it's up to you and whom you elect,
So vote Labour.

XXIV

The smells of autumn and its solemn brown,
Thoughts that are lit like careless cigarettes
Illumining the figures at the gate,
Are memory of what I've seen and done.
Vanish in smoke, what I have seen and done.

Particularly wood beside a river,
In a stone building, boredom; father's anger;
Marching somewhere, marching and a banner.
These images recur, but not for ever.
I expiate by memory and for ever.

Malice I remember, to a friend,
Excitement playing games, the early teacher,
Suddenly clear the accent and the feature,
Beginning anxious and the happy end.
So burn these scraps in fire and make an end.

XXV

Political Poem

O communists with gradual inevitable chemical action
Turning this blue litmus people red,
As potent as acid, the good, we believe you have got it.
We believe that you are our enormous nurse
Helping us not to cry in the dark, not to steal sweets,
Kindly to many, a saviour of rearrangement.
We must believe in you as we believe in life.
Our faith flies over the world like an unassuming bird,
Peacock not nor nightingale but brown and confident,
No song having but the experimental magic call
Emotive as factory sirens, a caller to freedom.

Our contests held in the round amphitheatre of the skull
Mirror your fighting; pain and ideas of pain,
Fear and ideas of fear alike are enemies.
Our indolent mystical helping is done in the name of the
    summer,
In the name of landscapes, in an atmosphere of dancing,
Sensitive to you as the powerful throb of accordions,
We accept our world as your world upside down.

XXVI

We follow lives that twist like woodland paths,
Each having many lives; those in the sun,
External, are the best. The life that sees
Landscapes as beautiful and limbs in clothes
Crying for delivery, the anxious sexual children
Confined in warmth and tired of their peace.
Also the life that throbs with music's rhythms,
A Nordic boy with an accordion.

He is a good one. Also good the life
Content to listen, patient, the poised hawk
In powerful withdrawal above the dovelike words,
Stronger by mercy, the active intellect.

The lives are bad that conscious of impressions
Push tentative roots, feel for depths, can talk
Only to mirrors; mirrors all for them.
Impress an image, theirs, on face and note,
Four words impressing, 'How do we react?'
Their paths are circular within the wood.

XXVII
The English Wife

He had a steady hand
  And a clear eye,
He was gay, he was bland,
  And as straight as a die.

I was never frigid,
 I was never coy,
But O he has left me
 For a pretty boy,

For a gay mechanic
 Unbuttoning overalls,
More dangerous than movies
 Or the music halls.

Once he longed for me
 And my lovely bed
And in these hands have rested
 His tired head.

And the soft exertions
 Of the velvet night
Were the bold assertions
 Of my ancient right,

The language of the body,
 The sincere saying,
No winner in the game
 That we were playing.

I was significant form
 And the fabled city,
Who now am torn
 With anger and self-pity.

I was the Ideal
 And abstract beauty,
More powerful than power
 Or sense of duty.

By accident I saw them
 In the little car,
Urged with love's secrecy
 Behind the garage door.

The wind, how it did blow!
  And the rain drumming
Delayed the bitter snow,
  The crisp snow coming.

I sheltered in the doorway
  But my heart was in the storm,
While in the azure coupé
  They were warm, so warm!

With their kissing and their fingers,
  In love's aerodrome,
At the controls I left them
  And walked home.

For hours I sat in silence
  With my numbness and my pain,
But his car was stumbling westwards
  Through the bounding rain.

He drove my happiness away
  Into red Devon,
He took the brightest angels
  Out of my heaven,

Down the motorist's roads
  To the teashops and the cream
He left me sad and single
  With a sexual dream,

An unreal incubus
  And a real sorrow
Not for to-day only
  But for to-morrow.

And in the dim city
  And the aching vein
The true reality is pity
  And the pain, the pain.

XVIII

Song

The waves of tenderness beat still
On a shore of solitude,
Behind the sail the wind is ill
And melancholy the mood,
Haunted the motive and the will
Confused for what is good,

And passers-by are passers-by,
Shop-windows are for show,
No signposts on those roads that I
Have never dared to go,
The passionate question in the eye
Unanswered long ago.

A childhood image on that screen
Perturbs the charming face,
A city on the rustic scene
Has put me into a daze,
Only the thought of what I have been
In such another place.

XXIX

Jazz Song

Life is short and time is money
And 'Push' is written on the door to success,
So come to me now, I feel so funny,
Down the road of wisdom and the path of excess!

Nobody knows where we'll be to-morrow,
The future's likely to be a mess,
We can't keep things but we can borrow,
So always try to answer 'yes'.

Even censors are only human
And their daughters dance in suggestive dress;
So learn to Rumba and be Cuban
And I'll teach you things you'd never guess!

XXX

O girl beneath the exploring hand
    Silently quivering,
Enter with me that monotonous land
    Where the eyes are sovereign,
Forget what you say and what you see,
Your twenty years of living and me
    And the sun and the rain.

Everything but that particular spot
    Where the eye is a mirror,
The palm trees and the desert so hot
    And the midnight terror.
Forget it, baby, it's all a dream,
What it may be or what it may seem,
    All those people together.

Only the eyes can shine through all,
    The country houses,
The family jokes and the May Week Ball,
    The transparent blouses,
The pointed look and the printed page,
The disturbances of this day and age,
    That amazes, amuses.

Take my affection, you know it's yours,
    And the hugs and the kisses,
Curtain the windows and shut the doors,
    Whatever life misses
Here it is in our arms, my dear,
Heaven on earth, yes, our heaven is here
    And in no other places.

XXXI

Summer Time Ends Today

My nervous energy spent
And summer in retreat
I think my autumn thoughts
As I walk down the autumn street.

Equable and sad
With a delicate melancholy
I trace the lips and the eyelids and
The beautiful supple body.

The curls on her neck and the kisses
Warm and moist and tender,
Part of my mind now, only mental
That perfect surrender.

All changed and the leaves are falling
As the year moves to its end
And she who was my lover
Is only my friend.

XXXII

Cambridge

Imagine all the dons in the attitudes of buggers
With their complicated neurotic simplicity of learning,
Something comfortable, something not quite real,
The life of the tea-table, the book-scattered study,
The manuscript under the magnifying glass
In that white, cultured hand, deserving of pity.

Dons live on with occasional satisfaction,
Hand on the shoulder of the promising pupil,
Attracted but envious of the coming young men,
Middle age has caught them and the night comes after,
No soothing books and no charming companions
To quieten those nerves that cry for satisfaction.

What was their desire? Was it known and never realized,
Behind the lines and bathed in yellow lamplight?
In the world where their young men fight and are
    wounded
They suffer neglect like a curtain or a picture.
Pitying themselves they are never wounded,
Suffering quietly with a book in hand or smoking.

XXXIII

Verse from an Opera –
The Village Dragon *

1 Prologue

This is a story of dragons and in putting a dragon before
    you
We don't want to bore you.
Directors of banks and you who work in a bursary
Remember your nursery
When toys were real and wallpapers told stories
Of simple glories,
The gallant knight and the lovely lady,
But also the shady
Villainous dragon with the arrow-tail
Drinking from the sea or your seaside pail.

---

* *The Village Dragon* was written as the libretto for a jazz opera
(heavily in debt to Auden and Isherwood's *The Dog Beneath The
Skin*). One or two numbers were actually written by Frank Scholl, a
contemporary of mine at Cambridge, but it never got farther than
that.

People, think backwards, suspend your disbelief!
Like an autumn leaf
Dragons lie hid to-day in the secret foliage,
Beyond your knowledge.
All forest fires and motor accidents
Are their experiments,
The couple snapped up in the bluebell wood
Would tell if they could,
The cigarette-ends and the girl's dress found in the gorse
Mark a dragon's course.
Yes, they are clever, with their crimson tongues
And their powerful lungs.
They are very seldom seen
In that protective colouring, being green.

A girl called H is the lady fair
With carmine lips and golden hair.
The dragon's name is Old Sir Percy
Who disregards appeals for mercy,
The hero's Christian name is Giles,
A traveller over many miles,
Liberating from ghost and flood
The happy common and sinister wood.
Ring up the curtain on our captain actor,
The neighbourhood's future benefactor!

2 Love Duet
Giles:
A thought of hills to one walking on pavement,
The captive's dream of the end of his enslavement,
   An escape from prison.
   Like these is our vision.

H:
Night and the light and the promise of the city
Offer us prizes of tenderness and pity,
   The death of the dragon
   And a sleeping waggon.

Giles:

Flying away to an unvisited country
Where caresses shall lack the accustomed sentry,
  Joy be unconcealed
  And love revealed.

H:

Where no dragon's tail shall whisk at a corner,
Vanishing suddenly like a literature-scorner,
  And the breath of fire
  Shall forget its desire.

Giles:

After the sea-fight the promised landing
With increased pleasure and understanding,
  No flag at half-mast
  And the past past.

H:

What has been weak and what has been rotten
From then onwards shall be quite forgotten,
  The lesson learnt
  And the letter burnt.

Giles:

After this singular public service
We shall never despair and never be nervous
  But be safe on deck
  With no thought of a wreck.

Both:

Constantly happy, not depressed or elated,
We shall be perfectly integrated,
  Living as lovers
  On what love discovers.

3 Sir Percy's Song

O vice is nice
And virtue won't hurt you
   In the amoral world,
Whatever you do
So long as it's new
   And even if it's old.

Supposing it's funny,
Supposing it's money,
   But always if it flatters,
If it makes you happy
Then make it snappy,
   There's nothing else that matters.

If it's boys or girls
If it's ropes of pearls,
   If it's motor cars or gin,
You'll soon be dead
So go ahead,
   Don't hesistate, begin!

If it's an heirloom
Or a slim volume,
   A virgin or a widow,
If it's the flesh
Or a champion fish
   Or the cottage in the meadow.

If it's night-starvation
Or saving the nation
   Or an unexpected cheque,
It's the same to us,
We don't make a fuss,
   What you have or what you take.

Is it Mrs Besant*
Or shooting a pheasant
   Or the Rosenkavalier,
Is it social conditions
And East End missions
   Or the Ritz and caviare?

Is it Ezra Pound
Or Dorothy Round†
   Or ecclesiastical calm
And reading *The Times*
Or pantomimes
   Or a cricket bat under your arm?

Is it Budapest
Or an eagle's nest
   Or a week in gay Paree,
Is it Chaliapine
Or the Golden Mean
   Or the moonlight on the sea?

Is it loaded dice
Or a strawberry ice
   Or a prep school on the Downs,
Is it Beverley Nichols
Or hammers and sickles
   Or Mrs Belloc Lowndes?‡

Is it reading Homer
Or William Plomer
   Or Sir Arthur Quiller-Couch,
An Old School dinner,
A Derby winner
   Or practising the Mooche?

* A spiritualist

† A well-known British tennis-player.

‡ A novelist.

Is it saving your soul
Or birth-control
    Or scoring the winning try?
Is it budding genius
Or pet gardenias
    Or the beautiful evening sky?

Is it Maurice's* hat
Or a furnished flat
    That makes your pulses beat?
Is your paradise
In Garbo's eyes
    Or Ginger Rogers' feet?

Is it Colman's smile
That makes life worth while
    Or Crawford's significant form?
Is it Lombard's lips
Or Mae West's hips
    That carry you through the storm?

Whatever you choose,
And it might be news,
    Whatever you wish or dream,
If it's far or near
You can have it here
    For we're nicer than we seem.

O vice is nice
And virtue won't hurt you
    In the amoral world!
Whatever you do
So long as it's new
    And even if it's old!

* Maurice Chevalier.

4 Song by Giles

Giles:

The body is a reservoir of strength,
Intellect above and love below.
Some say the intellect is love
And only loves what it can know.

'Below there is not, but Above,
And that is where those waters flow,
Darkened and arrogant with pride.'
But they are wrong who say it so.

Chorus:

Can love sustain
Summer lightning and winter rain?

Giles:

Honesty once was a signal virtue
And only used one-syllable words
But it is love that is now the scarecrow
And the intellect sends its curious birds

To peer at this single ragged survivor,
Rooted in the rich, heavy fields,
Of soft and warm and moist and tender,
That conquers chiefly when it yields.

Chorus:

O, beware of sex
With its thousand necks!

5 Chorus of Villagers★

There are timber logs
And musical chairs
And fucking dogs
In the genteel squares

★ I have restored the adjective 'fucking'. In 1939, when *Poems and Songs* was published, such words could not be printed. Similar blanks have been filled in in the poem 'Fed Up and Going Down'.

Where comfort lives,
But in Tonytown
Nobody gives
And the leaves are down,

A depressing sight
For the chap-lipped poor,
And the saviour knight
Passes by the door.

When the lights are low
And the town is far
How should we know
Of that Eastern star

Leading us on
To the sacred hay,
To the mystic One
And the lovely day?

Why should we care
For that bitter death
And the songs in the air
And the ancient myth?

Doors are locked
And fires are out
But we are mocked
By the Great Without.

We have no pride
Who have no doubt
That there outside
Dragons move about.

In the hostile night
Windows can slide
And the horrible sight
Makes us open-eyed.

The hand on the plough
And the hand on the spade
Both know how
But are both afraid

In the complex act
Without a friend
But the friendly fact
Death is the end,

The final villager
Equal and free
With the highborn pillager
For eternity.

6 Question and Answer

Question:

Is it the hostile grouping of two hockey teams
That the gaiety of parties hides us from,
Behind the curtain what is it it seems
That keeps us sullen and nervously at home?

Answer:

In the country and in the town
It is the future that is getting us down.

Question:

Tell us about this sinister insistence
On our aphasia and our shrinking eye,
Never remitting and clouding our existence,
Tell us if it shall happen bye and bye.

Answer:

The shadow on the floor
Is the longest shadow, cast by war.

Question:

Can any feminine influence soothe us,
The hand on the arm or the tongue in the kiss,
Can these redeem before death shall remove us
Or is there no way out of this?

Answer:

The girl shall read but not understand
The poems of the loving hand.

But there are ways if you would take them,
Subtle and dangerous, hard and crude,
Of politics and education,
To overtake what you and time pursued.

Question:

There was a door
But you have been the key, not known before.

7 Night-time Chorus

The hard shapes of the day-time and the light
Are washed by waves of darkness and the all-pervading
    night
And gradually the young are learning how to live,
Learning what to take and what to give,

Finding their feet, to gradually recover
From that wicked century's hangover,
From art as art and work as work
Where the sensational spectres lurk.

Making full use of their talents
They begin to achieve the long lost sense of balance
Returning step by step from the twilight lands,
Eagerly caressed by pink and trembling hands.

Happiness has an unfamiliar feel
To those unused to the even keel,
Familiar with birds and dreams and mornings
Dazed with the thunder and the storm-warnings.

61

But now no hesitation in the motor-bus wheels,
In their huge rubber circles, shows what pride conceals
And we can sail in an ocean however deep
Who go now to a sound and healthy sleep

With no thought of the beautiful, persecuted head
Or simple martyrs since forgotten and dead.
In our ignorance we put questions but Giles was the
    answer;
He played the music but Reality was the dancer.

8 *Wistful Song*

In the eighteenth century gay young men
Had all the housemaids to practise on
But nowadays the bourgeoisie
Seem to be meaner and not so free.

And always the footstep on the stair
Keeps the loving hands from the lovely hair;
While things are safer but not so pleasant
For the beautiful town-attracted peasant.

It's the class-struggle in a final stage
That makes the intellectuals rage,
Beating their heads against the doors,
Like ships cast off from the friendly shores,

So far away from the harbour bar
And not quite certain where they are,
Some of the flags are flying half-mast
And what they long for is the Past.

And sorrow, once proud and elemental,
Only makes them more sentimental,
Turning from quarrels with the Mater
To tender readings of Walter Pater.

Hopeful voices are hard to hear
In that oppressive atmosphere
And no plain speaking and well-planned marriage
Are like being sick in a first-class carriage.

Until the mistress or the wife
Their sorrow seems as large as life
And sympathy's all that we can do
When they're feeling randy or feeling blue.

9 Chorus Leader
Pity the individual
For ever divided,
Breaking down and
Cracking up
The world at his feet
And he undecided.

Pity the young ones,
Their sexy dreaming,
Moody, uncertain,
Expecting only
A doubtful future with its masked scheming.

Pity the old ones,
Going gay or silly,
Cynical, sensual,
Oh, what
Of the night when the evening grows chilly?

Mechanical world,
Embraced by lovers,
Turner untroubled,
Tell us
What each one living has done or suffers!

XXXIV

Miss Twye

Miss Twye was soaping her breasts in her bath
When she heard behind her a meaning laugh
And to her amazement she discovered
A wicked man in the bathroom cupboard.

XXXV

Fed Up and Going Down

Goodbye to all the fucking English Tripos,
   Goodbye to fucking silly girls in Girton,
Goodbye to all the scurfy, doddering dons,
   And let the virgin Newnham keep its skirt on.

Goodbye to young neurotics in their beds,
   Sleeplessly planning how to save the Nation,
Goodbye to all the bureaucratic reds,
   Goodbye to cocoa and emancipation.

Goodbye to spectacles and to straight hair,
   Goodbye to all the mannered pathics,
Goodbye to Boat Clubs drowned in seas of beer
   And spotty scholars reading Clathics.

Goodbye to all the flowers of culture,
   Goodbye to all the local whoredom,
Goodbye to lectures early in the morning,
   Goodbye to flicks and blinds and boredom.

Goodbye to river parties in canoes
   And miserable, frustrated dances,
Goodbye to all the bread-throwing Blues,
   Goodbye to the depressed romances.

Goodbye to Christians carnally degraded,
    Or worrying about their wretched souls,
Like children that can hardly walk unaided,
    Or overgrown Boy Scouts with hats and poles.

Goodbye to horsey toughs in racing cars,
    The pop-eyed pimps who fill the Bath and Pitt,
Drunkenly yelping, leaning on the bars,
    Whose every second word is fuck or shit.

Goodbye to Cambridge architecture,
    The academic life, so false and clever,
Goodbye to don and lecture-room and lecture,
    Goodbye for ever!

XXXVI

O listen to the band excite the dancers,
    Walk over the lawns, admire the architecture,
Be like that flower expansive in your leisure
    Or reading Auden in a Cambridge theatre.

Be the highbrow, be the lowbrow,
    Imagining your Spain with all its rivers;
Exams as distant as a call from sirens,
    Play tennis with the men in faded blazers.

For life runs on, excusing us who live it;
    Even the prep school with its early terrors
Wears the bright halo of forgotten nightmare,
    The face is different in the different mirrors.

Be comfortable while you can, be bored,
    Be gay, be undergraduate, be clever,
Smoke cigarettes and flick the ash away,
    Either be mean or be the generous giver.

Do as you please, for time runs on to London,
    Where girls will finger you and life be different,
Cambridge forget you like the Isle of Thanet★
    Or the black rock the single cormorant.

XXXVII

From mass of enemies, group of friends
Or in indifferent world the young man lives,
Ambition turning to the higher buildings,
Tracing the dream in architectural mouldings,
Among giant flats arranged like hives.

What unsuccessful love, what hidden whisper,
What doubted talent on the hidden shore,
Prompt him to make a doubtful future certain,
Spy on the scuffling heard behind a curtain,
The childhood voices crying for more and more?

Simply to compete, establish value,
Say to the self You are not weak or small,
This turns him to the earnest conversations
Where to impress is wartime decorations
And failure to be shot against a wall.

Like magazines, like sipping drinks and smoking,
This life is useless and the words a strain,
So much to bother, so much to be haunted,
No morning take its afternoon for granted,
These are his days till life runs smooth again.

★ My preparatory school was in the Isle of Thanet.

XXXVIII

Days of Contempt

Bring me light verse to liquidate my sorrow
And make it really light – not dull or shoddy!
My life may be much happier to-morrow,
Hunger and love that press against the body,
The two eternal needs we recognize –
Desires that so relentlessly pursue one –
May get me down or raise me to the skies
And make me a Don Bradman or Don Juan.

Freud said that writers always compensate
By fantasies of power and love of women
The inadequacies of their lonely state,
Till dreams come true and then they rank as he-men.
I think that Freud was wrong and ought to know it.
I always find it wiser not to let on
For somehow girls avoid the simple poet –
Verse isn't stuff it's really safe to bet on.

I may be happier, as I said before,
But at the moment I am unemployed,
Love unrequited makes my life a bore
(To complete Oscar's jest – 'I'm unenjoyed')
And skies are dark but don't rain love or money
As I sit eating ginger nuts and smoking.
Somehow I don't think life is very funny –
More cause for a complaint than jolly joking.

But still, I won't turn nasty like Laforgue,
Who renounced Lerve – or odd like Baudelaire,
Or stretched out on a table in a morgue
Lie still in mute reproach – I like free air,
I like the girls and strawberries and cream
And I like Groucho more than I can say –
Life isn't just exactly love's young dream
But somehow I get by from day to day.

I'm fond of parties and I'm fond of wit,
I simply love the Eighteenth-Century Novel,
I think Shakespeare was great, yes, every bit –
Before such genius I'm prepared to grovel.
I'm keen on modern poets – Yeats of course
And Auden's variegated splendour,
I think MacNeice is rather a dark horse,
There's something very Nordic about Spender.

Life has its pleasures, few and far between;
But there's a danger, that is, as I see it;
Poets try hard to tell you what they mean
But mostly tend to analyse, not be it.
And life split into watertight compartments
Isn't quite what life once used to be.
To meditate in bachelor apartments
Has somehow never been my cup of tea.

Yes, in the Spring a young man's thoughts grow
    warmer –
Or used to once. But now he seems to falter
And wonders if it's an erotic trauma.
A double bed might lead him to the altar
But short of that there's nothing that's much good.
Some know the words and practise on their friends,
That only lands them further in the wood –
Amateur psychologists can wreck week-ends.

The reasons are so clear just why I'm fed up –
Perhaps old Father Time will take a hand
And help me when I'm blue to keep my head up
Or even lead me to my promised land,
Soften the hearts of advertising agents
And turn indifferent glances to a smile,
Beguiling beauty with its sexual pageants –
Oh! one deserves some luck once in a while!

Other Pre-war Poems

Home*

How awful to live in a horrible house
Where there's nothing to eat but cold chicken and
grouse
And there's nothing but barking and horrible noise
And the sound of a harsh, unpleasant Voice;
Where a really fine couple of beautiful cats
Are kept in the basement as though they were rats –
And a permanent wireless to keep us in error
By means of continued false humour and terror,
With everything run to a penny and mean
And everyone asking you 'Where have you been?'
Or 'Where are you going?' and 'What did you do?'
To make everyone nervous, bad-tempered and blue –
And there's nothing but illness and feeling rotten
And worrying over what's better forgotten,
Sadism, anaemia, anxiety neurosis
To make our dear home such a sweet bed of roses.

How awful to live where a horrible Dog
Is pampered and petted as though he were God
And all love is destroyed but not malice and fear
Though a code of good manners still flourishes there
And our laughter adorns such hysterical scenes
As a meal off cold mutton, potatoes and greens.
How awful to see the same faces each day
So full of self-pity, disgust and dismay,
To hear the same voices that say the same things
And the dog having fits every time the bell rings –
O could one imagine an atmosphere fitter
To make one depressed, antisocial and bitter?

* Written in 1938, unemployed and living at home, full of
adolescent rebelliousness and bad temper.

John Betjeman's Brighton

For Charles Rycroft

Lovely in the winter sunshine lies the Haslemere Hotel,
Near the Homeleigh and the Sussex, home of ex-King
  Manoel.
Lager in the West Pier Tavern, cocktails in the
  Metropole,
Who can spot Lord Alfred Douglas – not the gross and
  coarse of soul!

Stained our hands, our lips polluted, with a sinful
  cigarette,
We who saw 'The Dance of Love' – we are not likely to
  forget
Those moustaches and those knickers, seen through that
  machine of shame.
Palace Pier, beloved of wavelets, hushed the breath that
  bears thy name!

We remember shouting breakfasts, old men who forgot
  their teeth,
Exchanging photographs of nurses, symptoms, means
  to gain relief.
We remember that Pavilion, Moorish, with chinoiserie,
And the Ice Rink and the High Street, Fuller's layer-cake
  for tea!

Still we see those sugar-daddies flashing by in
  terraplanes,
On the Hove Lawns lonely colonels fight again their last
  campaigns;
Wickedly we drank our coffee in Sherry's where the bad
  girls go,
From the balcony we watched them bathed in purple
  light below.

O Finlandia, heavenly music, played by massed bands on
    the pier,
O those automatic palmists, how I wish that I were there!
O pin tables, Russian billiards, where the ball melodious
    clicks,
And the languid coloured postcards, bathing-girls of
    1906!

O voluptuous! O ecstatic! O that convalescent air!
In the sun those terraced houses, wonderful wonderful
    Regency Square!
There among the winds of winter we were gay in spite of
    gales,
Still a memory we cherish though the recollection pales.

War Poems (1940–46)

Sonnet, 1940

The point where beauty and intelligence meet,
Where intersecting lines cross and divide –
Happy were I to lie between those feet
Or by that rare and warm and lovely side –
You are the centre of my moving world,
The cold ideal to which I daily move
Although iron flags of battle are unfurled –
You are not yet, though might still be, my love.
And I, before the happy tough battalions
Engulf me or the frozen seas of Norway,
Have still my dreams of cities and of dalliance,
But most of you as standing in a doorway,
Who might, though I so dissipate my life,
Be mistress or, fear of the young, a wife.

The Bofors A A Gun

Such marvellous ways to kill a man!
An 'instrument of precision', a beauty,
The well-oiled shining marvel of our day
Points an accusing finger at the sky.
– But suddenly, traversing, elevating madly,
It plunges into action, more than eager
For the steel blood of those romantic birds
That threaten all the towns and roads.
O, that man's ingenuity, in this so subtle,
In such harmonious synchronization of parts,
Should against man be turned and he complaisant,
The pheasant-shooter be himself the pheasant!

Officers' Mess

It's going to be a thick night to-night (and the night
    before was a thick one),
I've just seen the Padre popping in to 'The Virgin's
    Womb' for a quick one.
I don't mind telling you this, old boy, we got the Major
    drinking –
You probably know the amount of gin he's in the habit of
    sinking –
And then that new MO came in, the Jewish one, awful
    fellow,
And his wife, a nice little bit of stuff, dressed in a flaming
    yellow.
Looked a pretty warmish piece, old boy – no, have this
    one with me –
They were both so blind (and so was the Major) that they
    could hardly see.
She had one of those amazing hats and a kind of silver fox
    fur
(I wouldn't mind betting several fellows have had a go at
    her).
She made a bee-line for the Major, bloody funny, old
    boy,
Asked him a lot about horses and India, you know,
    terribly coy –
And this MO fellow was mopping it up and at last he
    passed right out
(Some silly fool behind his back put a bottle of gin in his
    stout).
I've never seen a man go down so quick. Somebody
    drove him home.
His wife was almost as bad, old boy, said she felt all alone
And nestled up to the Major – it's a great pity you weren't
    there –
And the Padre was arguing about the order of Morning
    and Evening Prayer.

Never laughed so much in all my life. We went on
   drinking till three.
And this bloody woman was doing her best to sit on the
   Major's knee!
Let's have the blackout boards put up and turn on the
   other light.
Yes, I think you can count on that, old boy – to-night'll
   be a thick night.

Sonnet

We make mistakes, my darling, all the time,
Love where we are not wanted, sigh alone,
Simply because our passions are not tame.
No fairy story dragons to be slain,
Our living difficulties are not so simple.
Huge effort cannot bring a love to birth,
The future offers no instructive sample
Of what's to come upon a warlike earth.

O, if I had time back and you to kiss
I would not now reject your wasted sweetness,
But meet the tide and fullness of your love
(If some invisible god would stoop to bless
And cancel my love's blindness and its lateness),
That now ebbs from me daily, wave by wave.

For Whom the Bell Tolls

Aircrews have had it and the war goes on
And I have had it if I die to-morrow,
Not needing the marvellous conceits of Donne
Or any word of fear or sound of sorrow.
Love I have had, the climax of all lives,
Traditionally the enemy of death,
That like an Old Testament prophet power-dives
And takes away the hard-drawn, precious breath.

Yeats read much in old poets all his life
And prophecies and dreams of golden sages,
Condensed past wisdom into a few pages,
But in his passionate intellectual strife
Had not the art new generations praise,
To cram a lifetime into seven days.

Sonnet

Armies, like homes once hated, feed and clothe
And occupy with certain dull routine,
Are Fathers, strict, and cannot ever soothe,
Nor see what lovers with clear eyes have seen.
Good at its job, the soldierly, keen eye
Combs fields for gun sites and the sky for planes;
Landscapes suggest campaigns – but you and I
Are too fine detail on those endless plains
Where generals are romping. 'Personnel'
Would be our label; we are on their files.
And where you are no flag will ever tell
Although my love for you should cover miles.
Known to the wise, for you I write it out –
There are two worlds, within us and without.

Oxford Leave

'The Lamb and Flag' was closed, so I went to the
  Randolph Hotel
And saw there several faces that I remember too well,
War-time and peace-time faces, R A F operational types,
Girls who were arty and tarty – and several blokes with
  pipes.
Young undergraduate faces and over there by the door
Under a smart and once fashionable hat what might
  (perhaps) be a whore.

I stood there like Charles Madge, observing, with the
  ginger beer I had bought
(The war had done away with the beer) and to myself I
  thought
Et ego in Arcadia vixi and wore undergraduate clothes,
No one here is different from me essentially,
  I suppose. . .
Plus ça change . . . and a donnish type, a rather
  middle-aged queen,
Gave me a look, not a dirty look, I knew what that look
  could mean.

Behind my back was a shocker with a handlebar
  moustache
Treating a blonde to a *Dubonnet sec* and his laugh was loud
  and harsh.
A rather passé arty woman invited a boy to her home
'We're going to have fish and chips, my dear, really we'd
  like you to come.'
On my left two rich young men were busy discussing the
  tart,
Two well-fed minds without, I should say, a single
  constructive thought.

Ah, youth! and how time passes! Was it really five years
  ago
That I left my Alma Mater? Yes, time is not so slow.

It takes the loves and the parties but nostalgically in the
    brain
And even in the Army, their memories remain
And these are all real people, not the distortions of
    dream,
And though one might not believe it, they're all of them
    what they seem.

Cigarette for the Bambino

Hey, Joe! Cigarette! Cioccolat'!
Egg and chips?
Wanna eat, wanna drink?
Vermouth a very good
Very nice
Wanta girl? Wanta woman?

In the filthy streets of handsome towns
Black Market kids accost the soldiers –
Under the pictures of the Virgin Mary
Whores give themselves for tins of bully
And still amidst a starving population
The priests ecclesiastically waddle
As fat and sinister as any gangster.
Catholicism, black market of the soul,
That holds this wretched country down,
Corrupted state, corrupted crown,
Dangles its tarnished tinkling Heaven
Above this maze of medieval squalor.

Gone all the good of European culture,
The hangover of 'taste' in tawdry chapels,
Fat cherubs and madonnas puffed like clouds,
A throbbing, over-sexed and maudlin music –
O, that the centuries should show so little!

The beauty of the girls and children
Shining through rags, their friendliness,
The easy kindness of a Latin people,
Lacking the hardness of the French,
Brutality of the conceited German,
Deserve a better heritage than this.

Naples 31 May, 1944

When a Beau Goes In

When a Beau goes in,
Into the drink,
It makes you think,
Because, you see, they always sink
But nobody says 'Poor lad'
Or goes about looking sad
Because, you see, it's war,
It's the unalterable law.

Although it's perfectly certain
The pilot's gone for a Burton
And the observer too
It's nothing to do with you
And if they both should go
To a land where falls no rain nor hail nor driven snow –
Here, there or anywhere,
Do you suppose *they* care?

You shouldn't cry
Or say a prayer or sigh.
In the cold sea, in the dark,
It isn't a lark
But it isn't Original Sin –
It's just a Beau going in.

Poems (1946–64)

Young Blondes

A religious poem

Young blondes are tempting me by day and night,
Young blondes in dreams trouble my restless sight.

With curly heads they rampage through my thoughts,
Full-bosomed in their sweaters and their shorts.

Or lie sunbathing on an impossible beach
Naked, aloof, continually out of reach.

On the mind's promenade, above the rocks,
Young blondes go sauntering by in cotton frocks

Or flatter cameras with their negligent poses
Or drenched in moonlight gather midnight roses.

While I am eating, smoking, working, talking
Through long romantic gardens they are walking.

Protect me, Lord, from these desires of flesh,
Keep me from evil, in Thy pastures fresh,

So that I may not fall, by lakes or ponds,
Into such sinful thoughts about young blondes!

Spring Song

Efficiency in offices is found
And love in basements and in two-room flats
And death traditionally under ground.

There are no new equations to propound –
Although we get as drunk and blind as bats
Efficiency in offices is found.

The Life Force, always, pushes us around
Until they lay us out like table mats
With death traditionally under ground.

Perhaps a parson black and trimly gowned
Will speak of us while friends remove their hats –
Efficiency in offices is found.

So get the girls and get the whisky downed
While we're alive we're luckier than cats
And death traditionally under ground.

Let love and beauty dance and music sound
The land be gay with lambs, the sea with sprats –
Efficiency in offices is found
And death, traditionally, under ground.

Extravagance

Extravagance must have its day
So that one learns the easy way
That overspending doesn't pay.

Much buying compensates in part
For inferiority in art
And failure in affairs of the heart.

We know that fortune is a bitch
But the illusion of being rich
Keeps us content and stable, which,

Like drinking wine with every meal,
Prevents the Guilt we ought to feel
And dulls the lack of the Ideal.

To the Muses

In the fat butteries of the South
And in the North unknown to fame
The words are dead in the god's mouth,
The priest forsakes the sacred flame.

Language, once vital to our lives,
Maintains a perilous underground
With peasants and in jiving dives
Where transatlantic musics sound.

Old English with Old England dies
And dim Whitehall restrains the tongue,
The broadcast word's civilities
Infect the breath in every lung.

Fair Nine! Return to us again,
Return with pentecostal fire,
Revitalise the voice and pen
That now are starved of their desire!

Hymn to Proust

For you Time Past could not forget
   Nor alter what had been –
And Time has still its lost Odette
   And Love its Albertine.

We worship under different names
   The figures of the past,
Like characters from Henry James –
   But not designed to last.

For we know many a Charlus still
   And many a Verdurin,
Gilberte as Swann and de Forcheville,
   And M. Legrandin.

Each, an ambiguous Saint-Loup,
   Carries Françoise within,
And sex comes to its Waterloo
   In Jealousy, not Sin.

For all know Vinteuil's little phrase,
   The brilliant Balbec day,
The Méséglise and Guermantes' ways,
   The greyness of Combray.

Each one has tasted as a child
   Madeleines dipped in tea
And loves that drove the reason wild
   But set the fancy free.

A Music Lover

I listen to my gramophone
Proclaim a masterwork
Unhindered by the telephone
Or memories of Dunkirk.

Nobody can admire me,
My neatly-tied bow-tie,
And no one can desire me
For so alone am I.

My cigarette and holder,
My little polished feet,
Smoke floats above my shoulder
Oh so effetely sweet!

I am the priest and priestess,
My nightly cult is sound
At altars where the least is
By contemplation crowned.

After Heine

With an Irish accent

The old malicious stories,
The hymns of love and hate:
Oh, let us see them buried
In a coffin huge and great.

For much will I lay in it
(But what, I will not say).
The coffin must be larger
Than the whole of Dublin Bay.

A monstrous bier bring also
Of boards both strong and thick;
It must be long, much longer
Than the road to Limerick.

And bring me twelve great giants –
They must be stronger far
Than Greek and groaning Atlas
Or wrestling angels are.

They must drag out the coffin,
And plunge it in the waves;
For coffins so gigantic
Must have gigantic graves.

Then say why is the coffin
So heavy and so vast?
It bears my loves and sorrows
Together in it cast.

British Guiana *

When the blue sackies fly down from courida trees
And the jumbies are out on the Corentyne coast,
When the cabbage-palms stir in a Caribbean breeze –
This is the moment that I miss the most!

When the vicissi duck fly high in the evening light
And the rough trunks of samans loom into the sky,
Black against sunset, mysterious, scented night!
Jasmine envelops me, warm the wind's sigh!

   * This piece of imaginary nostalgia, written in London in 1953,
draws its colourful flora and fauna entirely from one novel by Edgar
Mittelholzer.

Mournful the call of the big yellow kiskadees,
Tempting the tarts at the Viceroy Hotel –
Mango, jamoon, sapodilla and breadfruit trees,
Dark Demerara that I love too well!

What am I here but the slave of the businessman?
Who knows or cares what exactly I am?
Carry me back on the wings of a chicken hawk,
Carry me back there, to New Amsterdam!

Huckstep

Huckstep was the groundsman at my prep school.
He put the heavy roller over the pitch,
Dragged by a horse in large flat leather shoes,
In those long-vanished summers.
A handsome smiling man and sunburned; quiet;
The brownest man I'd ever seen,
Dark oily hair and powerful arms in shirt sleeves.
He played, somebody told me, for the Kent Second
    Eleven,
Certainly he bowled at us in the nets,
Left arm medium, round the wicket,
With a beautiful action, a back-tossed lock of hair.

Now that I've been 'literary' for so many years
I recognize him. He might have been
Lady Chatterley's lover, Ted in *The Go-Between*,
The natural man. A Kentish yeoman
Who even then charmed me with his grace –
So that for ever I shall see him bowling,
Picture the wheeling arm, the fluent action.
His name is one of those like 'Adlestrop'
That, once absorbed, can never be forgotten.
Huckstep. We all admired him.
And who, if he was as I think he was, would not?
There is a place in life for simple people.

Londoners (1964)

Chelsea in Winter

It's a long pull down the King's Road and down to the
   Pier Hotel
To the Thames where the turbulent seagulls float
   backwards on the swell
As muffled in my duffle coat
Unruffled in my duffle coat
I walk the streets of Hell.

Intellectual introspective streets of the higher income
   brackets
Trodden by Mr Eliot's feet and the leaders of the rackets*
Where artists in their duffle coats
Feel smartest in their duffle coats
Like cigarettes in packets.

The Carlyle statue, pondering, sits wrapped in gloomy
   thought,
And warns that Human Wisdom still may be too dearly
   bought –
When duffle coat meets duffle coat
Each passes like a river boat
Towards its final port!

* Refers particularly to portrait painters.

Tennysonian Reflections at Barnes Bridge

The river flows before my door,
Sad with sea-gulls, mute with mud
Past Hammersmith and Castelnau,
And strung with barges at the flood.
Pink rowing girls by eight and four
Gently stroke the tide of blood.

A railway runs from side to side
And trains clank over on the hour.
The rowers strain and stretch and slide,
Hair like chrysanthemums, the flower
Of girlhood not yet opened wide,
Each happy in her virgin power.

The dying sun, the dying day
With sunlight charms suburban reaches,
The hackneyed river flows away,
And Time runs too, experience teaches,
Nor for the boring bard will stay
Or rowing girls as fresh as peaches.

South Kensington

1 The Natural History Museum

What man is
In a vast Gothic cathedral devoted to Life
Sit Darwin and Huxley like twin, uncomfortable saints,
More serious than the stuffed and innocent animals
At bay yet serene in their clean glass cages,
Cleanly divided into separate species
By omnipotent Man in his function as Providence.

At the top of the stairs, however, is evidence
That for some animals there was no surrender
To the clean shot and the heroic eye –

No less than the bust of a Victorian hunter★
With a name, a date, a place and above them
Words now grown too familiar – KILLED IN ACTION.
And Natural History, like all History, has its martyrs.

To feed the young with knowledge, some animals must
    suffer.
To feed some animals, some animals must suffer.
Not animals alone in permanent Apartheid
Are regarded by man (an animal) as different –
The list has been long and is being extended:
Huns Jews Poles Czechs Japs Reds Blacks Whites.

Life is less passionate in Museums of Natural History.

★ The inscription reads: 'Captain Frederick C. Selous, DSO,
Hunter, Explorer and Naturalist. Born 1851. Killed In Action at
Beho-Beho, German East Africa, 4.1.1917.' It is easy to misread this
memorial statement. Having regard to the date and place of his death,
I should have realized that he died from human 'enemy action' and
was not struck down by the vengeful paw of a lion.

2 The Victoria and Albert Museum

What man creates

Over a huge arched doorway stands Albert
And at his feet in capitals the one word ALBERT.
Inside are pots, paintings, prints, pincushions,
Every imaginable artifact by which Art is honoured –
But nothing primitive or pornographic.
(For the creative output of primitive man
One must go, as parliamentarians say, 'to another place'.
For pornography, to the British Museum Library
Or the royal collection of drawings at Windsor.)

No, this is Art. This is sophisticated. This is what Man
Has made for his pleasure and for his use.
Not entirely free from Sex and Religion,
But innocently, in general, serving the senses.
From India, for example, a many-armed goddess
Does penance till forgiven by Siva.
Chinese, the vases are proud of their coloration.
Greek, the vases are proud of their shapeliness.
And Moslem art has eliminated man entirely
In a profusion of pure patterns
Pleasing to geometricians (and perhaps to God).

In a room on their own the Raphael Cartoons
Are glorying in their Renaissance splendour,
Turned long ago into looking glass tapestry
(So that here the Apostles bless and curse left-handed).
On one wall is an English example,
The Miraculous Draught of Fishes,
Made at Mortlake in the Seventeenth Century.

Art gives with many hands, a many-armed goddess,
Gives that we may take, in the joy of creation,
In our varying degrees of contemplation.
Only here, Music is absent – except in the evenings
When the late quartets of Beethoven
Shrill the calm air with their grasshopper stridency.

Man is alone not an art-hating animal
(Where is the dog that can whistle you Mozart?
Or the cat that fully appreciates Picasso?).
Better to say: most animals are indifferent,
Except to the peacock displays of their courtship
(Art with a Purpose). Although Darwin
Once played the bassoon to some earthworms
And observed a reaction.

Art, from religion and magic, a divine child,
A child of necessity, a many-armed goddess.
Art is Art
And she lives in South Kensington.

3 The Brompton Oratory and Holy Trinity, Brompton

What man believes

Close to the Oratory – a good building, for a change –
Cardinal Newman is leading a kindly light,
Testifying to the Faith in all winds and weathers.
Hidden beside it, the antiphonal Protestant
Voice of Holy Trinity is raised in protest:
'We shall this day by God's grace in England
Light such a candle as (I trust) shall not easily be put out'.
Was it Latimer or Ridley? The light is fading,
The figures grow dim. The figures in firelight,
The burning zeal of Smithfield, the army of sectaries.
Through a pall of smoke, from a far hill of time,
We observe the ambiguous drift of the action.
What were they doing? And why did they do it?

There are many paths that lead to Believing,
The heart of man is criss-crossed with so many
That the original motive is wound like a spool,
Wound with the many-coloured silken threads of action.
Fear of Death? or Fear of the Future?
(And the Future in any case means Death).
The comfort and calm of a Father Figure
Big enough to protect a deplorable universe?

Who can see? Who can know? The spool remains hidden,
The thread is never completely unwound, until
Time pulls it clear – and the answer is Death.

'Let us leave Heaven to the sparrows',
But let those that believe continue to believe,
Continue to extract the old (false?) comfort
For the one situation that never changes.

4 The Science Museum

What man knows

The deities here are Galileo, Newton and Einstein.
Galileo has a full-length statue,
Newton and Einstein are, more modestly, busted.
They are the big wheels.

Wheels within wheels. Stephenson's 'Rocket',
Watt's Beam Engine and 'Puffing Billy',
The Blenkinsop Locomotive (this one a model).
Like the skeletons of prehistoric animals
The earliest engines have a kind of pathos,
Survivals in a more sophisticated age.
Steam, electricity, and (now) atomic energy.

But the wheel. Whoever invented the wheel
Was the greatest and most original mechanical genius.
This, one may say, was the beginning
Of man's intermittent raids on the vastness
Of Time and Space, changing the here and now
For a new and surprising there and then.

Wheels within wheels. But what man knows
Is more than the quickest ways to move himself about.
Human knowledge is never regrettable,
Although its uses are often regrettable.
It is better to know than not to know,
As, in other words, said Dr Johnson.

We are like the children who turn the handles
And press the buttons. We accept without question
Discovery and invention of our brainier fathers.
Throughout our world the wheels are turning –
But the man who invented the wheel is forgotten.

5 Excavation Road

Man is a political animal

In Excavation Road the traffic crawls.
Progress is slow. The street is full of words
Like HALT and MEN AT WORK. On the long hauls
The diesels fume and fret. Above, the birds
Show no regard for what goes on below.
The family cars, the lovers' scooters come
All to one common stop. The fast, the slow.

There might well be an answer in the sum
Of small progressions to infinity
(Some praise the closed captivity of trains) –
Meanwhile, in holes, the men work carefully,
Avoiding the sky-high-blowing, dangerous mains.

Madame Tussaud's

1 The Grand Hall (First Floor)

Past the waxwork girl at the publications desk,
Past the waxwork attendant at the turn of the stair,
To the first floor, to the Grand Hall.
And we have ascended into a heaven of Top People –
Historic Ministers, Royal Group, Conservative
    Government Group,
Labour Opposition Group, Famous Warriors,
    Ecclesiatical Group,
American Presidents and Statesmen, Modern Statesmen
    and Notabilities. . . .

What is one's first impression? A musty smell.
Not like the damp dusty smell of books in libraries,
Nor like the dry central-heated sunshine in museums.
Something to do with the robes and the regalia?
Some chemical to protect the clothes from moth?

Be that as it may, here is Churchill,
Sad and lonely in the Order of the Garter,
Set apart in the eminence of an Elder Statesman.
Macmillan, with his Cabinet around him,
Like a bored walrus in an Old Etonian tie.
Gaitskell with his lips pursed.★
Antony Charles Robert Armstrong-Jones†
On the edge of the Royal Group, and looking
As though the modeller had been tempted to impart
Something of the features of the late King George the
    Sixth.

★ This was written in 1960.

† Now Lord Snowdon. 'He was educated at Eton and Jesus
College, Cambridge, and received his rowing Blue as coxswain of
Jesus College's first boat, also directing the Cambridge University
eight to its victory over Oxford in 1950' – Madame Tussaud's
Exhibition, *Guide and Biographies*. Throughout the poem there are
many 'references' to this valuable document.

Khrushchev gives solidity. de Gaulle gives height.
On the raised platform he seems about ten feet tall.
Is it the platform? Or is it Company policy
To add some dignified inches to the possessors of status?
Certainly the great are great – but here they seem
   enormous.
And certainly the murderers in the Chamber of Horrors
Seem relatively tiny (but then they are standing
With their feet on the ground, at exactly the same level
As you and I).

2 Hall of Tableaux No. 1 (Second Floor)

Waxworks that neither eat nor sleep,
Make love or feel that they are human,
Can freeze in action, freeze so deep
They shame those fidgets – Man and Woman.

Here Mary kneels and waits the axe,
Ready to kneel and wait for ever,
Nelson dies under French attacks
And grapples Hardy in his fever.

Napoleon (death mask) lies in state.
'When did you last see your Father?'
Question unanswered. They can wait.
Time is no object, Life no bother.

Guy Fawkes is playing a children's game
Like 'Hide and Seek' or 'Hunt the Slipper' –
Slow matches, touchwood, but no flame –
No spark of life in that dead cellar.

Forrest and Dighton moving in,
Lantern held high, draw near the Princes.
No beating hearts, no thoughts of Sin,
No apologias, no defences.

No words. For waxworks, unlike us,
Possess their souls in perfect patience.
They make the minimum of fuss,
Happy to keep, and know, their stations.

A self-portrait of Mme Tussaud at the age of eighty-one,
Dressed like Mrs Grundy, obtrudes among the
    Tableaux.
Here also is The Original Guillotine Knife
Used for cutting aristocrats down to size;
Used, in fact, on Louis and on Marie Antoinette –
'The gruesome paraphernalia of History' – another
    reminder.

And (Culture at last!) a Literary Tableau
Where Walter Scott stands (modelled from life
In Edinburgh in 1828). 'The last outstanding liabilities
Were cleared on the security of his copyrights.'
And, sitting at a table, an improbable group:
Wells, Barrie, Kipling, Hardy, Shaw.
Shaw in the chair. As though a public meeting
Were about to begin, or a team photograph,
Or even a Brains Trust. But no living writer
Confronts us with his genius. No Eliot, no Forster.
And Yeats, Joyce, Lawrence are not represented –
As though Literature came to a full stop in 1910.
Here, there is no doubt, the sword is mightier than the
    pen.

3 Top Landing (Hitler and Stalin)

Roped off in opposite corners, unexpectedly mild and
    peaceful,
Alone, with nothing but the ghostly
Cheering and suffering multitudes of the years of power,
Stand Hitler and Stalin.

95

Mussolini has vanished – melted down, forgotten
Like the junior partner in a cross-talk act
When one survives the other. Hitler and Mussolini!
Names once as close as Sullivan and Gilbert,
Layton and Johnstone, Flotsam and Jetsam.
Alas for fame! for infamy! for both!

Hitler. Stalin.
Great crimes were once committed in these names;
Jews, Kulaks, Party Members, millions
Died when these voices spoke, or when these hands
Put bloody pens to paper. It is right
That they should now stand meekly in this Limbo,
Not in the Hall of Kings nor even yet
Among the dumb defenceless murderers
Whose crimes were trivial.

They were a different sort, who in the mass
Knew that a lie could work and thrive like yeast;
Leavening their doughy, sheep-like populations
With hates and fears until, like bitter bread,
They rose. And followed them
Into a hell where men burned down like wax
And personality was charred away
To leave obedience only to these names:
Hitler. Stalin.

4 Hall of Tableaux No. 2 (Second Floor)

Here are the VCs. Whose names are known
Mainly in the Regimental Histories. Whose bravery
Many would like to share (and I for one).
Eighteen of them, and all from World War Two.

No memory returns from World War One;
Those earlier heroes are reported missing,
Choked in the mud or scarecrowed on the wire,
Sprawled in a trench, lit by the Very lights,

96

Shelled, mortared, gassed.
They have achieved no immortality
Among these men whose names are writ in wax.

–As though the heart of man can only hold
One war, and that the latest, in its grasp.
All others as remote – places and dates –
As Wellington's and Marlborough's campaigns.

Takers of life. Yes, Murder has a way
Of putting his sly hand on deeds of honour,
Is never far from politics and war.
Like saints and martyrs these were brave. And yet
In cooler minds a peacetime thought is heard:
Surely a man has better things to do?

Pass to Celebrities of Past and Present,
To Radio, Stage and Screen (Dors and Monroe –
To cheer us with a fleeting glance at Sex).

Sports Section. Here one sees how flesh
Is merely parodied by flesh-in-wax.
Wax legs of tennis girls and footballers
Have a smooth dusty look. Fine hairs and veins
That give real legs their living dullnesses,
Their softness and their warmth – these are not here.

Faces in suits – all right, and real enough.
But not the body, not the man himself,
Still less the woman, object of desire.

5 Hall of Kings (First Floor)

Down to the Hall of Kings, those effigies
Come round out of a Children's History.
Noteworthy only Cromwell (with his wart)
And Charles', his victim's winkle-picking beard.
Note how, quite reconciled, they stand and stare
Across a chasm of three hundred years.

6 The Chamber of Horrors

Down to the lowest circle. On the walls,
As mimicking the prisoners of the past,
Contemporary names are scratched and scrawled,
By the descending steps.
A notice here says 'Portrait Models of
Notorious Murderers'. All of them are numbered.
Look them up. Some of them you will know
From seeing their pictures in the Sunday papers
(Heath's too-good-looking, slightly foxy, features).

Begin at the beginning. Youngman, Mahon and
    Podmore,
Bywaters and Mrs Thompson (a bad business
For Law, for Justice, for Judges, and for her).

Medieval Tortures. A Diorama. Like an Italian
Cinquecento painting. Wheels and trees, galloping
    horses.
Sadists at work and play in a brown landscape.

George Joseph Smith – and, look, 'The Actual Bath
In which Smith drowned Miss Lofty'
Pleads with the dumbness of ironmongery
'Not guilty'. An instrument only. Never thought.
Dougal (Moat Farm) and Cream – neurotic knave
Who poisoned tarts in drugged euphoria.
And Mrs Dyer, the wicked baby-farmer of the ballad,
A strong-willed woman executive, a career woman,
Not caring much how many little bundles
Were thrown into the Thames. Business comes first.

'Notorious Murderers'. What marks them out?
Well, most of them are small, and this might be
Past malnutrition of a criminal class.
But then there are the bourgeois psychopaths.
They are small, too. Would this be contribution
To their conception of a great 'I am'
Doing what it likes and taking human life
To satisfy their own 'great' needs and wishes?
A Divine Right to treat themselves like Kings?

So much for theory. Back to the Catalogue.
The Mannings look distinguished.
Crippen is very mild, sad and respectable –
He had a raw deal from a ghastly wife
And cut up rough.
Charles Peace is black-faced like a nigger minstrel
('He is shown in one of his disguises').
Chessman, unlucky pawn,
Strapped in a chair ends twelve years' waiting.
The Torture of The Hooks. And Burke and Hare
Looking like a couple of railway porters
In their peaked caps. Ready and willing, both,
To knock off any old bags for a living
And spirit themselves away on whisky.
John Reginald Halliday Christie,
The Great Necrophile (my capitals). Responsible –
If you count himself – for the deaths of ten people.
His wife, five whores* and Evans, Evans's wife and
   child.
Here in the fatal kitchen he is monarch of all he surveys.

Landru, Courvoisier, Palmer, Wainwright, Haigh.
Dumollard and his Wife – French peasants who
With peasant cunning decoyed eighteen young girls,
Garrotted them.
And on the wall, framed like a Testimonial,
A letter from the Master. Jack the Ripper
To the Chief of the Metropolitan Police:
'Dear Boss – I keep hearing the police have caught me
But they won't fix me just yet.'

Ancient and Modern.
Louis XVI and Marie Antoinette,
Robespierre and Hebert, Fouquier-Tinville,
Carrier – mouth-bleeding, pallid *Têtes de Morts*.
And Marat in his blood bath, frozen meat.

---

* This is not entirely accurate. Miss Eady, one of Christie's victims, was in fact a 'lady'.

Iron Masks of Infamy to distort the features,
Spiked belts and thumbscrews – all the evidence
That man, to man, is crueller than the wolf.

So out. Into the open air
And pleased, at last, to light a cigarette.

Harrods

Harrods – stronghold of the Establishment!
Some people worship the Royal Family,
A kind of second religion. And for such
There's something sacred in the name of Harrods,
Divinity hedging every Royal Appointment.
Some make a pilgrimage each Saturday
To walk round Harrods, just to meet their friends.
Some women from a garment bought at Harrods
Will cut the name and sew it slyly in
The inside neck of (say) a cheap new coat.
Deceitful cats and snobbish, silly bitches!
Conservatives and *Daily Telegraph* readers!★

Enough (too much) of partisan abuse –
Enough to say that on such people's hearts
Harrods established a strong stranglehold
That now cannot be broken. And, at that,
One cannot say that it is Harrods' fault
If people buy their snobbery from them.
If not from them, they'd get it somewhere else.

I am myself, by virtue of descent,
An Old Harrodian,
Card-carrying Party member. On that first Honours List
Of those deemed worthy to buy on account
Were names of credit:
Lillie Langtry, Ellen Terry, Oscar Wilde.

★ *C'est un Jacobin qui parle.*

100

After the First World War
My mother, with myself, two sisters and a dog
Would walk across Hyde Park from Albion Street
To shop at Harrods. Bringing her small convoy in
As sheepdogs worry home the wandering sheep.

But the building?
Stevens and Munt (1901 to 1905).
The building in its way is very fine,
Symbolic of the Harrods way of life.
Imposing. Solid. Not to be knocked down
By any one 'conventional' kind of bomb,
And pinkish-orange in each perfect brick.

Harrods in 1849 – a modest grocer.
But after two initial Harrods (H.C., C.D.)
In 1891 upon the scene
Came Richard Burbidge, due to play a part
As the main actor in the time to come,
Important as his namesake on the stage
Once graced by Shakespeare.
Imperial expansion followed soon.

In 1894
'Lord Esher, Master of the Rolls,
Stated from the Bench that Harrods Stores
Was one of the most interesting and beautiful
    establishments
In the whole of London.'*

Close-carpeted within and warm,
Perfumed by many women.
With marble Food Halls – where once Wilde perhaps
Chose delicacies for Bosie's lovely tongue,
Bees' balls in butter, chocolate-coated ants
(Or are these fantasies of later date?).

* *A Century of British Achievement 1849–1949.* Privately published
by Harrods.

Luncheon at Harrods! For me, a genuine thrill,
Still, now, in graceless 1961.
The Georgian Restaurant, A La Carte Café –
A well-bred accent on the final 'e' –
Like stepping onto any West End stage,
In drawing room comedies of between-the-wars,
The faces and the voices. Here, most gay,
The Silver Buffet sports a 'thirties' bar –
A host of brief encounters, gay divorcees
Reflected in its mirrors.

Culturewise,
Tea With An Author in the Georgian Restaurant.
Commodore Thelwell speaks: 'At Home With Queens'.

Below, in the main hall with leather chairs,
The portraits on the wall can take it easy:
Three Burbidges, one Newton,
All knighted, all. And, but one, never knew
That they were taken over,
Or heard at all the powerful name of Fraser.

So fade – or change – the glories of the world.

Soho

Eighteenth-Century houses. Neat. Reasonable.
Three streets in alphabetical order
(Reading from West to East):
Dean, Frith and Greek.

Dryden in Gerrard Street, Mozart in Frith,
Prodigious infant. Johnson at the Turk's Head.

But look in Soho Square, the 'stately quadrate'
(A windmill turning then in Rathbone Place).
First resident: Monmouth. Lucifer that fell.

In a more lucid day
This was the heart of fashionable London –
With link boys, chariots, ombre, whist and tea.

Routs. Public Assemblies
Of the Nobility and Gentry.
Mrs Cornelys. Carlisle House. Casanova.
The pleasant titillation of (masked) balls,
The flaming candles, Chippendale Chinese.
And at the gates the rough unlettered mob
Ready to throw the old four-letter words.

Now a few only of the first remain,
The original houses. Cowed and small
Beside competitors. These parvenus
Disdain that world of wit and cultured charm,
The pearls of wisdom. The world of Commerce
Is *their* oyster.

This is the architecture dedicated to the proposition
That all that matters is to show a profit.
And on the Soho houses that remain
From that Augustan Age are signs
Of the times. Neon invitations
To eat, drink, watch the girls strip,
Outraging modesty of mild façade.

The streets are full of Mediterranean life,
Italians, Greeks and Cypriots, Maltese,
With Huguenot-descended French.
And, as exotic, furtive blooming, BOOKSHOPS.
For here, before the deluge of the Act,
The connoisseurs bought 'doubles' – 'singles' too,
The happy snaps that could debauch the eye
Of schoolboys, sadists, or the very queer.

And still the trade in flesh continues here,
The warm, compliant flesh that knows no Law,
– but more discreetly. (Every kind of lust
Is more a kind of love than Judges think.)
And on the notice boards tarts' cards proclaim
A change of language, not a change of heart:
ACCOMMODATION
FOR GENTLEMEN ONLY, YOUNG LADY SEEKS
INTERESTING OCCUPATION, even PRIVATE STRIPTEASE.
Below, the cryptic cyphers only the dial fully
    understands.
Telephone numbers! magic in their power
To serve the twentieth century's good time myth,
The talismans of Northern businessmen.

Less modest once, such cards had photographs,
Vital statistics, and the hidden words
That called the initiates to the Mysteries.
Rainwear. High heels. Bondage. Correction. All
Like jungle drums to lonely fetishists
And those whose impulse learned to deviate.
And this is still a jungle, where at night
The infantile desires may roam at will
With Tarquin's ravishing strides.
Here, in the glistening rain, the mac men come;
A pack of masochists each night whipped in,
Slaves of the 'models' with the hunting crops.

Crooks, ponces, whores. You think: a world away
From eighteenth-century elegance and charm?
The wise (or cynical) have leave to doubt.

South Audley Street I

The Grosvenor Chapel

The prettiest chapel in town? Yes, I would say,
Who daily walk by that blue-painted spire,
Those heavenly proportions. 1730.
Raised by what Unknown Christian Soldier
For 'Real Estate' Sir Richard Grosvenor?
Tradition says a builder name of Price
(But non-committally adds 'probably')
Dug in, threw up defensive walls,
Fought the good fight.
Where in 1945 the American Forces
'Gave thanks for the Victory of the Allies'.
Lone outpost now of God. Much bombed.
Trinity Chapel, Hanover Chapel, Berkeley Chapel.
  Gone.
The Mayfair Chapel. Gone. Their very absence
In the consuming night of history
Adds brightness to this one star that remains.
An interior small, sober, decent,
Whose white and gold seems unemotional
Faced with the hanging Christ in agony
Of polychrome, of counterfeited flesh.
'Extensive alterations in the Chapel
Were carried out under the direction
Of Mr J. N. (now Sir Ninian) Comper.'

And here John Wilkes – 'A Friend of Liberty' –
Lies buried, darling of the mob
And rightly. The first four Georges
Were not above some very tricky stuff,
The Lords continually threw out Bills
To stop the hanging of a child of ten,
The Bishops could not see where it would end
If capital punishment were not retained

For picking pockets or for knocking off
Goods to the value of five bob or more.
(Say half a dollar and you might be right).

So long live Wilkes! Debauched, intemperate Wilkes,
Whose 'Essay on Woman' (if he wrote it) was
Death to all Virtue and all Chastity.
A demagogue who knew a thing or two
And did a thing or two for Liberty,
While moderate, unenthusiastic men
Looked down their long, cold noses, modestly.
Hurrah for Wilkes! For Wilkes and Liberty!
But Wilkes is dead. Gone as we all must go,
As eighteenth-century architecture is hacked down
By thoughtless navvies with the hands of Time.
Rubble and dust where once great buildings stood.

South Audley Street II

Thos. Goode & Co. (London) Ltd

Architects: George and Peto. 1876
In giant wrought iron figures clamped
Onto the fashionable red brick front.
Late Victorian richness. Granite pillars
Polished ecclesiastically smooth.
Behind plate glass, two china elephants
Stand huge and silent, both ignoring us,
In china contemplation. As a child
My mother took me to South Audley Street
For wedding present buying,
To Goode's. Those elephants
(And that was in the Twenties)
Were even then the tenants of the house,
Familiar landmarks. Like the Bourbons
They have learned nothing and forgotten nothing.

Between the elephants – the magic doors.
Stand on the mat outside and lo!
They swing wide open and you can step through,
But close again as your foot leaves the mat.
Symplegades, the far-famed clashing rocks,
Were not more dangerous or more wonderful
To that sea-girt, far-flung Odysseus
Than the glass doors of this emporium
To me, untravelled, shy, and under ten.

Within, a paradise of china, glass;
The colours bloom like flowers
Around the borders of each silent room –
For all is quiet, refined. Here, salesmanship
Consists in leaving customers alone
Until the pressure of the atmosphere,
The sense of what's expected, forces them
Exploding, into speech; a declaration
As difficult to voice as words of love,
And as irrevocable.

The purchase made, and deftly wrapped, what joy
To see again those intricate machines
That fire like cartridges their tubes of change
About from place to place!
Here, to a basement? or some higher floor?
The vulgar mechanism well concealed.

It was not always so. On tracks of wire,
Like trolleybus cables overhead (or New York's El),
In those far haberdashers of my youth
The quick projectiles rushed and whirred,
And landed with a satisfying thud.
A memory, again, of shopping trips
Made with my mother, and a Scottish dog.
To me those interdepartmental missiles
Were easily the best part of the shop.

Once more, departing, through the magic doors.
To leave one's childhood and step out again
Into the world of 1961.
Forty years on and all that jazz! Ah, yes
We grow more sentimental as the years go by,
More self-absorbed, like china elephants.

Earls Court

Earls Court – a bourgeois slum,
Well the wrong side of that dividing line
That runs down west of Knightsbridge, north to south,
Invisible but strong to separate
All those with Capital from those without.

This is the country of the single room,
The two-room flat, three single girls who share.
The secretaries who have families
In the Home Counties. (Young executives
Exhaust their nights with noisy male displays
Of potency in tiger-roaring cars.)
Home perms and frozen food.
Nail-varnished stockings where the ladders are!

And students. Indians and Africans, the sons of chiefs,
Intelligent and well-behaved and far
Removed from Notting Hill's black heart
Where the poor whites would carve you for a giggle –
Though just a mile north as the jim crow flies.

Australians too. In groups in Earls Court Road,
In solidarity that will not move for prams,
Like little clots in the pedestrian bloodstream
That flows along the pavements.

Sweaters and jeans. Some beards. For in Earls Court
Live bachelors (boys and girls),
The adolescents and the very old.
The families with children – very few.

The old, like refugees,
Into the hotels of the Cromwell Road
Have all retired. To leave the world behind,
With TV, knitting, books and cups of tea.

And what has Earls Court got? A Hall
For Exhibitions; and the Empress Hall
(For boxing, Louis Armstrong, and the rest);
New, high and mighty, looms
The Empress State Building – from Holland Park
A summer's landmark.
A Station (District and Piccadilly Lines)
Known to commuters as a terminal.
Victorian streets and squares
Like living memories
Of that Great Exhibition (1851).
Hotels for oldies. Restaurants a few.
Churches. Some coffee bars for student life.
Some hospitals (my son was born in one).
Some shops, some pubs. Nothing spectacular.

What Earls Court has is this:
A sense of free and easy. There are no Joneses
For anybody to keep up with here.
The negroes in the snow are beautiful,
And you can wear what clothes you damn well please.
No debs. No escorts. No tycoons. But life
In great variety. Eccentrics, too,
Who in a bus will tell the passengers:
'To-day's the Birthday of The Princess Royal.
I'm telling you because you ought to know.'
A lady neat, precise, a bit insane.

Yes, that's the nut-shell truth. Earls Court
Was never smart. Nor likely, much, to be.

The Marble Arch

Wars never end wars.
The monuments to old victories
As they stand, grow small. After the first
Orgiastic erection in youthful pride and hope,
Are over-shadowed by the later building –
As now the Marble Arch. The Odeon,
The Cumberland, have since the Thirties hedged it lushly
  in.
Degraded now, reduced in rank
To a minor Police Station.

First built to honour Nelson,
A tribute to that lucky one-armed bandit,
His victories that turned a French sea British,
Kept the map pink.
1828. John Nash. And modelled on
The Arch of Constantine. Till 1851
Stood to at Buckingham Palace as main gate.
Moved then to Tyburn, entrance to Hyde Park.

Where, till the recent reconstruction,
A triangle of stone set in the road
(X marks the spot on plans of murders)
Showed where the gallows stood – that Tyburn Tree
Providing spectacle and entertainment
Free for a fun-loving, drunken public
All in favour of Capital Punishment.

Here in 1305
Died William Wallace,
An early martyr to the cause of Scotland.

And still, across the Odeon's wide screen,
Chase coloured fantasies of lust and pain,
To prove that violence is part of life
And for the young a licensed way of love,
Approved by Censors.

In the cold Thirties here, the unemployed
Hung sadly round the alleyways and doors,
Round the fat neck of a rich and stuffy nation –
A useless, guilt-inducing albatross.
At Speakers' Corner, no further than a shout
In a high wind would carry, the frenzied agitators
Cried out for vengeance on the status quo.
Mass Rallies. Mounted Police. But Politics died
Of overspending in 1951.

The speakers still speak; each one a universe
Bounded by the theory he proclaims,
Where only the admissible evidence is admitted.
But the audience sits at home,
Its senses cosy by the warm TV.

And now, under the immutable lovers' trees,
Where folded like chairs in one another's arms
They kissed away the summer; under, still,
Is a giant garage for 1000 cars.

Park Lane

The *douceur de vivre* had a good time here
In the days when to be rich meant that you had good
    taste,
And even now a few bow-fronted Regency beauties
Sadly confront the Park,
Short of paint, short of care,
Elbowed aggressively by the boorish squareness
Of the freebooting modern office blocks.

Here with the flats and business 'Houses'
(Indistinguishable and undistinguished)
They stand reproachful of a way of life.

Note, perhaps, among such mediocrity:

1. Fountain House, reverse of No. 80,
Has, in replica above the door,
The Dolphin Fountain, Once on my childhood walks
A landmark. The fountain is removed,
Disgraced and parked a mile to the North East
In Regent's Park. There ought to be
A Society For The Prevention Of The Removal Of
   Fountains.

2. Two huge rival hotels – the Dorchester
And Grosvenor House. Both built in 1930, the
   Grosvenor first.
The Dorchester, though, proudly bears the date
Of 1930. If one has to choose,
Perhaps it is the better building, more cocksure
And truly of its period.
In 1937 I had a girl friend
Who worked at the Dorchester as a shorthand typist.
She was sometimes lent
To visiting celebrities for typing.
And Maharajahs with their purple lips
Made passes at her.
The staff (she said) referred to Grosvenor House
As 'the jam factory'.

3. At the far end of Park Lane
The new Hilton Hotel is a gigantic phallus
Rising like a monster on the boundary of Wolfenden
   country,
Mayfair – which once was residential.
And till late 18th Century the May Fair
Was a scene of unexampled debauchery.
To-day we are more discreet.

Hyde Park Corner

London is full of gates; gates through which nobody
    passes.
The Marble Arch; the Wellington Arch at Hyde Park
    Corner;
The triple gateway entrance to Hyde Park.
Statues do better, within the gates.
Permanently fulfilling the function of statues,
To stare and to be stared at.
As Byron, pensive on his chunk of marble,
Achilles, mutilated,★ with his lifted shield
(The slings and arrows of outrageous fortune),
A warrior, beaten from the bronze of cannon
Silenced for ever by Wellington's campaigns.
The monument to Milton is also silent,
Its heavenly trumpeter now far removed
From the entrance to Hamilton Place. An island site
Swamped by the tide of progress.

Enjoy what still remains.

The Wellington Arch is 'crowned
By a large bronze quadriga representing Peace'†
By Adrian Jones, MVO.
A group unique, as guide books will suggest,
'Because the silhouette is practically the same
From both sides of the arch.'

The wonderful Screen Entrance to Hyde Park
Was erected in 1826,
Designed by Decimus Burton.
The reliefs copied from the Elgin Marbles.

★ This was written when Achilles' fig leaf was not in place,
removed by an act of vandalism. It has since been restored.

† All quotations are from *London* – Ward Lock's Red Guide.

Both sad and beautiful, in London weather
They have their dreams of Attica
But keep them to themselves.

Here Apsley House, the Wellington Museum,
Faces the equestrian statue of the Duke
Mounted on Copenhagen (work of Boehm).
Great Apsley House, a perfect beauty,
Built in the 1770s by Robert Adam
On the site of the old Lodge that watched Hyde Park.
Two years after Waterloo
Was bought by Wellington.
In 1830 'the freehold was purchased
By the trustee of his parliamentary grant',
Gift of a grateful nation.
Now houses spoils of war,
Including a vast statue of Napoleon,
White marble, by Canova – the last captivity,
Outlasting Elba and St Helena –
The conquered as an *objet de vertu*
In the home of the conqueror.

Here also note
Goya's huge equestrian portrait of the Duke,
Too big for stealing.
Enough Field Marshal's batons
To fill a knapsack (one for each
Of the Allied Armies). The table centrepiece
In silver-gilt, with nymphs, from Portugal,
Laid for a ghostly banquet never finished,
Never begun. Murillos. Flemish *genre*.
A rape of Proserpine, her tits escaping
Immodestly from the Grecian drapery.
Dinner services, each plate portraying
A victory. Great Wellington
Who never lost a battle!

But once, at orgies, when the gentlemen
Were drunk on elegant wines by candlelight
A panel would slide back to show a line
Of crested silver chamberpots.

Hyde Park Corner is a nest of monuments.
The Artillery Memorial
Points the fat finger of a howitzer,
Underlines the agony
Of manhandling the guns.
The Machine Gun Corps has David,
Reminiscent of Florence, Michelangelo,
And marble heroes with their neutral eyes.
Here his inscription reads:
'Saul hath slain his thousands,
But David his tens of thousands'.
A smug, sadistic epitaph – but happy days
When cross machine guns meant a megadeath!

St George's Hospital in its new paint
Revives its dignified incumbency,
The finest hospital building London has,
A bust of Hunter underneath one wing.

Drive through the underpass – you miss a lot.

The Museum of British Transport (Clapham)

If train-spotters are voyeurs (who see their love in action)
Then a Transport Museum is a collection of dirty
    postcards,
Static and involving the exercise
Of the imagination only.

This is most true of the prints and the pictures,
Less so of the models; least of the life-size specimens.

The models are beautifully made –
The B Type omnibus (1910),
A Trolley-Bus of 1931,

Shillibeer's first omnibus, that ran
From Marylebone to the City
On 4 July 1829,
A real Independence Day for Public Transport.
G. F. Train's Horse Tram Car (1861)
Preserves the elegance of horse-drawn coaches.
Largest and most impressive
The First Class Coach EXPERIENCE
(Liverpool and Manchester Railway) –
A model made by a 16-year-old boy.
For us, and Freud, and Tennessee Williams
Only perhaps what we had expected.

Upstairs – a Ceremonial Wheelbarrow
'Used by Lord Palmerston in turning the first sod'
In the construction of the Andover and Redbridge
    Railway,
20 September 1859.
Dark wood, and grand enough for any drawing-room.

Walk on
Past fittings, lanterns, crests
Worn by proud engines like the figureheads
On sailing ships. Some smooth Victorian painting,
Where ladies in crinolines converse with gentlemen
In the upholstered salon set on wheels
Behind the Iron Horse.

Then out. This was a day★
When 'Small Exhibits' only were on view.
But as a treat, to satisfy the fans,
A guide conducted us into a huge garage,
Fit setting for the gems of the collection –
The old originals, the genuine thing.
All real (except a replica of the 'Rocket',
Coupled however to true rolling stock).

Trams of nostalgia! So lately with us, now
One with the Giant Tortoise, Dodo and Great Auk.

★ Early in 1963, before the whole Museum was open to the public.

116

Locomotives unnaturally preserved,
As mammoths in their thick Siberian ice.

Note 1). A vintage tram of 1907,
Belonging to the Sheffield Corporation.
2). A horse tram, well-designed, before
They skyscrapered to tin collecting-boxes
For profitable fares.
Deserted they stand (and round them metal signs,
Platform ticket machines, slot machines for chocolate)
Bearing the advertising of the vanished brands,
Whose passengers are long in silent graves.
This is the final terminus. The burial ground
Of elephants that roared and trumpeted.

The little sawn-off double-decker buses,
Types K and S (1919 and '20)
Are most pathetic. More like toys
Than adult motor transport.
Here, under glass, the dog
That, stuffed, for years at Wimbledon Station
Collected for the blind – 'Wimbledon Nell' –
Looks as though it had been co-opted
From the Natural History Museum.
Faithful unto death, and knew its station
Better than most.
When one has Transport in one's blood
One can never have enough.
Disregard the small meannesses of the bus queue,
The rush-hour madness. Guilty conductresses.
Take the broader view:
How one can sit behind a Chinaman
On a Routemaster going down Oxford Street
And, looking over his shoulder, note
That he is reading a pornographic book:

> 'Her face had that screwed-up look that the faces of
> middle-aged nymphomaniacs often have'.

A few stops later:

> ' "Where did you learn to drive like that?" I asked.
> "By watching the hot-rods on TV – but natch!" was the
> response.'

How, on a long journey, in one seat, the people change –
So that next time you look, man has moved on
From infancy to dim old age; or else flashed back
From middle age to giggling girlhood,
Changing his sex as well as occupation.

How once in 1941 at Swindon
A Troop of Light Anti-Aircraft lived on the junction,
Guarding the workshops from attack by air,
Lewis guns mounted on the highest buildings.
A brother officer and I (one pip each)
Lived in a Coronation Coach
(Edward VII's, was it?) in a siding.
Each morning for our early morning tea
The batman cadged hot water from some great Express,
Impatiently boiling. Its life-blood turned to steam.

Transport, like Time and Life, is seldom still
And well deserves the honour of Museums.

Strawberry Hill

*'a very proper habitation of, as it was the scene that inspired, the
author of* The Castle of Otranto'

HORACE WALPOLE

This was the home of a literary man,
The son of a Prime Minister,
Who wrote many letters to many people,
Including the Countess of Upper Ossory,

118

An urbane, intelligent collector
Who stimulated an architectural revolution
And refused to be introduced to Dr Johnson
Because of his 'blind Toryism and known brutality'.

About two thirds of what remains are Walpole's.
The later building – Lady Waldegrave's,
A rich, attractive Jewess, blossomed out
In entertaining and Victorian splendour.
The legend says that Shaw,
Visiting the house long after she was dead,
Refused to enter her Blue Breakfast Room.
He said it was 'vulgar'.

Perhaps the velvet ceiling put him off.

And certainly she favoured Tudor doorways,
While Walpole's ended in a Gothic point.
(She also pulled down Walpole's larger cloister.)

A Catholic Training College now inhabits
The Gothick structure Walpole slowly made
Out of his 'little play thing house'.
Purchased for fun in 1747.

Behind the nailed and Middle-Aged front door
His fantasy, involved with screens and ceilings,
With suits of armour, monks and chivalry,
With Dutch stained glass and golden antelopes
Set on white-painted stairs by Chippendale,
Ran headlong after all those 'last enchantments'.

Here everything is 'after' something else.

A chimneypiece from the tomb of John of Eltham,
A screen from the gates of the choir at Rouen,
A ceiling from the Queen's Dressing Room at Windsor,
One from the side aisles of the Henry VII Chapel,
A fine Adam fireplace in coloured marbles,
Pinched from the tomb of Edward the Confessor.

Outside, the 'Prior's Garden', where he wrote,
And further off, his Chapel in the Woods.

An ecclesiastical fireplace (of his own design?)
Was possibly his first attempt at Gothic.
Restored: the Entrance and the Sanctuary,
The Little Cloister. In the Gallery
Are portraits (copies) of the ruined boy,
Chatterton; Dryden; and Pope,
Whose villa's only one bus stop away;
Sir Robert – in one hand the Civil List.

The Gothic Library held two pink priests
The day I visited; extremely clean
And young and Irish in quiet-spokenness.
High ceiling. And the books
Encased in soaring woodwork – but elsewhere
The ceilings, all are low, most rooms are small.
Contrariwise, the Waldegrave rooms are large.

As old as I am (47) he
Dreamed up – and literally – the first
Great *roman noir*.
The bogusness of these surroundings still
Could bring to life that first surrealist prose,
Where a giant helmet kills the sickly son,
A foot in armour fills a moonlit room,
A giant's hand in armour haunts the stairs,
A hundred knights bear an enormous sword,
Three knights have one as spokesman for them all,
A giant speaks out and throws the castle down.

Majestic symbols. Now the little villas
Crowd round. The lawns no more run down
Clear to the Thames. The gesture has been made –
But what we make of it is up to us.

Pleasures of the Flesh (1966)

Anti-poem

A small talent, like a small penis,
Should not be hidden lightly under a bushel,
But shine in use, or exhibitionism.

Otherwise, how should one know it was there?

Like the extant portions of Sappho
These lines are fragments –
An arm, a foot, dredged from the warm Aegean.

They hint, nothing more, at other existences.

If they were written out in boring fullness
They would be as long as the lost plays of Euripides.

Money.

My wife has only two pairs of knickers
To bless herself with. The curse of Eve
Was always lack of clothes. See the
Frescoes in Italian churches, depicting
The primal Pair in Eden's innocence.

Money.

The children squall and fight on a wet, windy day,
Diminutive pirates.

Money.

At night comes home
The sour-faced husband.

Literature.

At the Royal Court and at the Arts: two 'modern' plays
Set in the bogs, the waste land, old backyards:
My Old Man's a Dustbin and
What A Way To Do Wee-Wee!

Literature.

Little Red Riding Hood – grandmother to
A small bed-wetting wolf.

Literature.

Critics. Blind dogs
Leading the blind.

Literature.

A large proportion of letters to the Press
Are written by lunatics.
Lost poets, they sadistically pollute
Reams of defenceless paper.

But what has all this to do with the Royal Family?

You may well ask!

Serious Matters

A thin girl with an Earl's Court cleft
Has promised me remission of my sins.
I can't afford to die. My family need me.
What would they do if I suddenly stopped earning?

That bowler-hatted major, his face is twitching,
He's been in captivity too long.
He needs a new war and a tank in the desert.

The fat legs of the typists are getting ready
For the boys and the babies. At the back of my mind
An ant stands up and defies a steam-roller.

Striptease

They sit round us, hot from the Motor Show, these
   imagists.
They'll carry home a pack of coloured snaps
To be fingered over when the wife is lying asleep.
The young pink nipples, not yet stained dark
By maternity. The small patch of fur
That brings the eye down, makes long legs seem short,
Disturbing the centre of gravity.

The frantic metal music
Slices our head-tops like a breakfast egg.
Young girls. Old routine. A business
Like any other. Everything shakes like a jelly.
Oral or phallic, here the law keeps us visual.
The eyes devour – but are soon satisfied.
After a time you can get very tired of chicken
(Though they'll never believe that, back on the farm).

Wanting Out

They're putting Man-Fix on my hair. And through the
   window
Comes a naked woman with a big whatnot. Oops! I'm
   away
To a country where the fantasies can be controlled.
Modestly I want to live, modestly. Where the Herr
   Baron
Takes an Eiswein from the cellar, cradles it gently
In the tiny frozen hands of an echt Deutsch Mimi.

123

Where the quiet roebuck surround the hunting lodge,
Where the peasants, if they wanted, could shave with
  their hats.

Take me down to a Lustschloss in the year 1900,
Give me tea on the lawn of a vicarage garden,
Put me in a punt with all my little girl friends,
Let the dreams grow into the leafy sex-books.
I want a magnifying glass and a knowledge of Coptic
And a box in the British Museum for the last
  performance of Hamlet.

S.F. (Vienna, 1901)

I am at the height of my powers.
My brain like a searchlight penetrates darkness
And sometimes the whole landscape is lit
By a blinding flash of unlooked-for insight.
I have achieved considerable success
As an interpreter of dreams.
I have solved the riddle of the Sphinx.
I am beginning to be recognized by my colleagues
And I have written a book that shall stand unaltered
For fifty years. The last word
On a complicated subject.

I have overcome my fear of train journeys,
My occasional dread of dying.
I am free to travel and explore.
My life is quiet (but the work is rewarding)
And my wife and family exist in my love.
My pleasures are simple. Wine, but no spirits.
Twenty cigars a day. An infrequent
Visit to the opera – but Mozart only.
In my opinion *The Magic Flute*
Is not to be compared to *Don Giovanni* –
The story is such rubbish.

Money is important. And at last I have enough
To devote myself to what I have to do
Without the time-consuming chores that pay the rent.
I am ambitious, a pioneer, but contented.

In and Out the Dusty Bluebells

'In and out the dusty bluebells'.
A children's game, a singing dance,
Rite of an urban Spring in wired-off playgrounds,
Clear voices dancing over traffic sounds.

'Tap-tap-tap on Someone's shoulder:'
With childishly expectant menace
The phrase stands up, and round it they all dance;
An antic frieze of children, they advance

Into a sinister future; where no rhymes
Hold up the threatening English sky,
Where clouds no bigger than a man's dark hand
Hold darker rain than they can understand.

Short Time

She juliets him from a window in Soho,
A 'business girl' of twenty.
He is a florid businessman of fifty.
(Their business is soon done.)

125

He, of a bright young man the sensual ghost,
Still (in his mind) the gay seducer,
Takes no account of thinned and greying hair,
The red veins webbing a once-noble nose,
The bushy eyebrows, wrinkles by the ears,
Bad breath, the thickening corpulence,
The faded, bloodshot eye.

This is his dream: that he is still attractive.

She, of a fashionable bosom proud,
A hairstyle changing as the fashions change,
Has still the ageless charm of being young,
Fancies herself and knows that men are mugs.

Her dream: that she has foxed the bloody world.

When two illusions meet, let there not be a third
Of the gentle hypocrite reader prone to think
That he is wiser than these self-deceivers.

Such dreams are common. Readers have them too.

Tittle-tattle of an Emotional Dwarf

Fantasy I

I in my frigged and gold-laced fuckcoat,
She in her tulle. I in my executioner's outfit,
She in her naughty Victorian hoops.

Fantasy II

A great critic lies stranded like a whale
On caviare pebbles of a champagne sea.
All literature round him shrieks and passes
With the derisive defiant cry of a seagull.

126

Fantasy III

The literary life. A dishy young poet
Talks to a very queer fish with a chip on his shoulder.
Butch Lesbians applaud.

Fantasy IV

In the evening we came to the land of No-Feeling
Where not even the dripping Chinese tears
Could wear away the stone, or Faith move mountains.
In the dark solitude we tethered our bric-a-brac
By that never-to-be-forgotten shore.

Fantasy V

The office lies quiet like an old-fashioned battlefield
With only the cleaners still scavenging for paper.
One thwarted, solitary telephone
Rings with the message that will never be delivered.
But there is a time-bomb ticking in the basement.

Fantasy VI

The children are playing with the swings and the
    roundabout
In a hot unbelievable summer
When suddenly the sun explodes with disaster,
Language dies, and the words
Go dim for ever.

Barbary

I pace the Fourth Floor like a quarter deck,
My windows square portholes on the sailing traffic,
My executive suite littered with charts.
From raids on the surrounding country
I bring back the new business
Sailing close, close to the wind.

I am surrounded by captured beauties,
The sexy secretaries come mincing in,
In it for the money.
And this is also the Good Ship Venus
Where fantasies are playing in the rigging
Like St Elmo's Fire.

I shall have a memo sent to all the staff
Prohibiting collections for those who leave
To go to other agencies.
I shall bank a good many thousands
This year. I shall stop my ears
When they fire an old copywriter from a cannon.
After all, I am an alert, brisk trader –
And everyone can recognize the Jolly Roger.

The Middle Years

Between the pale young failure
And the bloated purple success
Lie the works on the life of the dahlia
Or the shrewd financial guess.

Between the love and the yearnings
And the fat indifference of age
Lie the greatly increased earnings
And the slick best-selling page.

Between the romantic lover
And the sordid dirty old man
Lies the fruitful wasted lifetime
Of the years that also ran.

Dream of a Slave

I want to be carried, heavily sedated,
Into a waiting aircraft.
I want to collapse from nervous exhaustion.
I want to bow my head like Samson
And bring down with me
The ten top advertising agencies.

I want to see the little bosses
Vanish in the limelight like harmless fairies.
I want the pantomime to be over,
The circus empty.

I want what is real to establish itself,
My children to prevail,
To live happy ever after
In this world that worships the preposterous.

It is better to be a scribe
Than hacking in the salt-mines,
Heaving the building blocks.
Everybody wants to be a scribe.

But I want out. I want non-existence,
A passive dream, a future for my children.

The Back Streets of Fulham

Nobody knows very much about
The people who live in these rows of little houses.
They are mysterious. There are some respectable
    criminals.
Some pay lip service. Some are outright wild.
It is even suspected that witches are worshipped.
The women are up to their eyes in folklore.

The wars start in the boredom.
Like mushrooms growing in cellars
They push up through the darkness, packed with
  violence.
If anything were known, it would disgust the
  neighbours,
The married women are genteel and may be neglected.
A husband knows that if he were a Roman Emperor
He could force a slave to suck him.
You could torture him, and he would never admit it,
For if such things were known, they would disgust the
  neighbours.

Nothing is known. It's all painted over
With do-it-yourself and efficient repair work.
When it cracks and the wars get out
The 'small public for poetry'
Is amused and disgusted.
And, it may be, dead.

78s

First come the Twenties. The jogtrot rhythms
Of the Savoy Orpheans; Paul Whiteman;
Yearning saxophones, ragtime pianos. Jack Hylton;
With the genteel slightly Cockney vocalists.
Arrangements that close with a cowbell.

On the white body of the dog is lettered
My mother's initial. These were nursery days
For an over-shy, mother-fixated boy
Proud of a snake-clasped belt.

An old music. The house is now pulled down.
I know exactly where the scratches come
In jazz that moves me like the poetry
Of Pasolini (I have 'grown up' too).

And later, in my teens, I knew (and know)
Where the unnatural breaks came in the symphonies.
Beginning with Beethoven I worked my way up
At 78 (and 80) revolutions per minute.

The speeds change, the nostalgia builds up
Into a fury of neglected life.
Looking back, it all seems very simple.

Climacteric

When the love goes out of the act
   And the brightness out of the eye,
When the thriller turns into a tract
   And the roaring bars run dry,
When life is sage, and dull, and moral –
That is the time to take up the quarrel.

When the heat goes out of the sun
   And the colour out of the flower,
When there's nothing new to be done
   And the kisses are turning sour,
When good men's bones change into coral –
That is the time to take up the quarrel.

When the time runs out of the clock
   And the music stops in the band,
When the crowing forsakes the cock
   In silence throughout the land,
When the roses leave the mourning laurel –
That is the time to take up the quarrel.

Lepidoptera

The butterflies are leaving.
Brown and drab, they have it –
Industrial melanism.
The beauties are rare,
Delicately sipping
You sometimes see
A Pot-Bellied Purple
With a primping White Lady
In a flower-banked
Expense account restaurant.

The nettles are tidied away,
Disturbing the life cycle.
It's goodbye to the Red Director,
The Diamond Duchess
And *Meretrix superpicta*.

An Old Song

For those who fancy themselves
A big let-down is coming.
It may be the work of the elves
Or the Phantom Drummer drumming.
But however it goes – it goes,
The gorgeous eye, the nearly perfect nose.

There's a magic that works and works
And charms away the talents,
Like the infidel Terrible Turks
That overthrow young gallants.
Yes, however it goes – it goes,
The mighty line, the dedicated prose.

The Loves and Cupids too
Where the lovely bosom is heaving
Find other work to do
And cry 'We must be leaving!'
Still – however it goes – it goes,
The girl in flower, the folded summer rose.

A Secular Saint?

Tell
How his father taught him to shoot
Rabbits straight from the shoulder.
How he went on the great Educational Pilgrimage,
Suffered under Caesar and Cicero
And was unjustly beaten.
How he underwent the terrifying boredom of war,
The tantalizing sorrows of impotence
When every girl was a mantrap.
Tell
Of the five years' analysis in the wilderness,
The marriage and the two children,
The crowded flats in unfashionable districts,
The continual spreading of The Word,
The three books of poetry in the British Museum.
Tell
How he was sacked in the takeover city,
How he discovered Italy and a foolproof method
Of killing time in North London,
How his goodness was never recognized,
How he died and was translated.
Tell.

A Christmas Message

In the few warm weeks
   before Christmas and the cold
the Toy Department is organized like a factory floor.
They're using epitaxial planar techniques
   in the labs. The toys are sold
and there's rationalized packaging and at the hot core

of the moving mass
   sweats a frost-powdered Father Christmas
in a red dressing-gown and an off-white beard.
What he wants most is a draught Bass.
   On a dry Hellenic isthmus
Zeus was a god who was equally hated and feared;

England is a Peloponnese
   and Father Christmas a poor old sod
like any other, autochthonous. Who believes
in the beard and the benevolence? Even in Greece
   or Rome there is only a bogus God
for children under five. Those he loves, he deceives.

The Law Allows Cruel Experiments on Friendly Animals

I don't feel very well. I'm the head of a rebellious
Family, where everybody's shouting. Shall we ever find
The particular island where we can all be happy?
Put up the huts, shoot the goats, plant the corn.
But I'm not Mr Fix-It, the Handyman Husband,
I'm not forceful or even a Leader.

Youth is the happiest drunkenness. Sober, we see
The problems that, young, we never guessed at.
No longer drinking black champagne with blondes,
Spinning with them the desert island discs,
And bathing naked in the sparkling deep blue water.

If I hit a child in anger I feel ashamed.
Weak kings are subject to flashes of temper,
Ruled by their emotions. So are strong ones.
We're in a test tube, say the theologians.

Someone is watching. His tremendous eye
Glares at us, held up to the light.
We are a few decimals in a book.

Nobody can get out, all our behaviour
Goes down against a date and time of day.

He'll publish his results – and maybe soon.

Witchcraft

Last night you were being ridden by a governess,
A tall dark girl. Her transparent blouse
Showed the fat round nipples – all she wore.

She rocked on your pintle like a rocking-horse winner,
Squeezing so tight with elegant long thighs.
After five minutes, you began to change.

There were sulphurous fumes. Your sex curved inwards,
Your bosoms began to slowly plump and swell,
Your hair kaleidoscoped to new dispositions.

At last, in your plump thighs she triumphed,
With her new member and a hunting cry,
Whipping you towards the Sunday papers.

The Good Money

You were a success. You were pouring
Out showers of gold in the Directors' Lavatory.
Everybody smiled as you passed down the corridor.
Rimbaud was left standing in his Gallic *conneries*.
Lighting a Gauloise, you went into a meeting.
Your voice was firm. The good money
Rested smoothly on some upper-class vocables.

Never throw it after bad. When the crows' feet
Walk round your eyes, ready to peck,
You will need it. In that field you sowed
Where the little voices come up fresh
From the dark ground: children.

You will need it. Though dark birds
Are pecking at the seeds
You can buy them off. A scarecrow
You may be. But the money keeps its virtue.

Warm to the Cuddly-toy Charm of a Koala Bear

It's dull in the huge palace where I live.
The basement's stuffed with seduced handkerchiefs.
A global war would do, or a new revolution,
To dissipate the gloom of early spring.
Everything's wet – but most the men and women –
Outside, where the long rains drip from the trees.

I'm lonely. There's nobody here but me.
The vintages go round and round in my head,
A merry-go-round I suppose I ought to call it.
Cobwebbed bottles and a thousand dirty glasses,
One in my hand.

Enthusiasm belongs *outside* – and mostly it's bogus.
I live in a mood, with a boozer's conk,
I'm no Prince Charming,
But I'm genuine, genuine, true to my dirty self.

Crossing the Bar

My ambition is to live to be eighty,
To die quiet, surrounded by branded goods,
In perfect harmony like Oxo and Katie,
In a gamekeeper's cottage in the woods.

I want to drift towards my last Bournvita,
My children happy and a room of books
With their lined agony to make comfort sweeter,
Remembering the girls and their good looks.

137

I want all my employment to have been gainful,
My life to be free of angst and nuclear war,
And my last illness not to be terribly painful,
As I float in towards that distant shore.

Spring

As I went down the High Street, it was pouring out of
   me.

Got some Dad's Cuban Cookies at Victor Value,
The children like them. The words began
To arrange themselves in my head. I shall never be a
   warbler.
Big clots, I can't suffer them gladly.
The pain and the words are like a sinus headache,
Always waiting, in the background, to take over.

Send up a few hymns to Joy,
I'm natural in my uplift. It's not all grey,
There's more colour than Greene has ever dreamed of.
Burying people in boxes is disgusting.
The client from out of town has a telephone as
   heart-throb
And his hand shakes as he begins to dial CUN 1234.

Secrets of the Alcove

Quand' ero paggio . . .
I must have been adorable (I was certainly stupid).
The then Provost of King's
Chased me down two flights of stairs at a party.
Nearly twenty years later
A girl ran a hundred yards down a platform in Paris
In high-heeled shoes to kiss me.

All answered with a coldish heart.

Who has not had their little successes?
Inner absorption breaks into a rash of pride,
Shows in the visible signs of bad behaviour.
I regret my calmness in the face of love,
It bothers me like an unopened letter
Returned to sender, that now will never be read.

Disturbing Incident at the Recreation Ground

Put in a lot of green. This is a child's picture.
Draw in the swings and the top-hung roundabout.
The sun beaming in the upper left-hand corner.
Scene set? Right. Now walk on a
Scraggy-legged grey-haired female loony

Pushing a pram. She moves bossy to the roundabout
Hung with assorted children, varied age and sexes.
It stops. She harangues my daughter
Who blushes at being singled out, so public and for what?
Keeping her feet on the ground, as I learn later,

139

While this hag is speaking. She collects two little girls.
A grandmother or mad old auntie?
Moving away they smile at me, abashed.
She bashes, now, the baby. Hard strokes with hands
For thumb-sucking or just for being a baby?

Draw in the baby (very small). To me
She turns two glaring spectacles. I glare back.
'*You* know!' she says. '*You* know!'
'I don't!' I shout, as hostile as I can,
But she moves off in triumph. Well she may!

Her madness sparks a madness deep in me.
I want to slam her like a tennis ball,
Smash her. My education tells me No.
But I am full to bursting with a rage
You'd find in textbooks. And it will not go.

The Dirtypot Decider

In my mind there's a Dirtypot Decider.
It comes from science fiction and the twenty-first century –
If you feed in a plus it comes out a minus;
When a digital computer really pulls its finger out
You get something of the same effect.
I use it on art and unsympathetic people,
It's like crossing oneself when one passes a nun in the
    street.
It combats black magic; it's a total negation.

It keeps me incommunicate and silent at meetings,
Makes me a silent drinker and a laugher at nothings,
Prevents me from joining in when the fun is other
    people's,

Gives me adventure stories to read, garbles fashion,
Plays curious tricks with time; so I find myself saying
'Do you remember the Beatles?
But that was thirty years ago!' It's no respecter
Of places either. China already has India,
Holiday resorts march backwards
And the debs are crowding the seafront at Clacton.
Prophetic, really. On art
Its workings are never so certain.
It hasn't yet made up its mind
About *Caro nome*.

To the Virgins, to Make the Most of Time

Now, listen.
I want you new girls, every morning,
To sprinkle an oral contraceptive on your corn flakes.
I've got my eye on you, I want to marry into you,
To fluffle you up a bit, then dive right in
Smoothly.

I'm a potentate. Don't be too girlish,
Don't bother to name those breasts Maria and Matilda
Or call your favourite ball-point Clarence.
None of this interests me. Wear a bra if you want to
And panties if you want to. It's immaterial.

In this establishment, my will holds.
If you are naughty, there's a cane in the corner.
I don't believe in God, I can do what I like.

Every morning there's naked bathing
And then at least two hours of horse-back riding
To promote a well-developed, rounded bottom.

The only lessons are Theory and Practice;
All my instructresses are big harsh Lesbians.
So watch your step.

Night Duty begins at eight. A roster will be published.
My favourite girls have a really marvellous time.
I hope you will be happy here. Never forget
These are the best years of your life.
Go to your rooms now. Goodnight.

Zeg's Fire Stick Spits Tremendous Power . . .

('Now I am Emperor!')

Hot stocking-tops! The frenzy of fat thighs!
The feminine smells that batter perfumes down!
The furry furbelows of pretty girls!

Male fantasies start at five, grow fierce at fifty.
The air goes hard around the sexual objects,
Shapes into the big attacking instruments.

The boys are brave and confidently shooting,
Destroying all enemies with water pistols.
From that destruction comes the later love,

Tender aggression of the animals,
Love bites, nipped nipples; throbbing soft but hard
The overriding urging of the gun.

After the Sex-bomb

The soppy scruffy girls are coming.
They wade over the pavements, full of glottal stops,
I am the last man in the world. They want me.
Desires bloom like the flora in a huge vagina,
Bacterial. In those dark red depths
Lie serfdom, nights in the sulphur mines.

That bomb, they should never have dropped it.
We could see it coming for months – for years.
Perhaps an illiterate typist made a mistake in spelling;
They were so anti-male they hardly cared,
But now breaks loose a dangerous rank and file
Rampantly female, disobeying directives.

They smell me out. From under my flat stone
They harry me into the open, into the streets
Where still, and cold, the poor male bodies lie
(Under the larva guns a son died too).
Hundreds are lynching me with their tongues.
They're closing in. They won't take me alive.

A Warning

A little fat genius is sitting there,
Small head, big belly.
A lot of brains under a little hair,
His sex organs – smelly.

That's the way it is with a genius,
He's always a bit odd.
He may have girl friends, grow zinnias,
But he thinks he's a god.

Don't expect ordinary behaviour,
Or a guide to morals.
A genius is never a Saviour –
He only looks to his laurels.

Tiger Rag

Make way for Lord Cyril Connolly, Sir Gavin Ewart.
Rein in that elephant. Track the sleek jungle beasts
That make us sport in London's dense square miles.
I'm a Native Prince, and interested in
Miss Lust of Letchworth. My chocolate fingers hold
Her future in my hands.

If literature were all, I might be rich.
If all the poems were strung out like pearls
I'd be a Maharajah in the sleep
Of all the beauties in the typing pools.

It won't work. The ruby gleam in Guinness
Is due to barley, so the copy says.
What's precious fades under the office lights.

War-time

A smooth bald head, a large white body.
No trace of pubic hair.
Raw, fretted and frayed by that rocky coast,
The flesh where the nipples were.

A woman drowned in war-time
On the Ligurian shore.
An Italian shouted *'E una femmina!'*
There seemed to be nothing more.

A suicide? A Resistance girl
From La Spezia floated down,
A murderee from Genoa?
The coast road into the town

Led me back to Livorno
And a British Army tea.
The war got hold of the women,
As it got hold of me.

Twenty years later, in the offices,
The typists tread out the wine,
Pounding with sharp stiletto heels,
Working a money mine.

It's a milder war, but it is one;
It's death by other means.
And I'm in the battle with them,
The soft recruits in their teens.

Eight Awful Animals

1 The Dildo

The Dildo is a big heavy cumbersome sort of bird,
Supposed extinct for many years but its voice is often
  heard
Booming and blasting over the marshes and moors
With the harsh note of Lesbos and the great outdoors.
The Dildo wears tweed skirts and Twenties
  elastic-thighed knickers
And smokes black cheroots and still calls films 'the
  flickers'.
It wears pork-pie hats and is really one of the boys,
It has initiated many pretty girls into forbidden joys.

It has an eye-glass in one eye, and its bad-taste jokes are
  myriad,
Such as the one about Emily Bronte's Last Period,
And a good many others that are best left unsaid,
Buried in the old laughter, as the dead bury the dead.

The Dildo is quite frankly worshipped by some members
  of the community,
Who consider that even its name cannot be taken in vain
  with impunity
As it hops heavily about on its one wooden leg –
But most real Nature-lovers think it should be taken
  down a peg.

2 The Masturbon

The Masturbon is a sort of dirty great elephant and it lives
  in a cave.
It's terribly keen on Do-It-Yourself, but it never bothers
  to shave.

It spends all its time reading ads and clipping the coupons
  out
And addressing them to itself. It knows what life's all
  about.
It has five spin-dryers and a twin-tub and a dream house
  and a Teasmade
And a Special Offer beach ball, and a bucket and spade
But it keeps them all at the top of a very high mountain
A long way away, too far for checking or counting.
It reads the *Daily Express*, and nothing in its life is shared.
When it dreams, it dreams in French and often shouts
  'Merde!'
At the sexiest parts of the dreams. It is very close to God,
Though its personal habits to you or me would seem
  unmentionable – or at least very odd.

The Masturbon, I must tell you, is a perfect
  hermaphrodite.
It sleeps during the day and comes into its own at night.
It loves dirty photographs and paws them all over
And it reads whole Police Stations-full of dirty books.
  It's really in clover
At a big swinging striptease. The music and the tits
Send it into ecstasies and mild epileptic fits.
In fact, like George the Fourth who was known as
  Georgy-Porgy,
The Masturbon's life is one long delicious orgy.

3 The Panteebra

The Panteebra rhymes with zebra and is a very slinky
  cockteaser,
She goes round playing 'Let's do it!' on a little transistor
  radio. But if you try to seize her
She will quickly vanish, leaving behind a very tantalizing
  smell
That will stay on your clothes and make your wife
  suspect that all is not well.

147

This animal is only female and her body is white
With black stripes over teats and crotch. She comes out at
  night
Like a girl in bra and pantees, to solicit married men
And lure teenage boys into bestiality now and again.

Like other forms of life the Panteebra is quite
  parthenogenetic
And goes round stirring up lust till the men become
  frenetic.
Then she quietly retires and lays a sex-mad baby.
If you're unlucky you will see a Panteebra one day –
  maybe.

4 *The Fux*

The Fux lives in a dark hole with a bush at the mouth,
In the Martini Season it always travels South.
Its member has stood for Parliament several times
And it goes about committing the most interesting sex
  crimes.
Its tail is a small but efficient whip, used for flagellation,
And it has written several short treatises on the Art of
  Fornication.
It is highly oral and it goes about licking people all over,
Which is very beneficial and relaxing like the air of
  Folkestone or Dover.

The Fux works very hard manufacturing testosterone
Which it guards as jealously as a dog with a bone
Though it often gives it free to the very prettiest girls –
In exchange for the usual and a snip from their hidden
  curls.
It lives in Earl's Court and Knightsbridge and drives fast
  cars
And can be seen laughing its head off in the most
  expensive bars.

It wears no clothes except a big hairy false tail,
And the female wears only foundation garments such as
 excite the male.
In country districts it is quite well distributed
And thick woods and high places to it are very suited.

The Fux can never be hunted. It's too far ahead of its
 time.
Some day we may catch up with it, when we drag
 ourselves and the censors out of our primeval slime.

5 The Stuffalo

The Stuffalo is full of the most tremendous energy –
It was once very nearly tamed by an Indian called
 Bannerjee.
It rushes frantically about in suburban streets,
Bursts into the houses and sweeps the wives off their feet.
It is a greater rapist and seducer than the milkman or any
 commercial traveller,
When it sees an upright woman it is a great leveller.
It goes like a whirlwind through the semi-dets
Coming straight to the point (it never sweet-talks or
 pets).
Unlike the fridge in the ads, it is *all* moving parts
And it treats respectable housewives like a lot of old tarts.

It would have knocked Boadicea right off her chariot,
It 'betrays the trust of women' like Judas Iscariot,
Paying no attention to their white gloves and elaborate
 hats
And their nylons and their cups of tea. There's a strong
 smell of sprats
After it has passed through the lounge and laid them all
 low,
As they lie helpless and satisfied in the warmth of the
 Cosiglow.

149

But afterwards, when they get around to adjusting their
   dress,
They suddenly feel as though they couldn't care less.

6 The Word-Bird

The Word-Bird knows that everybody in Britain is
   frightened to death of *words,*
So it flies up to a great height and drops them on people
   like turds.
It always chooses large assemblies where all sexes are
   present
And some of the words it lets fall are very far from
   pleasant
To the Puritan ears they strike with a loud thud –
And among the genteel (for this reason) its name has
   always been mud.

When the first four-letter words float down you should
   see the commuters quail,
As it chants them confidently and firmly on a descending
   scale.
They shake the Church and Chapel-going housewives to
   the tits
And the policemen are rocked in their boots as each hot
   syllable hits
And knocks their helmets sideways. Each Magistrate and
   Judge
Looks as though he is choking in a sea of hot chocolate
   fudge,
With bursting purple cheeks and a heart-pounding
   waistcoat
And big bulging eyes like a lecherous old goat.

The Word–Bird eats dictionaries and any printed matter
Sufficiently scarifying to make the crowds scatter –
But it also has several medical terms up its sleeve
And their effect on those who understand them you
   would scarcely believe,

Words that excite with a wild music, like 'penilingism'
and 'cunnilingus',
That pierce the brain like the disturbing notes of Charlie
Parker or Charlie Mingus.

And each night when the day is over the Word-Bird
returns to the nest,
And teaches its chickens a few more juicy dirty words
before it retires to rest.

7 *The Insex*

The Insex is like a large black beetle, it is a professional
voyeur
And a consummate actor and a most terrible liar.
It is coloured a very dark clerical grey, with a white
collar,
It is a prize creep and worships the Almighty Dollar.
On luxury liners at night it can often be seen in the
rigging,
Estimating the co-efficient of friction and the volume of
the gin-swigging.
It is very well up in Debrett and knows how often the
Queen Regnant,
While actually sitting on the throne, has been made
pregnant,
It can sometimes be heard in the summer woods
interfering with a minor.
It has written two plays called *The Amazing Dr Clitoris*
and *Victoria Vagina*.

The Insex has a frightening call like an air-raid siren,
It hates all good poetry, but especially Byron.
It loves probing teenagers and telling them about their
lives
And explaining to husbands why they don't get on with
their wives,
In its time it has written a lot of articles for the *Sunday
Express*

151

And it likes nothing better than obliging the *noblesse*.
It lives in a little incense-burner's cottage by a cute
  wayside shrine,
Offering up the sins of the world (including yours and
  mine).
It has been sex-mad and bosom-crazy since the day of its
  birth.
And this is the peculiar life of the Insex here on earth.

8 *The Spirokeet*

The Spirokeet is a terrifying brightly-coloured bird with
  a flesh-tearing beak,
It spends a lot of time in the palm trees squawking and
  spouting Greek.
It can curdle the blood-stream and shut teenagers up in
  clinics,
It reads Ibsen in the original and its friends are all old
  cynics.
It mocks unmarried mothers whose parts are absolutely
  brimming with VD
And the effects of its attacks are not very nice to see.

Its loud cry can be heard in the woods throughout the
  mating season,
When the boys and girls get together for a very
  traditional reason.
You may have only a second before finished the act of
  love,
And you look up to see it chuckling, quite near, on a
  branch above.
Once it gets its claws into your brain, you will probably
  go mad,
And not be able to distinguish between the Good and the
  Bad.

Some say the Spirokeet is a moral bird, with an acute
　　sense of Sin.
Others say it is a complete idiot and doesn't know where
　　to begin.

Office Friendships

Eve is madly in love with Hugh
And Hugh is keen on Jim.
Charles is in love with very few
And few are in love with him.

Myra sits typing notes of love
With romantic pianist's fingers.
Dick turns his eyes to the heavens above
Where Fran's divine perfume lingers.

Nicky is rolling eyes and tits
And flaunting her wiggly walk.
Everybody is thrilled to bits
By Clive's suggestive talk.

Sex suppressed will go berserk,
But it keeps us all alive.
It's a wonderful change from wives and work
And it ends at half past five.

On Seeing a Priest Eating Veal

(A Sectarian Hymn)

Put down that calf, thou Man of Flesh,
Put down that veal, thou Bloody Man,
God's creatures are the wheels that mesh,
And He will eat *you*, when He can.

Unfrock thyself, thou Man of Blood,
Thou art but meat, and so are these,
And have been since before the Flood;
Go down on thy unbasted knees

And ponder on Eternal Fires
And battered fish and slaughtered lambs.
Restrain thy animal Desires,
Be cured – or God will smoke thy hams.

A Handful of People

1 Sandra

What bosom tapped me on the shoulder?
           Sandra.
What blooming beauty made me feel much older?
           Sandra.
What sweet Italian English made me flinch,
Then made a man of me, yes every inch?
           Sandra.

My eyes! Who dazzled them and pulled the wool over?
           Sandra.

Whose nippled joys were born to swell a pullover?
                    Sandra.
Who lives in stereo (and I in mono)?
Who is the most beautiful Bondonno?
                    Sandra.

Queen of the bus queues! Saint of the dark glasses!
                    Sandra.
Teetering on murderous heels, aloof she passes!
                    Sandra.
Sweet poison, secret, venomous as Borgias,
In young sophistication O how gorgeous!
                    Sandra.

2 Weaslingham

You can't get hold of Weaslingham. He's slimy.
If he lived Stateside he'd be known as The Slimy Limey.
Let me put it on record, as firmly as (once) Thomas
    Edison:
He makes his living writing white lies about patent
    medicine.
The lies start black, and are discussed until they are grey.
They are usually off-white when they see the light of day.

But you couldn't make Weaslingham with anyone's
    scissors and paste,
Because he's a double-dyed villain and at least
    triple-faced.
He's an absolute backslider and obsequious to the
    Directors,
While to juniors and equals he's less kind than
    vivisectors.
In fact he spent years torturing his immediate inferior,
Saying 'I've saved you from the sack' (he felt good, and
    superior).

155

Weaslingham started off being trained as a missionary
In the far-off days before the world was nuclear or
    fissionary.
He could sidle into people's consciences in a way that
    would make you quite ill,
You could swallow it all without guessing the bitterness
    of the pill.
I don't believe in Hell or the cauldrons that seethe and
    bubble,
But if there were such a place, Weaslingham would slip
    into it without the least trouble.

3 Jerzy

Jerzy is an owl-faced Pole who needs very little
    headroom –
But he makes a lot of headway, particularly in a
    bedroom.
He was married to, but is now separated from, a
    charming person;
And all their relationship did was to steadily worsen.
For his wife had been married before and had a teenage
    daughter
And this daughter had a sixteen-year-old friend, like
    bricks and mortar
They were very close, and one night the friend stayed
And slept like a sixteen-year-old in the spare bed.

Now Jerzy's wife was pregnant (of their second son)
And it was obvious to Jerzy that if he wanted any fun
He must get down into the basement where the chick was
    sleeping;
So down the stairs in his pyjamas he was stealthily
    creeping
With his thick-rimmed spectacles and an owl-like look
Like a solid bird of prey in an illustrated bird book.

156

But Jerzy's wife slept badly, she was near her term,
She woke up big and ponderous like a good-looking
  pachyderm.
There was no sign of Jerzy or his sleeping head,
He was after that teenager (as she afterwards repeatedly
  said)
AND AT THAT VERY MOMENT HE WAS TRYING TO GET
  INTO HER BED.

There were two very loud and penetrating screams.
And now Jerzy realizes that teenagers are strictly for
  dreams.

4 Ian

It was on the hot dusty airfields of dry North Africa
That I first met Ian, who should have been a white slave
  trafficker.
He was full of tarting experience and when we landed at
  Napoli
He had scope to display his talents widely and happily.
We were both in the Artillery, and for tins of corned beef
We could shoot any girl in sight. It was beyond belief.
There were notices up saying WARNING. *New Type of
VD* –
You could buy more than you bargained for with your
  pounds of sugar and tea.

Dark sluttish beauties, they carried all before them,
Dirt outlining their bosoms where they wore them
Bulging their ragged frocks; and over the beds
Pictures of The Sacred Heart, above their olive heads.

The priests were always giving them the old Red
  Warning.
But there's a world of difference between Saturday Night
  and Sunday Morning.

157

Ian went into Tanks and the Allied War Graves
     Commission,
Jeeping about North Italy without any inhibition
After the hot war. With a girl here and a girl there
Just spread out waiting for the Capitano to appear.
In 1946, demobilized, Ian went medical.
His views on marriage were always fairly heretical.
He examined the girl students. A heretic likes to choose.
He converted a lot of nurses. He had very strong views.

When Ian had qualified he lived in Bayswater
On the North side of Hyde Park where each erring
     daughter
Stood to be picked up, a fallen woman. With a little soap
     and water
He washed them in his room; he wasn't worried by
     delinquency.
All he wanted was the satisfaction of their close
     propinquency.
When Wolfenden came he signed on as a ship's doctor to
     Japan,
To find out what the girls of the Far East could offer a
     man.

His praise of the Japs amounted to a paean.
But since I've been married I've seen very little of Ian.

5 Ursula

Ursula came to England from Germany; a rather odd
     thing to do.
In her late twenties, blondeish, blue eyes; average height,
     looks, IQ.
Mousy and friendly, she worked in the same office as my
     wife
And once, creeping up behind her, nearly frightened her
     out of her life
By slapping her hard on the back. When my wife said
     'Ursula! Don't be such a bloody fool!'

158

She was seriously hurt. She didn't know how to play it
  cool.
She had an Office Enemy, who finally got her the sack.
She was willing and efficient – I don't need to play it
  back,
Everyone knows the crooked ways of Office Justice
Which is probably most unfair where the most protocol
  and lust is.

Ursula was a natural outsider who tried to come in from
  the cold.
She liked my wife, and bought a small toy St Bernard dog
  for my daughter, who was about a year old.
She took a few typing jobs, then decided for better or
  worse
To go to a London hospital and train as a nurse.
All this time she had a boy friend who was a merchant
  seaman,
Wouldn't marry her, and popped up from time to time
  like a pantomime demon.

Ursula liked being a nurse. She read the medical books
  (her character was serious)
But the effect on her mind was mainly deleterious.
She developed some nurse-like techniques of abortion,
  and under her bed
She kept in a bottle a small baby born dead,
Pinched from the Maternity Ward. She also began to
  worry
That she was changing her sex (which can't be done in a
  hurry)
And explained to my wife on the top of a bus how her
  clitoris was growing bigger,
Which must have caused a lot of embarrassment or at
  least a faint snigger.

But Ursula's medical career was cut short, because out of
  kindness one New Year's Eve
She did someone else's duty at the hospital, and didn't
  leave

159

For home until one in the morning. A drunken car
  mounted the pavement
In the deserted street; broke her back; and ended her
  earthly enslavement.

The moral of all this is: Never be accident-prone.
But if by any chance I find myself alone
In the nursery or (where the children have left it) in some
  other place
With that little St Bernard dog, I can't look it in the face.

Young

I'm a young giggle. Teenage. Sharp
Claws and an undulating tail,
Packaged in bright dreams of leather and teasing.
I like to make the boys excited
I love it when the cocks grow angry
My pulse jumps to the razor-fighting.

Their hands have run over me like mice
And I'm not mean, I let them have it.
Books like *The Woman* promise something different
But I can't spend my lifetime waiting.
The things you miss, you never get again.

My Mum and Dad know one word: Steady.
I'd rather mix it with a dozen boys,
Ice cream in different flavours. No one
Really wants vanilla all the time.

You split a coke, like on the telly,
And the two straws suck up your lifetime.
The sharing makes it quicker finished.

On your own you take the full flavour,
Get the longer, as-advertised pleasure.

I'll change when I change, but not before I do.

Pi-Dog and Wish-Cat

When Pi-Dog and Wish-Cat sat down for a meal,
His and Hers on their bowls, there was a great deal
For them both to pronounce on, deny and discuss.
Their words were all taped and have come down to us.

Pi-Dog said he believed in a Man In The Sky
Who would end the whole world in a flaming great fry
Most delicious for dogs (who of course would be
    spared),
And the bones of their enemies equally shared.

Wish-Cat said, purring, how Love was the thing
And was easily captured by using a ring;
How Love would in rapture squeak louder than mice
And live happy as dreams. And wasn't it nice?

When the meal was all over they both wanted more –
And Pi-Dog dragged Wish-Cat down onto the floor.
Pi-Dog bit hard and deep, and she clawed at his eyes.
Now they both of them sleep where it says HERE LIES.

Variation on a Theme of K. Amis

Sooner or later, most women poets
Get locked in a lavatory with God.
Quietly they knit their little poems,
Receptive and contemplative and sad.

They are seldom raped by imagination
Or highly excited or screaming for lovers
Or drunk with the mad, leopard-spotted phrases;
Domestic virtues fit them like loose covers.

Perhaps words come to women too easily,
Pouring out regardless like coffee or tea
Or like the uncritical fountains in Renaissance palaces?
Nobody values what is given away free.

Diary of a Critic

Had two poets for lunch. This afternoon
Got my teeth into a fat biography.
Went down quite well. I always try
To taste the pages, savour line by line,
Remember what Richards on a Cambridge blackboard
Slyly wrote out in his peculiar spelling.

Reviewing dulls the palate.

'Placed' a few contemporary writers.
Took Auden down a peg, moved up Lowell,
Established a new End of Term Order,
Prizes to Eliot Major, Betjeman Minor.

Several new scholarship boys are coming on.
Must be ready. Never be left behind,
A fuddy-duddy wound in a black gown.

Beyond the pleasure principle. No more enjoy.
Never get plastered on the fine new wine.
Mem. The Meaning of Meaning. Stand firm.

Variation on a Theme of A. Huxley

Some fat pigs are actually eating
And do not hesitate to name the parts:
Rumps, breasts and legs. It's revolting –
And done in the name of Science and the Arts.

They even describe the use of the instruments:
Knife, fork and spoon. It's bad for the Nation,
And can only lead to a terrible decadence
When they write a forbidden word like mastication.

See them revel in their beer and their beastliness,
Egged on by sherry, the bit between their teeth,
Ginned up for chambering and wantonness,
As round a hot frilled leg they garter a parsley wreath.

Manifesto

I'm Old Brown, sitting in an oak tree,
And all you little squirrels can bugger off.

As soon as I read the print-new poems
Of Raul Quintela I knew I was marked out
To be the ground plan of a giant palace,
The not inconsiderable architect of a school,
A prophet with honour in another country.

I take myself seriously. How can I not?
My world like Milton's, the mind is its own place.
I spin new silk under that mulberry tree
That shall be worn by future generations.
I chart my progress, ship and captain both,
Down the unfriendly coast, a whole new world –
Known by the names that *I* write on the map.

A War of Independence

Run up the flag. Fire a shot across their bows.
Pour the Coca-Cola into The Wash, get going
On a Boston Tea Party in reverse.
Or try a new Pearl Harbor: surprise attack.
Tell them they're *all* no good.
Frost, Crane, Cummings, Tate, Stevens, Ezra,
Berryman, Lowell; and most no-good of all
Walt Whitman (the faggot who burst into flame).

Make an honourable exception of Emily Dickinson –
After all, she was a lady.
Tell them the greatest all-American poem
Is 'Miniver Cheevy'.
Get those fat-bummed Marines
Across a barrel. Make it clear
An Independence Day is coming soon –
The Union Jack for ever!

A Partly Smoked Cigar

(Sleeve Note: SAGA XID *5216)*

When the King offered you a partly smoked cigar
You had to refuse. Though the Queen
Strongly urged you not to decline the honour.
You were a non-smoker. Nobody was offended.

So much for patronage. Great corporations
And agencies and potboilers pay the rent,
Expense accounts allow a little boozing.
It's not the Court of Spain. I'm not Rossini.
I wouldn't try to write a *Stabat Mater*.
There's probably nobody called Ferdinand
In the whole of the Arts Council.

Try me for pride. That partly smoked cigar
Is bitter smoking – down to the very end!

The Deceptive Grin of the Gravel Porters (1968)

The Black Box

As well as these poor poems
I am writing some wonderful ones.
They are all being filed separately,
nobody sees them.

When I die they will be buried
in a big black tin box.
In fifty years' time
they must be dug up,

for so my will provides.
This is to confound the critics
and teach everybody
a valuable lesson.

1 The Life

Gentlemen v. Players

They're playing Queer Croquet, Midget Cricket,
   High-Speed Golf.
The orange trees stand in tubs outside the tiny expensive
   mews houses.
Inside is so much taste the eyes feel sick.
Just what's their little game? There's money in it.
A fourth child, a third car, and Daddy gave her
Two houses for a wedding present.

I won't get in. I'm Lazarus the Leper,
Thrown out for poverty from their rich dives
Where even the jazz has a high social tone.

Back to the family; to keeping warm
In a flat full of unfashionable love,
To kisses ignorant of capital gains,
And Africa stuffed with the liberal nightmares.

Anniversary

We must keep out the animals, they're getting on top of
   us.
Book a twable for twoo. Often I'm wonderwing
How the simple lispers commemowate their love.

I can talk straight, my heart is stone-hard,
My nose has the bloom and the colour of the grape.
In my steel curtain of hostility

There are two little holes, no bigger
Than a child could stop by inserting a finger.
Kindness. I melt like a lolly

As six blue-green eyes keep the love standing.

Eternal Triangle

My left foot! It's serious.
It knows the ways of a man with a maid
And how the ways of God are equally mysterious,
It's outspoken and quite unafraid.

My right foot is gay, and swerving
After the pumping haunches; it will clench
Its toes in ecstasy when the drinks are serving.
It's frivolous and talks a little French.

Between my feet I live, so pulled both ways
I can't walk straight, though straight is what I see.
And to the end of my hard-walking days
There'll be this trinity of my feet and me.

A Bad Moment

I'm frightened. I'm on a rock face and I can't climb.
I've got a toe-hold, just. My fingers are failing.
Below me is a vast amount of nothing.

In advertising a man of fifty is expendable.
The yawning sack holds economic murder
And wives and children fill it with their clamour.

A 22 bus goes whizzling past. Home to a tea and toast.
The star Betelgeuse would hold so many million suns,
The sun so many million earths. I'm nothing but a
   nothing.

Notes on the Way

That girl looks wriggly; she's been bedroomized.
Too many stick insects in the BBC.
Shorthand for Artaxerxes Longimanus.
A new Italian diva falls from heaven,
Orina Farinacci.

Put one tulip in a grey stone vase
and stare at it for a week.
How were they happy, the great Chinese drunkards,
who floated out with the tide so long ago?

June 1966

Lying flat in the bracken of Richmond Park
while the legs and voices of my children pass
seeking, seeking; I remember how on the
13th of June of that simmering 1940
I was conscripted into the East Surreys,
and, more than a quarter of a century
ago, when France had fallen,
we practised concealment in this very bracken.
The burnt stalks pricked through my denims.
Hitler is now one of the antiques of History,
I lurk like a monster in my hiding place.
He didn't get me. If there were a God
it would be only polite to thank him.

The Garden of the Clitorides

In the walled garden of the Clitorides
there's a paradise for middle-aged men
where the teenage girls come when they're called
and turn their eyes upwards in bitch-like adoration,
so perfect in their beauty of sleek prize-winning animals
it seems they never could die.

Perfect nakedness, perfect temperature, perfect idleness,
these are the dreams of middle-aged men.
Give or take some wines named by the gods.
Give or take some sleep in the perfumes of women.

Outside the garden lies a city of satire
peopled by parodies of garden behaviour –
the teasing stripshows, the expensive drunkenness,
the *noli me tangere* of vexatious virgins,
the falling into disrepute and destruction.

No one ever finds the gate to that garden.

The Decomposition of Management

It's too late. The oligopolistic companies,
the major enclaves of dynamism,
have done for him. In backward Britain
only 600 out of half a million anyway
have graduated in management studies.

The market rules us all. A Shakespearean City
has tight control of money, money, money.
It won't let that cat out of the bag
for a thousand Whittingtons, industrious apprentices
or all the copywriters in the agencies.

A computer would do his job x thousand times as well.
He lies there in the last exhaustion of death,
already a greenish tinge is creeping over him.

All managers are dying out, one by one.

Venus in Furs

There's a new opera called *I Masochisti*
With words by Freud and music by Bellini.
The first night's full of scented, furry women,
You can't have them. The conductor's baton
Puts an embargo on all base desires.
Under gold lamé the big nipples swell
Into crescendo. You're the muted horn
That sings of knighthood in the foyer bar.

Bullish, a stalled industrialist. He has it made.
His big bass voice comes straight up from his balls.
Whipped by desires, you're the derided one.
Nobody wants you, loves you, likes you.
Such marvellous deprivation! Can it last?

A Cup Too Low

Put on some Mozart. Then sit down and cry.
The world is very sad, and doesn't change.

Too many terrible people are people still.
It all looks bad, sounds bad; but don't be fooled,

It *is* bad. Though some of what you wanted
Perhaps you had. The wishes grow like weeds

Hemming you in till you can't see the sky
Or what is steadily flying out of range.

172

It's everything, not just the mind, that's ill.
Perhaps if all experience were pooled

The house of life would not be quite so haunted?
And happinesses grow from these sick seeds?

Nameless

There's something in my bed, with two feet,
two legs, a body and two arms.
It also has hands, but it is faceless.
It never seems to have heard of sex.
Of course it has a head. Is it a person?

Nobody knows what goes on inside it,
whether it has organs or just a shell,
you can't get through to know if it's thinking.
I guess that it is very, very old
and that its blood is equally ancient.

It never moves much. Sometimes it frightens me,
it's too obscure to be parsed like a language.
Mostly it lies there, breathing a little,
full, I imagine, of some odd significance.
Whatever it is, it ought to have a meaning.

The Muse

A boy was kissing me left right and centre
But something nasty crept into his quatrains.
I left for thirty years. I haven't changed
Though he's grey at the edges. Now I'm back
We live together in uneasy joy.

My lovely mouth; his bitter, tainted kiss
On sufferance like an old and worn-out husband.
The boys are waving in the other bar,
I swing my skirts and go. A long goodbye
To all who woo me when they're past their prime.

Beginnings

In the vast antheap of the world
one little ant thinks differently.

In the snarled traffic of metropolis
a small family car crashes the lights.

Under a tailored and conventional suit
a heart beats out a naked rhythm.

Like a roomsize coloured balloon
a man blows up a religion till it bursts.

Somebody somewhere begins to unpick the stitches
in the bright battle flag of glory.

Prisoner of Love

Across the green carpet moves a hamster
shaped like a racing car in cream-coloured fur.
The heart moves so, for all small animals.
Alone in a room it certainly never made
its ears are tender. Hamsters have problems too.
My fingers are its god, to scoop it up,
give it the freedom of that dark green sea,
return it to its cage. Food and drink
come from above; for sharpening teeth
the ritual gnawing of the metal bars.
Eating the corner of a record sleeve
is sin. Punishment is withheld.
Even a hamster is a child of light.

So Far

Through the dusk come the hot potato men
and the Streatham Strangler.
There's gaslight. I'm cosy.
Though all the starving cats in Latin countries
would fill Hyde Park,
a family kitten sleeps beside the fire.

In every room before sledgehammers slam
hundreds of people have lived.
It's such a cliché.
The children cut their devils out of paper,
love/hate their parents,
the past supports me like an easy chair.

So far we have come through life, so far.
In a bland ignorance
the young are happy.
The shadows on the wall, art for art's sake,
comfort, protect us.
I must be marvellous, to have such thoughts.

In a Block of Flats

The summer suns a threadbare lawn
And fills the Court with dryness,
Where children just a few years born
Are learning about shyness,
Where the imaginary unicorn
Looks round for vanished highness

Only to find that gayer girls
Ignore the Middle Ages
And sigh for medieval curls
Not on the heads of pages
Or on the shoulders of gross earls
But on the tops of mages

Who contemplate a swinging scene
And love the swinging city,
Young men that hate the might-have-been
And think the past a pity,
As admirably tall and lean
As unicorns are pretty.

Businesslike

On a big office block is a monolithic smile
That never changes.
It smiles at inequalities of income,
At old political injustices.

A client may seem like a red plush teddy bear
Or a red devil.
His voice may come out as a shout or a scream
But yours must always be level.

If it's digging your grave quick with a knife and fork
Or drowning in wine,
The business lunches will help you no end –
That smile is in no way divine.

A Mystery?

28 February, 1966

The clerical drone.
In honour of an uncle, weak flesh, enduring bone.
'And we shall all be changed, in the twinkling of an eye.'
As the seed into wheat, chrysalis into butterfly.

I nod; and hibernate,
Asleep from long habit; past the churchyard gate
Surges main road traffic, the coffin is wheeled out,
We stand by the raw grave, I with my honest doubt.

At the last words
There are no thunderclaps, no omens from the birds,
But, settling on the parson's gown, one Small
    Tortoiseshell,
Deluded and untimely, woken by the warm spell.

Daddyo

My hearing deadens. My eyes
aren't good in artificial light.
The memory wobbles. But
that's enough of that.

So clearly I remember
what a harsh crass old man
my father seemed
thirty years ago.

But he was the bright boy
from Edinburgh, the medico who won
hundreds of pounds of weighty scholarships.
A big attacking surgeon.

My mind shrank under the barking knife.

Now it's my turn
to be the red-faced fool
that sons hate, tittered at
by sneering miniskirts.

It's strange to wear
a dead man's shoes, to know
exactly where
each one pinches.

The Real and Unreal

In my son's mind
the Mexicans are fighting the Texicans
and there are drawings to prove it,
the Martians eat Mars bars.
A life no one can share.

Always I find
the words confounded with the antiwords,
a bloc: the mind can't move it.
There are battles, but no scars,
nobody dies there.

His war, unkind
to no one, kills but doesn't really kill:
the dead rise to disprove it
and drive away in cars.
Killing would be unfair.

Some Second Ghest to Entertaine?

In London's twin beds, where everyone's re-marrying,
lie some pertinent questions and some genuine
    arguments
and the desire for change when everything's not
    satisfactory.
He has his eye on an increasing waistline.
She is in mourning for a youth of loves.

To change! To change! The dream at every window
persists through months of nights boring as Sundays.

The wetness of the drinks is an oasis
in a broad calm that is also arid.
Begin a log book of the old emotions

and you will find they all come round again.
Plot them on a graph whose peaks are children.
I'm out of such a world. Too old for changing
I hold to humdrum love – and I have promised
never to murder my wife, and never to leave her.

The Deceptive Grin of the
Gravel Porters

Through the rain forests, up a long river,
over greensand and clay and red earth,
they toil like ants in their long procession,
hacking at difficulties that grow and close again,
covering once more the path behind them.

Following these unimportant carriers of the
    unimportant,
we seldom see them. When we do, they grin.
After the bad patches they turn with a kind of smirk
and beckon us. There are large animals too
that rustle through the hemispheres.

Travelling over chalk to a familiar sea
is all we dream of where the trees are strangled
by the great sneering creepers. Sunlit birds
yakkety yak above our own deep gloom,
hundreds of feet over our inadequate heads.

How did they do it? We see the marks on trees
but made by what? teeth, weapons, little axes?
They don't communicate except to grin.
We know they're there but jungles grow so fast
and all we have are bruised and bleeding hands.

2 The Cryptics

Lines

The other day I was loving a sweet little
   fruitpie-and-cream.

He was flying an Avro Manhattan into a beady-eyed
   silence.

His little shoes were shining as he stood by the sea-lions.

Panting, she lifted her skirt in a classical gesture.

The darkness came on like an illness while we were
   debating.

The albatross yawed to the masthead,
   Coleridge-fashion.

The seven dwarfs were singing these mystical motifs.

Lifelines

In the rat race he won by a whisker.

Bitching and bitching in the double bed.

She came unexpectedly, while he was standing waiting.

A voice from a jar of vaseline: 'This too is love.'

A girl like a cat sits in the window of The Sizzling
Sausage.

In the great cities the ants are actuarians.

The lips of the Muse have the taste of beauty.

In a field of alien corn a girl was reaped.

The Great Lines

For bad men do what good men only dream.

The beauties warble down the tracks of time.

What could console is working like a watch.

After the banquet: 'Shall we join the dead?'

From the wild lands the precious food of cities.

A dream of adultery: two for the price of one.

Even the wolves, at last, will go away.

182

Hands

With her short squat (and greedy) hands she seized
  power.

Yesterday he set his hand and seal
to his final arrangements for frying Boy Scouts.

Meretricious Mayfair hands were bathing the
  Birmingham balls.

He wants God to lean down with an enormous hand
and slap on his back a label that says SATISFACTORY.

Above the wine-shop her hands enticed him.

The writing hand was wobbling over the paper.

Hymn

The names are written on the heart,
and, as one dies, which is the last name? Whose?

Tchaikowsky, with his brass, bats on towards
his nineteenth nervous breakdown.

There are islands (far and few)
where all the villagers have absolute pitch.

Such heavenly choirs are all concerned with Love;
and Venus is muscular (ischiocavernosus).

Falls

After a sloshing great lunch she fell over backwards.

In the towering city there was defenestration.

Wind-warped, one parachute failed to open.

His mood fell like mercury when she left him.

In her cups her breasts fell softly.

In the place of the pins you could hear a leaf drop.

Objects

A sadistic whiskyglass belonging to my father,
a hanged man patterned: 'The Last Drop'.

A letter from my mother mentioning a General Election:
'I tremble for the rest of the country.'

A blue dressing gown that my wife spends time in;
quilted and somnolent like a walking bedspread.

A plasticine stegosaurus fingered by my son;
vegetarian fool with a wooden tray for pasture.

A troll with a Beatle haircut attempted by my daughter.
Folkloristic grinning in the nursery.

Classical Disasters

The brazen bull was filled with his bellowing.

The wax was melting as the wings climbed higher.

At the big banquet the food was human.

The greedy cloth bit at his muscular body.

He clubbed the old man at the lonely crossroads.

They cut the tongue from her squealing struggles.

At the last strained heave the stone toppled backwards.

Lines of History

By a deserted road the Apostles were peeing.

The sun through the burning-glass tickled the warm hay.

The sea heaved with its burden of whales.

The antheap was teeming with cries of injustice.

Above the wineshop she cupped her hands and held him.

Past the window of the torture chamber flew the pigeons.

There was no silence, now or at any time.

Gnomes

The ten-year-old who dreams of being Miss World
has a face like a pig with toothache.

The spotted pages romantically admire
the quims of queens.

Never forget the civilized meanness,
the smelly bums and cheesy feet.

The respectable citizen longs to murder
a few good criminals.

You, in a world alive with snerges,
be careful when you walk on pavements.

Couples

The little married hands. The pinky nipples
Soft as a hamster's shyly twitching nose.

An unromantic man bursts in and shouts:
'Hot jissom! I'm a Touareg!'

Behind the bushes there is country dancing.
Full many a jig, horned heads, archaic flutes.

Upstairs Mr Goldberg has his secretary over a desk,
Her panties round her ankles.

Fifteen Days in a Banana Skin

The first week still unripe and reading Henty.
And in the second week the wars came true.

On to High Art, High Art and disillusion.
The cryptic words took shape upon the wall.

Love ripened on the tree, the fall of Eve.
Some seed was scattered on a city pavement.

The years of sweetness in a spotted skin.
A bunch of college boys exposed for sale.

What's eating you? Lips that are feminine.
Lips that can well ingest a golden beauty.

Existences

Living at Potato Point, and dying of Dog's Disease.

Living in The Blue Desert, and dying of inertia.

Alive in Quick City, and fading with the trendsetters.

The Statements

Arts are actually anthropomorphic.
Business is often bilaterally baleful.
Causality is a considerable cow.
Desires are delightful as well as desperate.

Energy in everything is everlasting.
Freedom is frequently fairly fallacious.
Growing girls go gay with gallantry.
History has some horrible hermits.
Illness is injurious only to idiots.
Jokes are jealous and jazz is jolly.
Kitchens are kinetic like kisses and kiwis.
Love is laudable and lately laundered.
Matrimony is mainly merry and miserable.
Names are numinous and never negligible.
Officers often open their orifices.
Palaeontology is particularly painful.
Quails are queer but quiet and queenly.
Restless rovers are rarely repentant.
Soles slide sideways in silent seas.
Terrible tornadoes torture the terrain.
Under umbrellas the uncles take umbrage.
Various virgins veer into vinegar.
Weary wallflowers wait wetly for wisdom.
Xylophones excel in extemporization.
Yelling in youth is yesterday's yawning.
Zen is as zealous as zebras and zinc.

The Headlines

No dice, as Rasputin flies in to floozies

Mean famine tempts 5 bits from Queen

Profs flee as city falls to Turks

Agitator executed on funereal hill

Limeys and krauts combine to flog the frogs

Sage corrupts youth, say City Fathers

Too much water spoils the tea

Norman Archer catches Harold's eye

Demagogue roasts books, heebs

Daughters claim Pop unfit to rule

Allies victorious, fry Troy by stratagem

The Eight Suits

A lightweight suit from Austin Reed,
good for the evil act.

A suit of black silk pyjamas,
flavoured with decadence.

A track suit bursting with muscle,
vitality breaks the tape.

A suit of hairy tweed, alert
to publish snobberies.

A business suit full of smooth words,
charcoal for the grill.

A diver's suit for old oceans,
fish are its spectators.

An evening suit dark as nighttime,
the mourner at the feast.

A white protective suit of science,
at home among the poisons.

The Twelve Slogans

Override the underwear with Penetro

Keep above bard with Shakespeare Shoes

Dig the decalogue with Dean Dubrovnik

Be baroque with J. S. Bach

Plug in to the Passover for peculiar parties

Let Love lighten your liaisons

Populo promotes political people

Go gay with new bright Girlie

Make your member mad with Mysticism

Increase your stature with new Buskino

Smarten up with Smattering

Learn to live and lay off literature

she shouting pigshit on the american books
he drown in the glass of a dry martini
one canny pig runs down the lane of lingos

a purple splurge is coming, cut it out
on all the sibilant seas the words are walking
no trust a woman, she split down the middle

a spear of light the black fogs of the brain
under umbrellas twirls a memory boy
go home go home the flatness of the dust

All Brave Men are Slightly Stupid

At the fart of a gourmet several ladies fainted.

At the sigh of a saint the postulants passed away.

At the wriggling of Venus no man was a worm.

At the end of the conference the table was talking.

At the sight of the sea the dressed crab was disrobing.

At the sizzling of bacon the pig was perturbed.

At the cry of the cannon the soldiers were shouting.

3 The Others

Magic

An old man with his sary lume
And the drugs of the future
May be led to lodge with the light-wit ladies,
Reclining royally.

Wonderful when a wlonk beckons
In array that is seemly
And all are swimming in the swan-white wine,
Lustfully lapping!

Though we were yeild yesterday,
Like a riotous ratbag
Now are we loosely light-heartedly laughing,
Portentous potentates.

A New Poet Arrives

A new man flies in from Manchester.
Frank Frittlewood.
Death to the Public Schools,
Ready to piss in the eye of the Old Universities.

A big woolly striped scarf round his neck,
The hunched antagonism of a left wing student.
How right he is!
Through immense spectacles he sees clearly

That only a New Movement can save our souls.
Wordsworth's great beak was pecking at that apple.
The tree of knowledge,
Dividing line between the past and future.

Take off those vestments, and those vested interests.
Show as a naked soul. You must admit
He's onto something.
Change, in the Arts, is nearly always good.

Arithmetic

I'm 11. And I don't really know
my Two Times Table. Teacher says it's disgraceful
But even if I had the time, I feel too tired.
Ron's 5, Samantha's 3, Carole's 18 months,
and then there's Baby. I do what's required.

Mum's working. Dad's away. And so
I dress them, give them breakfast. Mrs Russell
moves in, and I take Ron to school.
Miss Eames calls me an old-fashioned word: Dunce.
Doreen Maloney says I'm a fool.

After tea, to the Rec. Pram-pushing's slow
but on fine days it's a good place, full
of larky boys. When 6 shows on the clock
I put the kids to bed. I'm free for once.
At about 7 – Mum's key in the lock.

The Paling of the Clerds

(for Bruce Broadstairs)

He never saw the paling of the clerds.
Somebody kneed him in the bolls,
He straggled herd, a rising son, went dawn.
A musked men knafed him in the rippling beck.
Such vehelence! The blod ren every way.
He stoggered, lick an ecks they broke his skill
And sore he lay a-daying all the nate.

Thin fur his greve they tippled a huge stein.
Wrought on it: TUCK HIM IN ERL AND ERL
HE WAS A MIN. End their the big bland see
Kipped keening dewly on the rising cost,
His lafe was spant. A less! Oh sod
To no thet promise never march filfulled!
The sturm brust from the paling of the clerds.

Nymphs and Satyrs

(for 'Filthy' Prior)

The satyr's mouth is stained red with wine,
The nymph is beautifully white.
The nymph is resisting – all very fine –
The satyr is slightly tight.

But it isn't exactly as you think
For here's a remarkable matter:
The inside of the nymph is as wet and pink
As the lustful lips of the satyr.

Office Primitive

Me likum girlum. Hatum work.
Smokum. Drinkum. Strokum pussy.
Go bus every day. Lovum stockings.
Boss say workum faster faster faster
Childer school work faster faster
Wife home work mucher mucher mucher
Me workum daydream slow
Get pounds get big get fat
But always thinkum stockings.

Likum bester rum
Rum bester bottle
Me dreamum top dreams
Me dreamum girlum under
Me lovum skyman?
Me love me me only.

A Woman's World

I'm being raped by an apeman
when the egg-timer pings in the kitchen,
the excited kettle comes in steam.

My lover has blue scales instead of skin,
I grind against him like cheese under a grater.
There are birds seven feet high,
I ride them down the motorways.
All gooey with blood; and fighting.
I am an Empress, pop from the beds
of the warm soldiers like toast from the machine.

It's red-hot buggery for the cheeky secretaries
my husband plays with.

Disciple

All His beliefs I share.
The Jews are getting uppity. The Banks must go.
The Russian Novel's not significant.
His Christ-like sufferings I catalogue,
The years of captivity,
The charge of treason.

And I admire his old-world courtesy,
His struggles to take his hat off to a lady,
With one arm full of books,
His unselfishness and consideration –
As when, in a concourse of bores,
He turns pathetically to me and asks:
'How much more of this must I listen to?'
In a low voice.

He's old and very special.
By my discipleship I'm special too.

A Guttural Frigment

Contstrock in bordlond, at the meal with slavs.
Whon will the cot ond mous be reconciled?
A woorld we wish! no keeling, on the sond
No stip of horsh mororder; inversion non.
Bot blonk the sea ond onpertorbed the sky
In peace thot longthins so onfinished out.

Fishcake palaver! Woorlds are not so culm.
Voiolence laps oopon the tittering
Gulls as the say lofts op its creamy skorts.
Stobbing ond stobbing to the poolsing hurt
Moch morder feels the flot ond nukid lond.
Sailence was never, now or ony teem.

Geeve us som sleep, som end to rostlessness,
Som quoiet in the ercherd of oor lov
Onder the epples thot oor purents knew.
Lit us bee Odom ond receiving Eve,
No sorpent in the ploshy greening gross,
A sommer's day by ony gloaming loch.

A Refusal to Mourn the Death by Fire of Edgar Mittelholzer

An agony greater than I like to think of.

You poured petrol over yourself and put a match to it.
You went out in a blaze of glory.
(But already in the writer that fire was dead?)

197

You will be a powerful jumbie,
At midnight every 5th of May
Let the marauding minis of Farnham beware.

A gaunt West Indian ghost
Flaming with strangeness, with madness in the head,
Magic fire on the brain, lighting the woodland.

Your strongest urges to destruction
Turned at last on you.
You lived in a cage with a tiger
For years before you put a foot wrong.

Love Song

You've got nice knees.
Your black shoes shine like taxis.
You are the opposite of
all farting and foulness.
Your exciting hair
is like a special moss,
on your chest are two soft medals
like pink half-crowns under your dress.
Your smell is far beyond
the perfumes at parties,
your eyes nail me
on a cross of waiting. Hard is
the way of the worshipper.
But the heart line on my hand
foretold you;
in your army of lovers
I am a private soldier.

Georgic

His verse is accomplished and formal,
It's never been boring or flat.
His mind doesn't seem to be normal
But he's perfectly pleased about that.

It's just what's going on that's so puzzling
In these nightmares of death and disease;
There's a hellhound around that needs muzzling –
And a Gothic Pre-Raphaelite tease.

Like an elegant dandified Borgia
He offers a bright poisoned cup
And smiles – just a bit – at our torture
Until we confess we give up.

He's the dark one who handles the riddles,
He's ill-met in an intricate maze,
Quite content if we burn while he fiddles
With a bland and benevolent gaze.

Short Story

She bit his love-nuts, what a nasty girl!

Her two were always going before her
a perfect pair, so softly supported.

They met in a bar and he was explaining
how 'Baa, Baa, Black Sheep!' is about pubic hair
and how the clitoris is only really
the little boy who lived down the lane.

199

Stand in front of the mirror and let me lick you.

It was hot on the beach. Too many bikinis
and several hangovers were stretched out in the sun.

They drank a very cold white wine. It
was a great life. After a big lunch
they rolled about on a 42 sq. ft bed.
Some sand grated into their copulations.

There's a whole literature of the Mediterranean.

He and she and a sea that is tideless
and peaches that ought to be wearing frilly panties.

He was called Jan and she was called Paula.
The Loves were laughing when they got together,
they parted with a shrill cry and a strong backhand
that reddened with a line her bloated floaters.

One for the Anthologies

Herbert's a hard and horrid man
    And so am I.
He does as much harm as he can
    And so do I.
He wastes the time of Institutes
And spends his nights with prostitutes,
    And so do I.

Wilfred's a weak and weary man
    And so am I.
He's always been an also-ran
    And so have I.

He's been defeated all his life,
Too tired to end it with a knife –
  And so am I.

David's a dense and drunken man
  And so am I.
He's fond of glass and mug and can
  And so am I.
When these sad dogs have had their day
They'll all be glad to go away
  And so will I.

The Legend of the Lustful Lozenges

I'm busy collecting material for a new long poem
(so many novels have used up so many people).
This one is about a little drinking duck
like the one the *Daily Express* found on Guy Burgess's
    mantelpiece
dipping its beak forever into a glass of forgetfulness.

This duck is in love with a bird that proves unfaithful,
Donna sleal! it cries. *La bella del Re!*
It is overcome with a sense of dishonour
and plunges into a carafe of red wine,
Italian-style, a beak that is sharpened by bitterness.

This duck (which you might not have thought) is a tenor
and it lives under the weight of an English winter,
oppressed by sleeplessness and the love that consumes it.
It is fairly happy in its work, which is also its life, which
is dipping its beak into some life-giving liquid.

Its loved one has migrated with another mate
and is busy laying eggs, but the duck keeps drinking;

its hours are not fixed like an office worker's,
through the cold dark night it is sipping and sipping,
swinging its head back, then down to the wetness

which is the only fluid in a large dry room.
Its task is as dull as machines in a factory.
Only in between sips can it shout its revolted
awareness that a beauty has left it forever.
If it slept it would dream of lustful lozenges

promising re-unions and billing and cooing
and some quite different and perfect existence.
But all it can do is move its head forwards
and backwards; all it knows is drinking
and the cold of a deserted, disappointed winter.

Xmas for the Boys

A clockwork skating Wordsworth on the ice,
An automatic sermonizing Donne,
A brawling Marlowe shaking out the dice,
A male but metaphysical Thom Gunn.
Get them all now – the latest greatest set
Of all the Poets, dry to sopping wet.

A mad, ferocious, disappointed Swift
Being beaten by a servant in the dark.
Eliot going up to Heaven in a lift,
Shelley going overboard, just for a lark.
Although the tempo and the talent varies
Now is the time to order the whole series.

An electronic Milton, blind as a bat,
A blood-spitting consumptive Keats,
Tennyson calmly raising a tall hat,
Swinburne being whipped in certain dark back streets.

All working models, correct from head to toe –
But Shakespeare's extra, as you ought to know.

Thriller

I drove the hearse back at 70 m.p.h.

My worries flew away, a flock of black birds.
Some shots of rye and on to see Diane.
Complete release. Her legs locked round my back.

But that night wasn't so easy –
there's nothing easy about any money –
I mailed the ransom note and marked the tree.

For two more nights the fuzz was circling badly.
Killing the headlights. From my hide I saw
a fat pockmarked man, with the binocs.

As in the wood he brutishly waited, freezing,
I thought of shallow graves and how the boy
had cried all night about a teddy bear.

But finally I did it with a cushion
and half a bottle of Scotch. Buried him too.
My nerves were bad, the hearse was catching up.

At last the tin box with the elastic band,
nobody there but me. And if the notes were known?
Diane was threshing about, mad at my failure.

Isn't it marvellous how it all turns sour?
Money to burn and burning's all it's fit for,
and down the long black road I drive the hearse.

The Gavin Ewart Show (1971)

The Day of the Creator

After a first-rate breakfast I sit in my shirtsleeves
and begin work on my new long poem 'Yelling for
   Elspeth'.
It's a complicated story full of repetitions,
about a scattering, a dispersion, a diaspora.
It's a love story too and my writing grows curly
as it lingers over the details of that seduction
in the dark bean swamp. Outside my window
the birds are singing a page out of Livy.

Only one could climb the mountain, that is the essence.
The rest were led aside by trolls, their legs jerked like
   billy-o
as they sank in the viscous mud by the pathside.
I feel I am being split down the middle by an axe
and down the fissure runs the telltale of narrative,
in not too long I shall be as famous as a novelist,
sign copies in bookshops. Down in the garden
a cat is playing god to several sparrows.

I go into the kitchen for a cup of instant coffee,
not too much sugar because of my waistline.
In the cheroot smoke I sort out some characters.
Jacqueline must be like H, and the tall Rabbi
must tell the truth about life to Adrian Semester.
Will Fontainebleau make it? The sugar lumps ponder,
white in blue cardboard. All things are thinkers,
and an ant zigs quietly over the windowsill.

So undisturbed, though I deal with disturbances!
I really have created the pen and the paper.
To the nastiest characters I assign action,
the nice ones sit still in a quiet contemplation.
What colours shall they wear? Would a dialect comic
destroy the whole effect of the nineteenth Canto?
Or improve it? Or what? It's my typewriter
that glints so much knowledge of communication.

Though I write so many words, one thing is certain.
Nobody will shout 'Christ!' at a critical juncture,
there will be no obscenity of thought or deed or even
any long mention of anyone's knickers.
There's a great deal of morality in quietness
and a pure style belongs to a clear sunny morning
and the myth I am holding. Ever so gently
a little white cloud floats over the treetops.

At the lawnmower's purr I stop for a moment.
Would Alaric do anything truly despicable?
Yet when that mean action flowed out of my biro
it seemed somehow so right, so *natural*.
Soon I shall have lunch, then a walk on the Common.
Any sort of exercise is good for my diction
and always has been. That rough dog barking
is like a caesura in my line of neatness.

A Black Rabbit Dies for its Country

Born in the lab, I never saw the grass
or felt the direct touch of wind or sun
and if a rabbit's nature is to run
free on the earth, I missed it; though the glass
never let shot or eager predators pass,

while I was warm against my mother's side
something was waiting in the centrifuge
(the world's a cage, although that cage is huge)
and separate I lived until I died –
watered and fed, I didn't fret, inside,

and all the time was waiting for the paste
scooped with a spatula from the metal rim,
the concentrate bacillus at the brim,
and lived the life of feeling and of taste.
I didn't know it. Knowing would be waste

in any case, and anthrax is the hard
stuff that knocks out the mice, the dogs, the men,
you haven't any chance at all and when
they've finished with you, you're down on a card.
How could I know, to be upon my guard

when they pushed my container into line
with the infected airstream? Breath is life:
though something there more deadly than a knife
cut into me, I was still feeling fine
and never guessed the next death would be mine,

how many minutes later lungs would choke
as feet beat out the seconds like a drum,
hands held me on the table; this was a sum
with the predictable ending of a joke.
Fighting I died, and no god even spoke.

The Sea-pig

Five miles through forest from the bathyscaphe,
great tendrils flapping and the giant rays
lazily flopping past, no nights or days,
deep-water darkness, till we saw it, safe
in our mobility, turning different ways

its eighty metres of a blinded worm.
Far from our friendly shelf and humane surf,
from sky and sun and rocks and trees and turf,
we saw it burrow, the metre-thickness squirm,
great protein sea-pig wriggling like a sperm

into the sand, and throw up a vast mound.
This was the marvel and the flesh we sought,
the one we looked for, for whom we had brought
the para-guns, the cable – at last, now, found.
We looked; and swam, good hunting, but no sound,

our little points of light illumined it.
Perhaps in dim perceptiveness it felt
an alien presence, encircled by a belt
electrically alerted. The guns hit;
and sand flew in a flurry, in its pit

it hurried down, but losing consciousness,
more feebly moving no-head, no-feet, no-eyes,
we were the ant destroyers of its size,
the thinkers with the more, though so much less,
cold in our triumph of its giant distress.

Until all segments heaved into a rest.
We shot the cables in at several points,
the joy made movement in our awkward joints
that clockwork swimming put to such a test.
All old equipment, but we did our best

and after minutes had it well attached,
the cables in our gloves, and turned for home,
back to our hardened and transparent dome,
the effort by the happy outcome matched,
another legend into living snatched,

the Great Invertebrate at last secured,
food for the generations yet to come.
The long five miles that would make up the sum
seemed to us then a nothing, all endured
with lightness, like an illness easily cured,

Ella Mi Fu Rapita!

'Die Liebe dauert oder dauert nicht'
BRECHT

Her boredom took her away. So simple.
She just became bored with me. No other rival
experienced the entrancing smile with the dimple
or put down his drink in joy at her arrival
or loved her in taxis that stream like ants
through London, fingers under her pants

caressing her holy of holies. Oh, no
it wasn't someone younger, bigger or better.
She went because she had the urge to go,
without a phone call, telegram or letter.
From our last meeting she just walked out –
a few pretexts perhaps. What were they about?

Nothing too serious. A red bow in her hair,
as she lay naked on the bed, knees-raising,
stays in my mind. I know I had my share.
Love is all programmed, it's all phasing,
there's a beginning, a middle and an end.
A lover's life is not that of a friend,

who by and large is able to take it or leave it.
For love there's a critical path – it goes on.
It can't go backwards or sideways, believe it,
that's all; a dream, a tremendous con,
and when it's over, you're out on your own.
Most life, they say, has to be lived alone.

And what can the lover do, when the time's come,
when THE END goes up on the screen? Yelling,
rush into the street, lamenting her lovely bum?
Get friendly with men in bars, telling
how sweet she was, praising her statistics,
or admiring his own sexual ballistics?

208

No, that's no good. Love lasts – or doesn't last.
And all the pink intimacies and warm kisses
go into Proust's remembrance of time past.
Lovers must never crumple up like cissies
or break down or cry about their wrongs.
If girls are sugar, God holds the sugar tongs.

The Pseudo-Demetrius *

After the summer on the lovely island
came the pretender, the autumn of the city,
the Pseudo-Demetrius garlanded with blackberries;
the true young one had strawberries and raspberries
and the real love in the matchless bed.

After the moistness of the pink lips opening
came the equivocal, the Pseudo-Demetrius,
the one who told us he would make us equal
to what we were when the flowers were young ones
and we knew love in the matchless bed.

After the sun's hour, the failing succession
came with a turbulence but no tenderness,
the anger and envy of the Pseudo-Demetrius,
the one who stirred up trouble and caused the ending
of our best love in the matchless bed.

After the green and the bees in clover
came the new season when we were forgotten,

* In the history of medieval Russia there are two Pretenders.
They are called Pseudo-Demetrius I and Pseudo-Demetrius II.

the riot and sadness of the Pseudo-Demetrius,
brown leaves falling on the musclemen fighting,
and no real love in the matchless bed.

After the summer, after the sun's hour,
came the equivocal, turbulent pretender,
the Pseudo-Demetrius garlanded with autumn,
with lies and fighting in the darkened city,
and death, not love, in the matchless bed.

Abelam

The long-yams are being grown in honour of the moon
A critic recalls Plissetskaya's celebrated jump
Soman is somewhere in the worship of the deadly
The strikers show clever running off the ball
That harpsichord remembers Michael Haydn.

The rainbow, they say, is a snake of no importance
The audience is kinky about Khachaturian
A headline says Hendon Afternoon Dogs
Some secretaries regard themselves as debs
Caroline Quoin on Candlewick has a clear round.

The hornbill carvings are definitely phallic
Graveney is stroking the ball through the covers
A broken choirboy miscalculates some trills
Menstruating women are put in special huts
Blake is accused as a formless draughtsman.

At important ceremonies there are palm-leaf flares
The Porsches like a plague overrun the country
Some minds are tickled by the feathers of investiture
The gin is jumping from the bankers' fountains
The massed choirs are singing A.M.D.G

Moving on

If Love has been sitting for hours
on an Allen Jones girlie chair,
if I have been given a backscrubber
for my birthday, if a prominent
poet wants to kidnap our pussycat,
if publishers regard themselves
as Fishers of Men. . . . This
is all so cosy in the Year of the Dog.

If I am a selfish liberal
socialist, if the office coffee
tastes of tealeaves, if the
ice is still on the polar ice cap,
if I regard my two
children with tenderness,
this is the face-down card,
the life that was dealt me . . . .

If what is ordinary still stays
ordinary, why should I run
to peanut brittle, put the
record straight on a Western campus,
worry about the tweeters and woofers,
blockade the television with
a sofa or davenport?
I am the friend of a healthy ulcer.

If the double-barrelled names
are firing off platitudes,
if some smooth idiots are
nursing constituencies,
if a moneyed party wears
Enoch's albatross . . .
my life still moves into
its twilight, grey is the colour.

The Challenge to Interpretation

Deleterious substances
are hopping with energy/
I am severely
monocoque construction/
In the blue saucepan
tempers are rising/
Two sprauncy birds
inhibit the parkway/
The old movie has
a dancer called Laundrette/

Under the mistletoe
x-rays are working/
At the small breakfast
the bigness of music/
The men in the fields
containers for earthworms/
It is incredible
the smell of the fish–lake/
Je n'aime pas
le *spunk* dans ma bouche/

Crown us
all tenderly/
There are no
differences/
A black dog
is barking/
Love to
the Apostolate/
Goodbye
for ever!

On the Death of an Unpleasant Executive

When the heart attacks
we all fall
down.

And, as Milton thought of
Edward King, it might have
been me.

What will the son think
about Daddy, dead
on holiday?

You needn't really
like them, to
sympathise.

For example: imagine
a crashed car drawn
to burial,

the judge's black cap
draped over the
steering wheel,

moving solemnly
in reverse; transistor
music.

Black pall on the
cold radiator; the body
sable velvet.

I hate cars but
I don't like the
perishing.

I'm sorry for wrecks,
stray dogs squeeze
the heart;

even the end of a snobbish
inefficient idiot is
the end of

something.

People Will Say We're in Love

But seriously, as the marriage wears on, thanks
   for the mem-
ory of hauling prams and shopping up icy door-
steps, equally as for the kisses and the dem-
onstrative eyes. Wives work hard. Cathy and her moor-
land romance are fine in the mind, but the caring for babies is the real and most test-
ing fact of a union. The children are the sharing. It's always Housewives *v*. The Rest.

And it's always into big offices for the good provid-
ers, the traditional way to keep the bank managers happy. Families don't like outsid-
ers. This is men's washing and ironing, fanning up a little flame of money in the current account. Chores of the typewriter. Essential reading about Management. Not the true sweetness, sacc-
harine at best – a businessman's Creed.

So the success of a marriage can be seen in the children and, believe me, certainly yours is the credit, after the nappies, the orange juice, the pil-
fered hours of sleep they took from you, bedtime too often a night shift, and loving not the novelist's outspoken rand-
y young sprawlers, pushing and shov-
ing, but tiredness, the offered and the taken hand.

The Boss is Thinking

His secretary has a habit of scrumpling the top copies
like sheets of a bed she's slept in. Take
those office beauties further
back
and they're reading
'Bunty And The Boo-Boos'.
Before that they're little screaming things
crawling across the carpet, blue-eyed, in nappies.

Good ones, he thinks, are as rare as seven-toed tabbies;
and the Office Manager tells him: put
just ten girls in an unheated
room
and they're making
warmth like a one-bar fire; yes,
even the inefficient ones are assets too,
smiling and carrying into meetings the teas and coffees.

They like people, they're not sensitive to hierarchies,
they're a kind of undisciplined army. Give
them the lover or father
touch
and they're licking
the saucers and purring, on, on,
into the unpaid overtime and the cut lunch.
Boy friends at night with the Greek wine and the
    moussakas.

Victorian

Miss with the vapours.
The claret and the oysters.
The curling papers.
Fat clergy in the cloisters.

Heavy squires hunting.
Pints of port and porter.
Grumbling and grunting.
Gothic bricks and mortar.

Fog in the dockyards.
Decorum at the Palace.
Blood in the stockyards.
Murder in the alleys.

The Short Fat Poem

the secretary describes an Italian holiday/the Managing Director's a perfect idiot/there's a lot of spin-off from American advertising/someone's an expert on gallium arsenide/nobody knows what she'll do if I touch her/ Dittersdorf is slowly filling the kitchen/the ephemerides twirl in the sunshine/the New and Middle Kingdoms belong to history/in the big gardens the girls are blooming/the guns are firing for Major McMason/ everyone loves the bestselling novels/the parents are sacrificed to the charming children/a US poet displays the stigmata/masochists want to sleep with bicycles/ I dream of the Queen as a bus conductress.

The Song

I am a free ranging hen
and God put me on this earth
to pick up the crumbs of intelligence
I need for my artwork,
the old how, the variant where, the new when.

I am a Gauloise (blue)
for many years since my birth
I have been jumbling the words into elegance,
part pleasure, part work,
and I have been smoked by the many, bought by the few.

I am a sandwich fresh cut,
eat me aurally, near the bone
and juicy the ham was, desiccated
the pub clock will make it –
catch me by the vanishing rabbit's quick scut.

I am a bottle of wine,
the wrath in my grapes homegrown,
drink me; those who hesitated
were never able to take it.
Slup me rough and homely and I'll taste fine.

& Son

Even if he thinks
poetry is something made with a wheel,
and Art
somebody's christian name,
and never willingly
reads a book in his life . . .

eats hard, drinks,
turns into a layabout or a heel,
that's part
of life – the very same
that so chillingly
faces the world and his wife –

if too much love
floats the sons out on the main stream,
moves away
from what fathers did;
so does reaction
against a cosy family firm.

In the iron glove
is the velvet hand? and men cream,
goatishly gay,
result: a new kid
goes into action,
there's a future in sperm;

but what he *is*
doesn't matter. How can a father not
love his own
son? though you could call
it narcissism,
or otherwise analyse,

it's not showbiz,
it's genuine; a saint or a clot,
blood and bone,
he's holy, the source of all
heresy, schism.
But lovable by the wise.

The Select Party

Hands that wiped arses
are holding glasses,
lips that fellated
are intoxicated,
parts that were randy
have counterparts handy –

but the fact of a quorum
preserves decorum,
and the social unction
inhibits the function
of the natural passions
concealed by the fashions.

Tongues that licked scrota
don't move one iota
from the usual phrases
that the century praises,
the undisturbed labia
are deserted Arabia –

these cats are all mousers
but skirts and trousers
keep the lid on the kettle;
there are magnets, there's metal,
but they don't click together
thru nylon and leather.

The Sentimental Education

Wear your Thomas Hardy suit and sit with candles in the
   gloom.
Summon ghosts of years departed till they fill the empty
   room.

First of all call up the weather – heatwave 1922,
Wartime winters with the blackout, blossom on the trees
   at Kew.

Then the people. First, a nanny. Next, your father
   wearing spats.
Mummy with her pearls at evening, and her three
   amazing cats.

Childish captions fit the pictures – you were very childish
   then –
But you see it still as clearly as the present world of men.

Peter Pan was pulsing drama, green lights shone on
  Captain Hook.
Carroll's Jabberwock caused nightmares, till you had to
  hide the book.

You were one. Then came two sisters. They were
  different from you.
You liked best fried bread and cocoa, loved the zebras at
  the Zoo.

Then the schools – a bourgeois saga – we all know what
  they were like.
Minnows in a pond, a bully swam among them like a
  pike.

Squeeze them in? You'ld need a ballroom. Still
  remembered, many names
Cluster round in shorts and sweaters. Latin, algebra and
  games.

Chapel services. Then freedom, and the length of King's
  Parade.
Dadie, Anthony – and Classics, all the dons that had it
  made.

Cicero made ghastly speeches, elegiacs were a bore.
You had two years in the saltmines – how could you
  come up for more?

Next was English, Richards lectures, Leavis supervising.
  Fine.
English literature went down as stimulating as new wine.

After Cambridge – unemployment. No one wanted
  much to know.
Good degrees are good for nothing in the business world
  below.

In the end you were a salesman, selling lithographic
  prints.
Trade was stagnant after Munich. Hitler frightened us
  with hints.

War came down, a blackout curtain, shutting out the
kindly sun.
Jews went under, all the playboys somehow lost their
sense of fun.

Still, we always had the weather – freezing cold or hot as
hell –
Birds continued, flowers were rampant, life went on
through shot and shell.

Back at last to shabby London, tired and rationed, sad to
see,
With its tales of air raid wardens, siren suits and hot sweet
tea.

People, literary people, now replaced the roaring boys
Fond of vino, signorinas, dirty jokes and lots of noise.

Tambi, Nicholas and Helen. Come on in. You see them
plain.
Publishing will never, surely, be as odd as that again.

Money, said the British Council, I have money in my
hand.
Get your hair cut, keep your nose clean, live in Civil
Serviceland.

Six years later came the end game – middle grades were
axed. Goodbye!
They were victims of the Beaver's petulant persistent
cry.

Advertising. Advertising. Fatal Lady of the Lake!
No one opts for copywriting, they get in there by
mistake.

You absorbed those business ethics – not the Sermon on
the Mount –
Walked into that artful parlour, had the William Hill
account.

Let the room explode with whizz kids, dollies, every
   kind of Pop!
Only crematorium silence brings that mayhem to a stop.

Money. Children. Mortgage. Rat race. Anxious words
   that tax the brain.
Nagging fears of unemployment drive the middle class
   insane.

It's not pretty when they throw you, screaming, in the
   empty sack,
Filled with nothing but the cries of wives and children
   screaming back.

Does the working class get ulcers? No one worries much,
   if so.
They know jobs are hard to come by, and the pay is often
   low.

They're inured to thoughts of hardship and of being out
   of work.
This is life. It's no good blubbing, throwing fits or going
   berserk.

Moneyed men in Lloyds, the City, can't imagine what
   it's like.
To the driver of an E-type, what's the old penurious
   bike?

Workmen are a bloody nuisance – just a ROAD UP sign
   or two –
Obstacles that spoil their record from the Bank to Luton
   Hoo.

Keep your voice down. Don't start shouting. Let the
   candles burn up straight.
(Privileged and trendy diners stuff themselves with After
   Eight.)

All you learn – and from a lifetime – is that that's the way
   it goes.
That's the crumbling of the cookie, till the turning up of
   toes.

The Ewart Organization

The Chairman's a charming graduate.
He does no work. He just inspires everybody.

The Deputy Chairman makes a few decisions.
He's very good at speaking after dinner.

The Managing Director shouts down the telephone.
His worries affect the lining of his stomach.

The executives wear dark suits, collars and ties.
They live their lives in memos of meetings.

The sales force whizz round the country in cars.
They sell soap even when the roads are icy.

The men on the factory floor are bored to extinction.
They're not alive, they go through the motions.

The secretaries are picked for their nubile attractions.
They type, varnish their nails, tell everything often.

There's a lot of life in the Ewart Organization.
Needless to say, I am the Chairman.

The Young Seduction Poem

I chatted it up, admired it birdwise,
and smoothed it very gently wordwise,
I filled it full of gins and fed it,
it very sweetly smiled and said it
would come with me for the week-end.

I drove it down, its gear was swinging,
under its breath it started singing,
it fluttered its enormous lashes,
giving out with dots and dashes,
to morse me it was my good friend.

I gave it lunch, I gave it kissing,
it told me that its heart was missing
on several cylinders and after
it broke into loud girlish laughter;
I felt its will begin to bend.

I moved it out that night for eating,
the wine took a terrific beating,
I brought it back and overhauled it.
It kept its knickers on and stalled it –
money was all that I could spend.

Dean Swift Watches Some Cows

How, when they lift their Tails, the Shit shoots out!
A foul Volcanoe next a Waterspout.
The Anus and Vagina are so near,
Each lovely Dame cannot repress a Tear
To think she's modelled on the selfsame Pattern.
And so are Queens, and so is ev'ry Slattern.

'Twas the Propinquity of these two Holes
That made Divines doubt Women had not Souls.
They knew those Furrows that would bear the Tilth –
Men could not choose but sow their Seed in Filth –
And how from Ordure sprung could Life be good
Or Mystery be part of Womanhood?

2001: The Tennyson/Hardy Poem

When I am old and long turned grey
And enjoy the aura of being eighty,
I may see the dawn of that critical day
When my lightest verse will seem quite weighty.
I shall live somewhere far away,
Where the illiterate birds are nesting.
To pilgrim admirers my wife will say:
       Ewart is resting.

Instead of the heedless sensual play
And the youthful eyes of love and brightness
I shall see critics who kneel and pray
In homage – I shan't dispute their rightness –
And Supplements keen to seem okay
Will flatter me with fulsome pieces.
Scholars will put it another way:
       Ewart's a thesis.

When the aching back and the bleary eye
And the dimness and the rationed drinking,
The cold unease of the earth and sky,
Leave me no pleasures except thinking
I shall be warmed (but what will be 'I'?)
With the awe inspired by what's Jurassic,
And people will say, before I die:
       Ewart's a classic.

Soon comes the day when the stream runs dry
And the boat runs back as the tide is turning,
The voice once strong no more than a sigh
By the hearth where the fire is scarcely burning.
Stiff in my chair like a children's guy,
Simply because I have no seniors
The literati will raise the cry:
          Ewart's a genius!

The Language of Love

HARRIS. *Euphemia Dorothy. – In ever loving memory of our
darling Muth. We thank you sweetheart for all your love and
devotion. – Dadwad and Ossisy, Billy Buntnums, Jack,
Peter and Dickums.* The Times, *4 March 1970*

Like a baby-talking tea cosy,
how such names polish up the silver,
count the teaspoons,
lock up tight
with goodnight kisses!

That sunset is too rosy –
but all the nuclear power of Wylfa,
the magical runes
of the owl night,
can't keep cissies

from strongly inbred feeling,
and it's certainly very often better
to have than not
in a hard life.
The affluent families

227

perhaps are the most revealing
of the soft love that transcends the letter?
A meal kept hot
by a fond wife?
Battles like Ramillies,

with the indecisive victors
at the blasting domestic cannon,
are usual here
and the rough poor
can't afford lovey-dovey.

Strict as the iron lictors,
no imaged sentimental Shannon,
Time is no clear
stream past their door –
partridges in a covey,

harsh words fly up so quickly,
if there's chocolate it's likely to be bitter,
for most of us –
and we shun
loveterms like rabies

but one can react *too* slickly,
there's a slight nervousness in the titter.
Ridiculous?
It's sad fun –
and in some ways we remain babies.

Literary Unions

*I have met with women whom I really think would like
to be married to a Poem and to be given away by a Novel*
JOHN KEATS, 8 July 1819

When the husband and wife sit
typing their novels, back to back,
there's a dialogue as the letters clack?
One stops for a smoke or a bit

of advice is asked, an adjective weighed?
This would be extremely cosy
if there were no such thing as jealousy –
and writing's an honourable trade.

But when it's *writers* the girl wants
then one should start to run.
If she's dying to be married to one
you'll be treated like Mary Quant's

last year's creation; there's
danger of a change of fashion.
Watch when warning lights flash on.
It could all end in tears.

It's equally bad if each word
you speak is treated like Holy Writ.
Being worshipped is boring, it
can make you feel absurd

unless you're arrogant enough to take
it like when Venus flopped on Adonis;
there are some literary phoneys
who revel in it and no mistake.

So it's best when the girl's just
a girl, and reads the *Sun*,
hasn't heard of John Donne
and flaunts an illiterate bust.

The Sexy Airs of Summer

In the summer the sex comes –
　for even the greatest poets.
Gito and Tryphoena get
　ready for a long ride.
It's very natural, really.

There's a baring of soft bums;
　all simple, and we know it's
compulsory (almost), a set
　book, and open wide
to interpretation. Ideally,

the serious say, the best
　writers think it trivial.
But there's a Goddess – or two –
　who flaunts a divine gash
and takes no account of meanies

who won't admit the guest
　or splosh the wine, convivial,
as I do or as, probably, you
　do. She has an unfash-
ionable love of the penis?

Yes, she has. But it's not
　admitted by poetry-lovers.
They have animals and trees
　on the brain, sunsets, blue
sky, isolated images,

true love that simmers hot
　between the book's covers
(novels have tits and knees).
　Sex? Why, they'd sue
the Muse for damages!

From the Phrase Book

Surely it is only right to arrive
With a satisfactory sausage for Germaine?

He is very sick, he has taken an overdraft.
The label tells: Pour in two heaping teaspoons.

There is something wrong with my transmission.
I was slightly oiled at the Service Station.

Did you not buy it for two hundred florins?
You will not get much change out of him.

In this country it is not politic to talk
But our new prison is the best in the world.

Drive to the left, Sir, and take the motorway.
That is the fastest road to the Cemetery.

The So-called Sonnets *

Sonnet: Lifetime

I wear a big codpiece to show I am the King.
There's nothing more public than a private soldier.
My thoughts decorate the walls as crude as posters,
they're simple in their blazing primary colours
and flat, not subtle. Every weekday morning
the office smells of vending machine coffee
and warm paper. But outside it's cold.
One must do nothing to offend one's liege-lord.

The great generalizing poets of the past
run onto sandbanks in a land of detail,
percentage was a word they never knew.
Literature's full of tie-wigs and laudanum,
pen-pushers, typewriter-tappers, tape-decks.
We may be in at the burning of the books.

* Any poem that has its title prefixed by the word Sonnet is one of
the So-called Sonnets – fourteen lines divided into an octet and a
sextet, rough and unrhyming. Usually the latter develops, or
comments upon, the former.

Sonnet: Soho and West, Saturday Morning

A day when you can't see the top of the Post Office
   Tower.
A mild, oily precipitation. Overall.
In my milk bar the muzak wistfully plays
'Pennies From Heaven'. Outside it's a plague city,
few walkers in the streets. I move among them
like a secret man, my thoughts are phrases,
I am the agent of a foreign Power. My language
would terribly bore dog-fanciers tubed to Cruft's.

The words sit up and beg. I pat them down,
change trains at Earl's Court. It's a sort of play,
tail-wagging energy finally brought to heel.
Meanwhile on the roof of the Playboy Club
two Union Jacks, Old Glory, one Bunny Flag. Two ears,
like sensual man's two-fingers-up to Culture.

Sonnet: A Sectarian View

God is on my side. He will protect me
against the Holebrooks and the Whitearses who
go about like raging roaring lions
seeking whom they may devour. And against
all those who think that sex is dirty.
They have cast several snares for my feet
but I shall rise above them; levitate
into free air, in pure priggish apartheid.

Those demons, those deluded, those obsessed
with every innocent bodily function –
surely with scorpions He will drive them out?
Those lawmakers for others, will not He chastise them?
As they wriggle in their lewd imaginings.
Bad pilgrims, labelled NOT WANTED ON VOYAGE.

Sonnet: Poetry is the Dustbin of the Emotions

As invalids simply revel in invalid port,
so we love our disabilities. They go well into verse.
And that great cannon booming: Fear of Death.
Just pick up everything that the cat brought in
and throw it into the well-turned stanzas
or little pointless poems. Anything not very nice
or painful or depressed – the Muse likes these.
So poetry gets a reputation for being unhappy.

How can we make the unbelievers see
that what to them is only sad or bitter
for us is purging of the discontents
that ride us, spur us? Blood is in the ink,
but it's a kind of homœopathic cure.
Casting the runes on demons. Exorcised!

Sonnet: Away Games

Some agro from a Rumanian referee.
The ball bouncing unevenly. Skidding on the mud.
An acting-injured, jersey-pulling oppositon.
The crowd with klaxons, noise to blow the mind.
One unearned penalty. That, you might say, was it.
If it's against you, then it's all against you,
the gods of football haven't heard of justice;
like poetry, the word 'fair' won't translate.

For us the world is one huge object found,
random with art and wars and income tax,
the very lack of pattern is a pattern;
as it swivels through space, an awkward
high ball in the air, it's lucky or unlucky.
Lucky for some; for some, bad medicine.

Sonnet: What is Needed

A complete new sex. Not those dreary old men and
   women,
where the beautiful are so pleased to be beautiful
and the unattractive live in outer darkness;
but a real democracy where everyone's equal and
   opposite
and nobody's under proof. Satisfaction guaranteed.
That would be something. If jealousy and frustration
could be thrown into the everlasting dustbin,
what an end to sourness and the moulds of madness!

We live, however, in an unregenerate country.
There's no sign yet of that desired mutation.
Monsters are wearing briefs and ties and waistcoats
and filling the world with hours of quiet agony.
Sprightliness wears the bowler hats of boredom
and young difficulties fill the bras and panties.

Sonnet: The Days and Nights to Come

An immense ballroom. Thirties style. And hired
by an immense Company: annual Dinner Dance.
The girls are young and beautiful, so beautiful
you could light a cigar at them. They burn,
some hundreds of them, with traditional ardour;
   flaming youth.
Hairstyles; and tits displayed, old salesmen's jokes:
make a clean breast of it. They shake in joy,
so loving it all, so loving the young men

and (most) themselves. Give it just fifteen years –
or ten. They're kitchen-sinking. Eyes are underlined,
what love did once is now the old routine;
the joint is jumping, sizzling. It's a gas.
The kids have spread that body like a quilt,
A sad negro sings: 'It's a wonderful world!'

Sonnet: Queering the Pitch

They say this fattening body was given me,
with its partial tolerance of minor drugs –
so that it climbs out of a hangover into living
like a fly clambering up the side of a huge glass of gin.
They say there is a pattern in the carpet
and a grand design is being knitted on big needles;
they seriously believe this, like the people
who know their dogs understand every word they say.

And the last man ever to bag a Purple Emperor
and the first man ever to softshoe moondust
are working out something that was always
    programmed.
But I hold to a belief in what is random,
with a backward look at old stone gods in gardens.
At the latest tit-count J. Walter Thompson were leading.

Sonnet: Sentimental Journeys

Noel Coward has been handed down to us. Noel
    Coward
is a flower that's free. Where are the songs
we sung? Nostalgia comes so easy
at all levels, and usually mixed with music.
So even highbrows adore adventure stories;
they got us young, incipient critics, before so many
thousands of words poured through the ageing eyes,
the great works of the serious couldn't move us more.

Don't fool yourself. It's simply because they're *yours*
you value bad music, dubious books; they're emotive
    landmarks,
part of *your* life. So as you love yourself
you love the secret heiress, the brave cabin boy,
the first books self-read, self-chosen. Blackmore,
    G. A. Henty.
Literary merit would be by accident only.

Sonnet: Books

So many books are crying out loud 'Unfair!',
see themselves Bronte-wise, wronged governesses
who could tell the neighbours a thing or two. Injustice.
Novels are written to prove the world's a cad,
and every morning someone wakes up to the fact
he/she is married to an unpleasant person.
There's something in it. But what were you expecting?
No justice can turn back the springing tiger.

If the beleaguered heroine dies from the bite of a badger
or a wasp sting, that is tragic/comic
but a more likely cause of death than heartbreak.
Most of what happens can't be budgeted for,
cry-babies invite the joyful persecution.
It's a dog world – but still the only one.

Sonnet: Intimations of Mortality in the Lower Richmond Road

A poster says 'Buy Wandsworth Bonds', on a bookstall
is a copy of *The Slave Of The Lamp* by H. Seton
   Merriman, a
novel that warns against the Society of Jesus.
Buying bonds is also a warning. What is coming is the
   Future,
within fifty yards I pass two old blinding dogs
grey-muzzled as the grey of my earside longhair.
With them and with all the old shrivelled women of
   Putney
I have sympathy; we queue for something in common.

I don't want to die, I want to write more and
much better poems, a harmless ambition. Also, I don't
   want to leave
the sexual objects. They link so directly
with a dark-haired undergraduate who was nervous
and silly. We all want to get as close as possible to
that nice girl. But the skin is a barrier.

Sonnet: The Only Emperor is the Emperor of Ice Cream

I want a new half million pound account
that I can bash into with hammer-headed words,
revolutionize the agency's billing, put myself
among the greatest writers of TV spots for ever,
something so classical that books on advertising
will quote it for cub copywriters: a new King Lear
but bringing consumer comfort, a Verdi
of cornflakes or detergents consoling all.

That's the way the kids get fed and clothed.
Consumer goods beget consumer goods,
the god is eaten. Self-perpetuating markets
demand our sacrifice, my bending of the mind
I offer up to cans and aerosols and packs.
Surely someday those shining gods will speak?

Sonnet: Concert in Leighton House

Missed seeing his grandson by sixteen years.
We didn't get on. For textbook reasons.
My father a difficult man, with a difficult life.
Something of that disturbed adolescence
comes at me now with Schumann's Sturm und Drang,
violin and piano warring through the air
passionate hate, a bitter kind of love,
that close at last, resolved in tingling silence.

Bathing on walls Lord Leighton's bushless beauties
wear a Victorian calm, the spiritual Burne-Jones faces
invite a martyrdom as quiet as muted strings.
After the life, the artefacts are quiet,
a harmony under glass, dead piano keys.
What I regret is also fixed for ever.

Sonnet: The Last Things

Of course there's always a last everything.
The last meal, the last drink, the last sex.
The last meeting with a friend. The last
stroking of the last cat, the last
sight of a son or daughter. Some would be more
charged with emotion than others – if one knew.
It's not knowing that makes it all so piquant.
A good many lasts have taken place already.

Then there are last words, variously reported,
such as: Let not poor Nelly starve. Or:
I think I could eat one of Bellamy's veal pies.
If there were time I'd incline to a summary:
Alcohol made my life shorter but more interesting.
My father said (not last perhaps): Say goodbye to Gavin.

An Imaginary Love Affair (1974)

'All love affairs are imaginary'

The Lover Complains

Writing your name on steamed-up windows,
standing at bus-stops where you've stood.
Such things can do no harm, but they don't do much
   good.

Small presents treated like holy relics,
your words treasured like those of saints.
Such love is a religion that neither fails nor faints?

Drinking to you in pubs – but lonely,
without you, without the lip or hand.
Such are the contacts that bring comfort. Do you
   understand?

It's a kind of long-range worship.
I want it closer, very very close.
Such love would be real and solid, not distant and
   verbose.

Writing the Poems of Loss

Some poets even seem to enjoy
writing the poems of loss
that are so truly sad and affecting.

I've always preferred to keep hold,
loving the girl, though her loss
may be what I'm expecting.

A poem's no use on a bed
(though they talk of 'pleasing the eye');
it's a poor, very poor, consolation.
What's the use, when she just isn't there,
bringing the tear to the eye
of Eng Lit admiration?

There's a time for the masterly plaint
weeping the loss of the flower.
That time isn't yet; so don't rush it.
Keep the heartfelt iambics on ice.
Human love is a delicate flower –
a canto could crush it.

To a Plum-Coloured Bra Displayed in Marks & Spencer

The last time I saw you, as like as two pins,
you were softly supporting those heavenly twins
that my hands liberated before the gas fire
in the mounting impatience of driving desire,

when the nipples appeared with their cherry-ripe tips,
so inviting to fingers and tongues and to lips
as they hardened and pardoned my roughness and haste
and both had, like her body, a feminine taste.

You're a bra made in millions, promiscuously sold –
but your sister contained something dearer than gold.
Mass-production, seduction; you've got it all there
on that counterfeit torso so cold and so bare,

243

but you serve to remind me, as nothing else could,
of the heartbeats and touching, what's tender and good.
I could ikon you, candle you, kneel on the floor,
my love's symbol of richness – in all else I'm poor!

Cleft for Me

Ah! Cleft for me! the lover cries,
that simple girlish part
as powerful as expressive eyes
though further from the heart!
From birth ordained, o She divine,
existing only to be mine!

Existing in that little girl
beneath the tiny skirt,
as winsome as a walnut whirl,
a tireless, heartless flirt,
fashioned by Venus, made to be
open and friendly just to me!

Oh, lover, your romantic pen
has carried you away;
it has been loved by other men,
and that auspicious day
when that wet sponge assuaged your thirst
won't be the last, was not the first.

Hurried Love

Those who make hurried love don't do so
from any lack of affection
or because they despise their partner
as a human being –
what they're doing
is just as sincere as a more formal wooing.

She may have a train to catch; perhaps the
room is theirs for one hour only
or a mother is expected back or
some interruption
known, awaited –
so the spur of the moment must be celebrated.

Making love against time is really
the occupation of all lovers
and the clock-hands moving
point a moral:
not crude, but clever
are those who grab what soon is gone for ever.

The Lover Reflects: Hearts That We Broke Long Ago Have Long Been Breaking Others

You tell me about an old affair
with a painter, on a top floor, in Chelsea,
(perhaps there is nothing quite so silly
as retrospective jealousy)
that lasted for two years – a 'long affair'
you say – and I picture you
in love with a man who is unimaginable.

My desire is equally to have been him
and to have been you; even to hear of
shared love in past summers is soothing,
since I am a man who has never loved
anybody who loved him.
So it's nice to know such things can happen.
As of now I am flirting with the ugliness of age.

This feeling is wistful, a kind of sweet and sour
pork, in terms of a Chinese menu.
Perhaps if I could sit with half a bottle of vodka,
mixing it with water in a glass,
pouring it in slowly, some peace would come?
The truth is, I've never been good at sharing.
To describe you adequately, these dead words fall short.

The Lover Writes a Heterosexual Lyric

Far less than a hundred years from now
your glorious cunt will be dust (or ashes).
But how to forget you? Tell me how!
The thunder explodes, the lightning flashes,

the emotions drum up a romantic storm,
and *your* face smiles in that lurid light.
Love is exclusive, and that is the norm:
a central attraction, not left or right.

You are the one, and the tired old words
run slick off the biro, but still are true.
Nature is fine, with the bees and the birds,
but the only Nature I want is you.

Nobody else quite has your face,
or there's something wrong with the eyes or hair,
that's why nobody can replace
the you that is no longer there.

The more they're like you, the more it hurts.
They remind all right – but that right's still wrong.
He's a hard man who coldly smiles and flirts
when that siren is singing her undersong

and I'm not hard, and I hear each note
clear as a bell in that dismal grey;
like a tiny figure on a twilight boat,
smaller and smaller, you sail away.

Pushing the Boat Out

You didn't ever ask me
to fall in love with you –
I was just someone new –
yet the result's the same
as if you were to blame.

And I could never hate you,
you walk around so sweet,
between your hair and feet
you carry what to me
is Beauty and Eve's tree.

But when you push the boat out,
I know and understand,
you can't say where you'll land.
A girl took off a dress
for joy – and my distress.

The Lover Doesn't Complain

Although it's sad, of course,
when a love affair ends,
it comes as a relief –
mixed in with the grief
(for you can never be friends)
is the joy of the pastured horse.

Don't sing 'Abide with Me' –
though you miss that little room
and all her dark strong charm
you cosseted with your arm,
never relapse into gloom,
at least, in a sense, you're free.

The not knowing where you stand,
the lover's old despair –
only the greatest fools
pursue a love that cools –
are gone with her stirring hair
and her adored small hand.

But oh! (as the poets say)
how lovely if she had
loved you completely too!
When a girl is keen on you
and both together go mad
that will be the day!

A Dialogue between the Head and Heart

Of course, she's only a digestive tube, like all of us.
Yes, but look what it's attached to!

The Lovers Reflects on Consolation Prizes

When you tell me I look very nice
or give me a parting kiss on the cheek,
this all shows kindness and friendliness
but it's really harder to bear
than the weary fact of the separation

because I know, and you know,
that these are Consolation Prizes,
saying Sorry, you weren't good enough
and Better luck next time,
so at once I am saddened with envy

of a laughing beautiful woman
who can choose her men easily
and drop them without much trouble
into the deep pit of Loss –
my circumstances are exactly the opposite.

The Lover Writes a One-word Poem

You!

In the Saloon Bar

Each Cornish pastie on the bar-top
is ridge-backed like a stegosaurus.

As he waits he remembers
a muff-diver's treasure trove:
a piece of blue loo paper wedged between the lips,
the loop of a tampax.
Tonguing the wild expressions of his love.

Some words were said, of course:
I'm very fond of you.

When the girl's beautiful
you get frightened –
and too great love can lead to failure.
A lot of women
go for the men who are almost indifferent.

That garden gate is closed now.
Looked through but not entered.

An infinite sadness
swims in the wineglass –
like Housman's memory of blue hills.
The young beer-drinkers
are sloshing their pints to the sound of muzak.

The Lover Reflects: Afterwards

Perhaps I was greedy. I know I should be grateful.
You wanted a snack and I wanted a plateful.

Too Little Care of This

Too little to eat, a big chance
of being killed or wounded
(most countries are being run by Armies,
full of brave efficient unpleasant men),

unfortunates in millions;
and in my literate comfort I complain?
It's all the fault of the glands
that make me forget she's just an ordinary woman.

This leads, as it has always led, to
the talk of goddesses and eternal love;
the envy that, being beautiful,
her face can launch a thousand other men

on my same sea.
Conversely, though, I was the one
that felt the excitement of the adoring heart.
It could be a bore

to attract too many people. Vanity, yes,
might smile a bit, but this must make her life
complicated. Since nobody goes for me,
my love was at least a simple thing.

Hearing the Love Note

You never called me Darling
Except when you were coming.

Memory Man

I'm sitting drinking Guinness
in memory of you,
on the wall is written Finis
and although the love was true –
if I were more romantic I would say sublime –
it was not a love that lasted until closing time.

The glasses are being polished
as they shout 'Last orders, please!'
and illusions are demolished
with the same fantastic ease
as the ease with which Joe closes his democratic bar –
if I think of you now, it's 'you were' and not 'you are'.

Each man that loves a woman
must be prepared for this
for a sexual love is human
and betrayal by a kiss
is a commonplace and not just in the holy Book
and it all begins when your eyes take that first long look.

You must have the boldness
to overcome the moods,
the sulking and the coldness,
your love must feed on foods
which wouldn't keep alive a common tabby cat;
no one can have *this* without an awful lot of *that*.

So it's sadly time to drink up
and let them stack the chairs –
he's a wise man who can think up
a remedy that bears
much resemblance to an answer (Venus is a jerk?);
for that holiday is over – from now on it's back to work.

Be My Guest! (1975)

To the Gentle One

Hiding under the leaves, where the fruit grows,
I can see you, you horrible reader,
nibbling my poems, a dirty feeder.

I know your coarse appetite for prose,
how your tiny jaws cut the pages,
digesting fat books in your larval stages.

I understand how you go into deep sleep
in the middle of long American sagas
like a beer-drinker after fifteen lagers.

You're dazed and pupal, you little creep,
in your lepidopterous coma,
oblivous to fruit or flower aroma.

When you emerge from your illiterate night
your wings will take time drying
but your next interest will be flying.

So prepare yourself now for a genuine fright,
my non-loved one, my undarling.
I shall be there waiting – as a starling.

The Larkin Automatic Car Wash

Back from the Palace of a famous king,
  Italian art
Making the roped-off rooms a Culture thing,
At about five o'clock we made a start,
Six teenagers squashed in. And as I drove
North from the barley sugar chimney pots
They sang the changeable teenager songs
That fade like tapestries those craftsmen wove,
But centuries more quickly. Through the knots
Of road-crossing pedestrians, through the longs

And shorts of planners' morse, the traffic lights,
  Over a hill,
Down to the garage advertising tights,
A special bargain, fast I drove on till
I drew up by the new Car Wash machine,
Pride of the forecourt, where a sign said STOP
Clear on the asphalt. In front a smaller car
Stood patiently as brushes swooshed it clean,
Whirling its streaming sides and back and top –
A travelling gantry; verticals, cross-bar.

We wound our windows up and waited there.
  In pixie green
The moving monster lifted itself clear,
The yellow brushes furled and now were seen
As plastic Christmas trees. Its wet last client
Made for the highway and it was our turn.
In gear and under. Two tenpences fed in
A slot on the driver's side. The pliant
Great brushes whirred and closed. Like yellow fern
One blurred the windscreen. Underwater thin

The Science Fiction light came creeping through
  Alien and weird
As when the vegetables invade in *Dr Who*,
Something to be amused at – almost feared.

254

And as the lateral brushes closed our sides,
Sweeping past steadily back, the illusion came
That *we* were moving forward; and I checked
The hard-on handbrake, thought of switchback rides
And how the effect in childhood was the same –
Momentary fear that gathered, to collect

In joy of safety. The tall half-children screamed –
    The girls at least –
Delighted to be frightened, as it seemed,
By this mechanical, otherworldly beast.
The boys made usual, window-opening, jokes.
And soon, tide-turning, the brushes travelled back,
Put our imaginations in reverse,
Though we were still. Like cigarettes and cokes
This was their slight excitement, took up slack
In time that wound by, idle. Nothing worse

And nothing better. To me it seemed so short,
    I wanted more,
I wanted hours, I wanted to be caught
In that dense undergrowth by that wet shore.
This was an exit from our boring life,
A changed environment, another place,
A hideout from the searchers. Otherness
Was that world's commonplace, a kitchen knife,
Something so usual that it had no face –
As the car dripped unnatural cleanliness.

Yes, it was jolly, *Fun for the kids* we say,
    But more than that;
For if you look at it another way
This was a notable peak where all is flat.
Into the main road by the riverside
We right-turned past the pubs that line the route
Where cheering crowds watch boat race crews go by,
Travelling with the full incoming tide.
The roof, the sides, the bonnet and the boot
Shone with new wetness. Yet the dust could lie

As thick there as before; and would, in time,
　　This was reprieve.
Cars too grow old and dirty. Gin-and-lime
Perks up the guest; but all guests have to leave.
In through the main gate of the block of flats
I drove my giggling adolescent load,
And in vibrating door-slammed solitude
I parked. Under their different hats
Spiritual experiences work in a kind of code.
Did I have one? I, from this multitude?

From V.C. (a Gentleman of Verona)

Give me the Daulian bird and Locrian Arsinoë.
I want to arrange a protest in high places.
I just want to say to a few fat-nippled goddesses:
　　　It isn't fair.

It's your door that I'm complaining about.
It's far too neutral. It admits revolting lovers,
fast talkers and political nitwits.
　　　I hate it.

It never speaks but if it did I know it
would have an American accent, smacking
its lips and saying, glutinously: 'That girl's a
　　　cocksucker.'

If I had my way it would be closed for ever
against those pretentious people whose main crime
is that they aren't me. It should only open,
　　　youwise, mewards.

Doors are disgusting. They'll let in anything –
secret police, creditors, puritan censors,
men with eviction orders. They're great painted
        layabouts.

But that I know it can keep out competition,
I'd have it off its hinges. Don't talk about oiling!
It's a Public Enemy – to me, you, and Venus
        a complacent traitor.

For Lord John Roxton

Tell it all gently
there is no aftermath/
you in the Albany
poured the stiff whiskies/
the lionhunting gentry
covered the dinosaurs/

Cigars went with bravery
the yarns of the hinterland/
it was a policy
you had a stab at it/
you had no family
winging pteranodons/

Spotless the napery
women were virtuous/
where was the fallacy
you never guessed at?/
in the big library
beards had a theory.

The Mystery of Edwin Drood

(and Who Was Datchery?)

Mr Crisparkle
is absolutely
        masturbating with
muscular christianity,
a cornflake breakfast.

He is the commissar
who tells everybody
        what they have to
do. He has Neville
buttoned in 17 pockets.

Little Rosebud
swaps ST's with
        Helena. Edwin
is the goalless
unmarked footballer.

Mr Grewgious
is just another
        pure living wet dreamer,
Miss Twinkleton
inserts a ruler.

But stay! who
is this totally
        melodramatic
opium-smoking
tomb-haunter?

Who with Durdles
owlhunts the old ones?
        Down by the weir
he worships Kali,
J.J. to the boardroom,

the double-lifer
among the singles.
        He is the
real one, the true
hip hypocrite.

The Afterflu Afterlife

Life is so strict that every act must rhyme,
Centipede poem beating out the time,
While dry lips lust for ice, for ice and lime,
While plonking rhythm meets the hourly chime
To make the written mime a paradigm

Of journey through the sameness of its tense,
Where brightest cities give the most offence
And meaning runs on darkly past the dense
Forest of black hysterical no-sense,
A low unvarying fence, without pretence

To shine in sun, or even to reflect
The moonlight, where a man might stand erect
And from some possibilities select
The difference they told him to expect,
In this or that respect. We genuflect

Before such length of sentence; it is long,
And birds are bursting, not bursting into song,
But under foxes' teeth, and a dull gong,
Booms in an artform that is wholly wrong,
But right where we belong; the gardener's prong

Spears nuisances in the bad undergrowth
And slow and otherworldly is the sloth
That creeps with treelife, and we have them both,
Archaic too, as meaningless and loth
We heard the dead word 'troth' once in Arbroath.

To cross the ice before the ice can crack,
To tighten muscles now deformed and slack,
To straighten the curved-in bedridden back,
To run once more with the commuting pack?
To stumble with the hack? The answer's black

And harsher than the rook or raven's caw
And comes as quickly as the jay or daw
Flies the grey wolf's unheard marauding paw.
All are timebound and subject to Time's law,
That was the scene we saw. The wind is raw,

The angels don't appear to tell us: 'Lo!
This must be done, for it is written so!'
The gods don't answer the imploring O!,
Sad islands form this archipelago,
It's all no go, no go – a triple no.

Reading Keats on Holiday at a Rented Flat in Saltdean

John Keats's letters
have very few betters
and they're full of occasional verse,
so for holiday reading
they were what I was needing –
though they tell of the terrible curse

of Poetic Ambition
(when you switch the ignition
you expect to be able to start
for a literary Glory –
but that's not the whole story,
Fame doesn't accompany Art

as her natural companion,
there's a wide and deep canyon
between what we want and we get.
Time's the critical sorter,
if their name's writ in water
the ambitious end up looking wet).

So it's best to go easy,
for Saltdean is breezy,
it's relaxing to lie in the sun;
if the poetic peaks
are reserved for the freaks,
let them have them. We still have our fun.

There's a gnome in the garden,
a young man gets a hard-on
with a girl who is full of Romance.
Life goes on, ordinary,
milk comes up from the dairy
and a batsman's correcting his stance.

That Traffic Warden
hasn't heard of Auden;
reading is only for schools.
They wake up for the telly
like the soldier's reveille –
but they're not necessarily fools.

Though the Plain Man is sensual
he lives well in that tense you all
praise who think Sartre was the boy;
and to live in the present
can be very pleasant
and well worth a few Odes to Joy.

The kids on the beaches
are a lesson that teaches
how our Foresight can spanner the works;
they don't howl when with damp arts
the sea makes their ramparts
like the Parthenon after the Turks.

Even Arts that are greatest
must survive, at the latest,
as dead languages, part secondhand;
if the sea is eternal
we are annual (or journal)
and the best of our life work is sand.

Going To

Some say Peter Rabbit
is buried in Père Lachaise,
some men love operas
in barking German,
some sit up all night
with a sick joke
or fondle an LP –
The Beauties of Beethoven.

Some can write novels
on sheets of sandpaper,
some cannot bear
the smell of bananas,
some regard sex
as an eight-pronged octopus,
go out like a light
when The Terror is mentioned.

Some are so singular
they can never be plural,
live in their skins like
the gnomes of the Aftermath,
go underground
with computer salesmen,
at just one bad word
can sulk for two years.

Some are found wanting
Eternity timewise,
love their big appetites
for personal relations,
some have sparkling
eyes for what's wholesome,
some count the railings –
might even get there.

The Screen

This is the land where Stalin, like something out of
  Disney,
Snarls between clenched teeth: 'Get Trotsky!',

Where a paramour of Charles II smiles at him lightly,
Winks, whispers 'I'm mad at you, Your Majesty!',

And Keats says 'Yes, we better had!' to Shelley,
Wicked Cromwell has desthroyed Oireland entoirely,

Robin Hood calls the Sheriff of Nottingham a heel,
  naturally,
Ladies love outlaws and all the monks are jolly.

The further in time the more acceptable; but latterly,
Where we *know* what they might have said, a bit silly –

Like Coghill trying to make Chaucer read easily.
It stands like a wide screen between us and History.

If

If I ever came back (if we are speaking of impossibilities
and revenants and Scholar Gipsies
and belief in Time Travel and supernatural facilities)
if by some sort of spiritual ellipsis
my entire life could be compressed into one episode
current between the anode and the cathode,

I would choose you to come back to – not in the inanities
of a daily life spent as a reviewer
but in a centre of learning, a place where the humanities
are taught, though few and daily fewer
those who would remember me in its venerable streets,
while dons lecture on the language of Keats,

and I would meet you in a pub with a garden and
the academic background wouldn't matter
or the centuries in which undergraduate and ordinand
in rough-walled quads trod the flat stones flatter,
and for one hour we would talk, touch and look –
by heart, and not according to the book.

That pub still stands, where I celebrated my affinity
with you; and its trade doesn't slacken;
and the long line of lovers stretches to infinity
in the bed-sitting-room and in the bracken,
and in that walled courtyard with its trees
you and I are the ghostly absentees.

Found!

(McCall's, July 1969)

Even protects you on your first day. Your worst day!
(We took the inside out
to show you how different it is.)

It flowers out. Fluffs out.

How to keep the most girl part of you
fresh and free of any worry-making odors.

People who have had schizophrenia
remain very sensitive.

Sharing their entertaining ideas and their recipes
are these five Washington hostesses.

Everything from cheesecake to moose meat.

Wear it with two print-slashed scarves,
tied one atop the other.

In a frozen dinner . . . only from Swanson.

The Dell

My mother took us, when we went walking
    across Hyde Park, to the rural dell
where wild rabbits occasioned excited talking
    and a kind of rustic enchantment fell,
    a woodland spell,

over our London whose traffic, roaring,
  was distanced there; but never odd
did it seem to us that our spirit's soaring
  was at the command of a country god;
  and brock and tod

might too be hiding in that green hollow –
  this was our simple, childish thought.
Given the premise, conclusions follow.
  That was the magic we found (and sought),
  as children ought.

The great black rock that towered there only
  seemed unusual, out of place
we never thought it; barbaric, lonely,
  hiding a dreamlike Freudian face,
  removed from Grace,

or primitive; such thoughts came later,
  with knowledge. A darkly standing stone
didn't disturb us, our joy was greater;
  though in a railed, forbidden zone
  it stood alone.

Years, years after, in summer twilight,
  I stood there, before the dell, with you
and the stone gleamed black with a lamplit highlight,
  and then and there, at once, I knew
  yes, what was true.

That you, as rare as a four-leaf clover,
  wouldn't hurry now, as once, so gay;
that, like my childhood, your love was over,
  the dell an excuse for one more delay
  on our homeward way.

Experience Hotel

The alcoholically inclined
who live in this hotel
are often stoned out of their mind
and only ring the bell
for bottles of that special kind
they know and love so well.

The ladies in their mules and wraps
who haunt the corridors
are knowledgeable about Dutch caps
and more discreet than whores
though not so different perhaps
behind their numbered doors.

The staff is neutral in all this
and tired from too much work
ignoring every pinch and kiss
from drunks who slyly lurk
to grope the matron and the miss
and the Manhattan clerk.

Trafalgar Day, 1972

All bathed and brindled like a brushed cat,
with a slight hangover from a literary party
(and what could be nicer than that?)

on the day that one-armed bandit finally bought it
I celebrate your sixteenth birthday;
Who (one could say) would have thought it,

when I was a neurotic sixteen at Wellington College,
that I should ever be a girl's *father*,
straining after poetry and carnal knowledge?

But there you are and here I am, and let it be believed
it was during a broadcast performance
of Mozart's *Idomeneo* that you were conceived.

So the whirligig of time brings in his revenges
(don't quote me on that one)
and something as mystical as our lost Stonehenges

has added another link to the chain of being,
making you real and believable,
and believing is (believe me) rather like seeing,

as you get stuck into *Jude the Obscure*,
in the gear of your generation;
Hardy certainly thought that Tess was pure

and said so on the title page. Though this is a concept
and a word that doesn't apply
much nowadays, and words themselves are inept

to transmit a person's quality, you've got a womanly
feeling
of the kind men often lack.
That's what makes women, mainly, so appealing,

and when the hawks gather round to bully a dove
you'd be soft-hearted; and
the emotion you inspire in me could, loosely, be called
love.

Fiction: The House Party

Ambrose is an Old Etonian and he
is terribly in love with a girl called Fluffy
who has Lesbian tendencies and is very attracted
to a sophisticated debutante called Angela Fondling
who was once the mistress of old Lord Vintage.

Don and Vi come to stay at the Castle
and neither of them know how looking-glasses aren't
    mirrors
or what wines go best with fish or even how to
handle a butter knife or talk about horses.
Don makes a joke about being unstable.

Fluffy doesn't know where to look and Ambrose
chokes on his claret. His Lordship is thinking
about a certain incident in 1930
when 'Filthy' Fynes-Pantlebury rode a bay gelding
up the main staircase and into a bathroom.

Angela is writing a book about the middle classes,
she keeps giving Don and Vi gin and depth interviews
and trying like a mad thing to understand Bradford.
Lady Vintage is pathetically faded
but she loves a young criminal in London: Reg. Ratcock.

They sometimes meet in the afternoon, on Fridays,
and smoke a lot of pot in the tenement basement.
Ambrose is thinking of taking Holy Orders,
he usually thinks of Fluffy as a very young choirboy.
Vi wants to go to the loo but she's shy about asking.

Lord Vintage has vanished into several daydreams;
he remembers well how Frank Fondling once shot a
    beater.
Don is getting very tired of gin. Vi wets her knickers.
Fluffy says to Ambrose: 'But what *is* a chasuble?'
And Angela keeps her tape-recorder running. . .

270

Fiction: A Message

'My dear fellow!' said the great poet, putting his arm
    affably round Ponsonby's neck,
'I respect your feelings for Gertrude. I realize they have
    something to do with sec
or secs or whatever they call it. Of course in my little
    backwater I haven't moved with the times –
just listen to the bells of St Josef – how I love those
    chimes!'

Down below, the Austrian lake reflected his agonized
    incomprehension sleepily in the sun.
'I'm at the end of my tether!' cried Ponsonby. 'But you –
    your race is nearly run –
I look to you for a message. I know that behind her
    spectacles she has the most beautiful eyes,
I've heard her playing Chopin at midnight with rapt,
    adoring cries!'

'These things are sent to try us' said Anzeiger. 'You'll
    find something in Apollonius of Rhodes,
or one of the Desert Fathers, that proves fairly
    conclusively that women are toads.'
'I've told myself so, yet I often have the most
    incomprehensible puzzling dreams.
I dream of the Kaiserhof, of milk churns, of chocolate
    creams.

Sometimes I run into a dark wood of feathery soft
    perfumed aromatic trees
or I'm sinking in unimaginable sweetness like honey,
    right up to my knees,
or I see Gertrude waving from a cottage with a very
    attractive rose-circled door.
I'm wearing my Norfolk jacket and, I'm ashamed to say,
    nothing more!'

'That sounds like the Flesh', pondered Anzeiger,
　　fingering gently Ponsonby's fair curls.
'We know well that St Anthony was tempted in dreams
　　by demons and dancing girls.
Though these apparitions, old fellow, seem so irrational,
　　so disturbing, so unaccountably odd,
I think we can safely assume, in your case, they don't
　　come from God.

Though, of course, He has been known to work in some
　　really very mysterious ways.'
'But what shall I do?' cried Ponsonby. 'Offer it up. Just
　　pray and give praise.
We'll take the pony and trap and go down on Sunday,
　　dear boy, to Linz.
The Lord will lend a kindly ear to your account of your
　　sins.'

They turned and walked towards the house, arm in arm.
　　The sun had nearly set.
As they approached the pretty garden, by the last dark
　　sentinel pine trees they met
Gertrude in a light summer dress, confidently smiling,
　　friendly and demure.
Ponsonby smiled back. He was above her. Of that he was
　　now sure.

Fiction: The Definite Article

What was the mood? Calm. What was the
    weather? Rainy. He crumbed the
kitchen table with his hands, felt the
    caster sugar sandy on fingers, the
milkblots wet. Across the road the
    sign of the Blue Star Garage, the
blue and white letters, showed. The
    B and the S were obscured, the
message LUE TAR; if he moved the
    extra foot or so one way the
words became UE AR. He called it the
    message of continued existence, the
Great Affirmation, even the
    gateway had blocked the
words for its own purpose. This was the
    trumpeted identity, the

tall fact of heness; and the
    effect was to make him all the
more lonely. Each morning he woke with the
    cry: 'Darling!', with the
languid 'You made me stiff!', the
    hangover of old love, the
memory of big bosoms, the
    carbon copy of youth, the
result of education. Oh, the
    loneliness! Bland in the
huge city, he meditated the
    others; they moved the
legs and arms, they were the
    working clockwork models, the
human scenery his eye walked past, the
    tribes perfected in the sign of 'the'.

Consoler Toujours

All bright love that strikes like lightning on our so-so lives
        is a bonus,
like the honey bees are making in their secret hives
        and the onus
to enjoy it is on us as decrepitude arrives,
        each Tithonus

remembering the years-ago girls clearly in his heart,
        not forgetting
all those faces and those kisses, every sexual part,
        heavy petting,
and each happy ending from a slow or frantic start,
        and its setting

—all those rooms that now hold others or are bulldozed down,
        flats and houses
standing tall as ghosts and ghostly in a ghostly town.
        The mind drowses
quietly on the beds and sofas, red, white, pink or brown.
        This arouses

old emotions, recollected in tranquillity.
        Thought's assizes
try the case of W or beauties B and C,
        no disguises
hide the naked A; as she is sleeping there so peacefully
        the sun rises. . .

Women count and hoard their lovers for the days ahead,
        single-bedding,
long last hours in hospitals, know towards what bed
        they are heading
and what bells will ring for them at that lonely dead
        last wedding;

theirs and ours, the lovely bodies end up in a mess
        or disgusting.
Yet these are the hands that fumbled to undo a dress,
        young and trusting
we gave sexual adoration, love and tenderness,
        June was busting

out all over like a song (and that's a fairly old
        jazz song title)
so let's remember that we had it – something gleamed like gold,
        very vital,
something beautiful and better than time's creeping cold
        sad requital.

To the Slow Drum

Beat for Auden, Wystan Hugh!
Solemn musics sound, where you
keep funereal pace with Time,
showing sorrow in a mime.
Measured steps go best with grief,
fitting for our old belief:
hurry does not chime with Death,
mourners mayn't be out of breath –
dead ones lie in that sad state,
doomed by tolling bells as 'late'.

Muted trombones, fateful brass
help the slow procession pass,
black on black and grey on grey
in the twilight of the day.

Music moved him; it is fit
we remember him by it.
Talent such as his is rare
and our singing branch is bare,
where shall we find such an one
now the feeling voice has done?

In the brilliance of his Art
noble grace-notes held their part
bringing harmonies as clear
to the convoluted ear
as the masters in their time,
making flute and oboe rhyme,
furnished for the sister Muse.
Homage that we can't refuse
we must pay to that true sound,
though the singer's underground.

Beat, drum, in the colder night!
If hysteric nuclear fright
seize us, choking, by the throat,
rabbits hypnotized by stoat,
let this be a potent spell
countering the ne'er-do-well
childishness of martial Man;
let these calm him – as they can –
systems closed and so complete
that aggression seems effete.

In that Never–Never–Land
all we know and understand
is that fantasy is fact,
locked as in a sexual act
two are seen to be as one,
play is play and fun is fun.
He could do it, let us swim
in that pool designed by him,
happily ourselves immerse
in the medium of his verse.

All our sorrow, all our fuss,
is entirely now for us,
not for him; for he achieved
more than many once believed
could be in an anxious age –
nervous eyes desert the page.
Beat, then, as the clock-hands cross,
dramatise our sense of loss,
lights are down, here comes your cue –
beat for Auden, Wystan Hugh!

The Odes

The numbered translations of the four Odes of Horace that
follow were made on the principle that the word-order of the
Latin should not on any account be changed. This gives effects
that would not otherwise be obtainable in an English version,
and perhaps restores some of the strangeness of a foreign
language.

The Odes: Book I, 37

Now must be drunk, now with foot free
struck the ground, now with Saliarian
    to decorate the couch of the gods
       the time was banquets, comrades.

before wicked to decant Caecuban
from cellars ancestral, while for Capitol
   queen demented ruin
      sorrow and for Empire was scheming

contaminated with a flock of foul
with disease men, everything wishfully
   hoping and with fortune sweet
      intoxicated. but lessened her rage

hardly one saved ship from the fire,
and her mind drugged with Mareotic
   redirected to true terror
      Caesar from Italy, her fleeing

with oars pressing, the hawk like
soft doves or hare the swift
   hunter on plains of snowy
      Haemonia, so could give to chains

the fatal monster; who more nobly
to perish seeking nor womanly
   feared sword nor the wide
      with fleet fast sought again shores;

bold both fallen to gaze on kingdom
with face serene, strong and rough
   to draw to her serpents, to dark
      with her body drink in the poison,

than deliberate death more ferocious,
by savage Liburnians as it were scorning
   despoiled to be led in proud
      not a humble woman triumph.

The Odes: Book II, 14

Alas fleeting, Postumus, Postumus,
slide years nor piety delay
    to wrinkles and impending age
        will bring and to untamed death:

no if three hundred however many go days,
friend, you please unweeping
    Pluto by bulls, who thrice ample
        Geryon and Tityos with sad

contains wave, in truth by all,
whoever of earth by spoil we thrive,
    it must be travelled, whether kings
        whether needy we shall be peasants.

in vain of bloody Mars we shall lack
and the broken of raucous waves Hadria,
    in vain through autumns harmful
        to bodies we shall dread Austrus:

must be seen black with languid
Cocytus flowing and of Danaus stock
    infamous and damned to long
        Sisyphus Aeolides labour:

must be left earth and home and pleasing
wife, nor of these which you tend trees
    you beyond hated cypresses
        any brief lord will follow:

will take heir Caecuba worthier
preserved with hundred keys and with wine
    will dye the floor proud,
        of pontiffs stronger than at feasts.

The Odes: Book II, 20

Not with worn nor weak shall I be carried
wing biform through liquid air
   poet, nor on earth shall I stay
     longer, and the envy greater than

of the city I shall quit. not I of poor
blood parents, not I whom *you* call,
   dearest Maecenas, shall die
     nor by Stygian shall be bound wave.

now now settle on legs rough
skin, and white I am changed into bird
   above, and are born light
     on fingers and shoulders feathers.

now than Daedalean more famed Icarus
I shall be seen of groaning on shores Bosphorus
   and of Syrtes Gaetulan singing
     a bird and on Hyperborean fields.

me Colchian and who hides fear
of Marsa's cohort Dacian and furthest,
   will know Geloni, by me taught
     will learn Iberian and of Rhone the drinker.

far be with pointless threnodies
and grief unseemly and complainings;
   restrain outcry and of the grave
     put aside the empty honours.

The Odes: Book III, 1

Hate profane vulgar and ward off;
favour with tongues: songs not before
   heard of the Muses the priest
      to virgins and boys I sing.

of kings to be feared in own flocks,
kings of themselves empire is Jove's,
   famous for Gigantic triumph,
      all with an eyebrow moving.

is that than man wider bounds
woods with furrows, this one more noble
   comes down to Campus candidate,
      with morals this and better in fame

contends, to that one crowd of clients
is greater: with equal law Necessity
   draws lots for famous and low;
      every capacious moves the urn name.

drawn sword to whom over impious
neck hangs, not Siculan feastings
   sweet will bring forth smell,
      not of birds and of lyre song

sleep may bring back: sleep of peasant
smooth men not humble houses
   disdains and the shady bank,
      not by Zephyrs agitated Tempe.

him desiring what enough is nor
tumultuous disturbs sea
   nor savage of Arcturus falling
      impetus or of rising Haedus,

not of beaten by hail vineyard
and farm lying, with tree now waters
   blaming, now burning fields
     stars, now winters wicked.

lessened fish the seas feel,
thrown in piles rubble; here frequenting
   rough stones throws down contractor
     with slaves and lord of earth

bored: but Fear and Threats
climb there where lord nor
   leaves bronze of trireme and
     behind horseman sits black Care.

but if the sad nor Phrygian stone
nor of purples than star brighter
   comforts use of nor Falernian
     vine and Achaemenian spice,

why with enviable gates and in new
sublime style should I build a mansion?
   why valley change Sabine
     for riches more burdening?

Sonnet: The Picture on the Packet

I was once a Stupid among Cambridge Clevers
and boys from my prep school are now Lords and Sirs;
though not all seeds come up like the promise on the
   packet
you can guess a lot from the unseen background.
A boy is just a boy to the boys that know him.

A twit or a twerp or a weed; but a chauffeur
is suggestive to the adult eye, a swimming pool
or an MP for a father prepares you for something.

So some step into affluence like a pair of trousers.
Others go down. One woke from an illness
and on being told he had inherited an ostrich farm
gave up the ghost. Went out like a light at twenty.
I was never heir to a golden future.
That's why I live by this uneasy writing.

Sonnet: A Dream

The feeling tone was one of lost love,
bitter, as I woke with a cigar mouth;
but, as Bing Crosby and others have said and
sung, it's better, etc. You can't lose love
unless at one time, in some way, you had it.
As one grows older, one grows reconciled.
The names of the lost are at home in other beds
with difficulties of their own. Not including me.

Dreams work with a kind of neat backslang.
Love could be evol; and the boy a yob.
The approved thing is to be in love with Efil,
she's the girl you ought to fancy. She
is the warm abstraction books call positive.
I like her; but you couldn't call it love.

Sonnet: Be Satisfied with What You Have

You switch on the set and you don't get a picture
as you sit waiting. Or your talent is directional,
like a portable radio it must face the music
or it fades. Don't worry. Such things happen
to everybody. The blank canvas, the white sheet of paper
stare back at the creators of masterpieces
equally as at you. Too much facility
can be just as destructive. There are examples.

Take a sexual parallel. Men with small members
may doubt their abilities; but impotence can also
disturb those whose assets are gigantic.
The overlarge can be too big for women,
love locked out. Be modest. The Muse has compassion.
You will be able to rise to the occasion.

Sonnet: Doo Bist Dee Roo

One of the South London power stations
has a chimney at each corner and looks like
King's College Chapel – which somebody once
    described
as a sow lying on her back. Some love runs
on bottles of cheap wine, like cars on petrol;
clonking, it stalls to a sober end.
There's a terrific amount of love in London,
of all kinds and intensities, at every time and place.

Not so much has romantic or Gothic complexity,
it's mainly now straightforward and utilitarian
like a child's drawing of a complicated machine.

284

We talk of sexual loves – but there are others.
They don't inspire so much fascinating nonsense.
They're usually quieter, less talkative, more peaceful.

Sonnet: Cat Logic

Cat sentimentality is a human thing. Cats
are indifferent, their minds can't comprehend
the concept 'I shall die', they just go on living.
Death is more foreign to their thought than
to us the idea of a lime-green lobster. That's
why holding these warm containers of purring fur
is poignant, that they just don't *know*.
Life is in them, like the brandy in the bottle.

One morning a cat wakes up, and doesn't feel
disposed to eat or wash or walk. It doesn't panic
or scream: 'My last hour has come!' It
simply fades. Cats never go grey at the edges
like us, they don't even look old. Peter Pans,
insouciant. No wonder people identify with cats.

Sonnet: Cat Cruelty

Our cat brings a mouse to the window and drops it.
It hobbles a few feet. One leg is injured.
The cat in an excess of delicate energy
dribbles it like a forward. From now on
there is only one tortuous path for it to follow,
only one destination, and that one a dark one.

The cat mouths it and walks off.
They know how to maim and not to kill.

Cat Inquisition. Extraordinary questions.
From those claws – only the dark destination.
Urbain Grandier. Such things certainly
would go near to make a man hate Life.
For lunch I am eating a savoury stew;
the small bones crunch in my mouth with disgust.

Sonnet: Nature

Sssh! Don't move! Just look. A bullfinch
has just jumped onto a forget-me-not. That's Nature,
the way the Nature-lover sees it (though you needn't
be tired of life to be very tired of London).
It's an alternative society – those rocks and trees and
   birds.
But whatever occurs in nature is natural,
natural men made moon-walkers. These metals are ours,
from the earth's crust, a natural cooling loaf.

Birds, beasts and flowers have the beauty of finished
   things.
Everything's intricate and marvellous. But
   conservationists
come very close to idolatry. And can we afford it?
To worship some indifferent obsolescent warbler
· when the real hard case is burning up landscapes,
the blockheaded violent ragtime cowboy – Man?

The First Eleven (1977)

These eleven poems were not included in the collection
Be My Guest! *for reasons of space and cost.*

The Conventional Love Song

I want to be the blue veins in your breasts,
a small serrated knife handled by you,
the bath water lying on your belly,
a glass of red wine staining your tongue,
a pair of your panties or an expensive bra,
anything close or useful (love is so useless).

What *you* must want to be is simply you.

Tourneur out of Touch

I thought of how bad cooking murders meat,
violates vegetables, penalises puddings.
With private poisons in a fingernail
a cook can fumigate a family,
clear the clean rooms and send them howling
to beds as easeless as the turning spit.
He stabs them with sharp pains. Or, rather, they
use greedy knives and forks upon themselves,
offensive weapons in the war of food,
as each a Brutus runs upon his death.

I thought of prisoned chickens in the cage,
the Little-Ease of cluttered row on row,
close calves drip-fed, that suffer
hoof-rot. I thought of how
10 cm. needles kill a man,
pushed under the lobe of the right ear
into the brain; a little speck of blood
wiped off with surgical spirit. All unknown,
a cerebral haemorrhage guessed
in place of murder on the headlined town.

I thought of lustful crimes and love betrayed,
of cryptic hangings and the colour black
and in dark rooms the whistling of dark wings,
masked movement, treachery. See how the
curtain stirs and yet there is no wind!
A breath of carnage; and the rot of war
comes in conspiracy through centuries
clotted with innocent blood. I see no change.
The mirror sends back man's ambitious face
pocked with police state cruelty and pride.

Orchestra

Cellos are dark

          creamy toffees

smooth on the tongue.

Oboes are

        acid drops.

Drumbeats

      pepper the score

clarinets

      reed warblers

with a fat taste.

Flutes come

         ice-cold, clear.

Violins

      rush to the head,

white wine.

          Violas

liqueurs,

      mild vermouths.

Brass!

   all the harsh hot

curries that stir us.

Harps

     drop

        single

           notes

like water in pastis.

The Hut

That is the hut where she used to work; and there
    under the paint-peeled corrugated iron
with square small windows set in wooden frames
by thumb and spatula she played the old Art games;
    under the moon now, far from bright Orion,
in misty autumn, tenantless and bare

it stands so useless in the bleakly chilling air,
     nettle-surrounded, a falling garden shed,
and cobwebbed to the mean and spidered roof,
sad as great Abbeys – for Time is so aloof,
     indifferent to that life that once she led
when she sat smoking in that single chair.

The canvases have gone. Some empty frames odd-piled,
     African figures on the windowsill,
witness the young Slade student of shared youth,
paint-splashes hold a bitter kind of truth,
     the easel stands at ease in empty drill.
And with these things I must be reconciled.

The friends and sisters go; and all who had in that past smiled
     (and some had beauty, some were bright with wit)
must forfeit health and come to this one room
as dark with memory as a Victorian tomb,
     and we must wrestle with understanding it
until from life and hope we are exiled.

Nightflight

          vampires

        vempires

   vimpires

      vompires

         vumpires

For Samuel Palmer

The countryside is wet and cold.
The lambs are gathered in the fold.
Tax-dodgers run the funny farms.
The nightingale exerts its charms.
Those labourers are very thick.
The setting sun illumes the rick.

Clods are dull clods and loam is loam.
Peace blesses ev'ry cottage home.
The rural rapes ride after dark.
Lightly ascends the twitt'ring lark.
Beer is expensive and not good.
Badgers play in the moonlit wood.

Mindless Nature doesn't care.
Through fields of stubble runs the hare.
Village idiots are grotesque.
The humble cot is picturesque.
Most farming is a frantic fiddle.
Rustic life's a timeless idyll.

Charles Augustus Milverton

see The Return of Sherlock Holmes

Lady Eva Brackwell, the most lovely debutante
    of last
season, will be married (and who dares say that she
  shan't?)
    to the stern
    and mast-
erly Earl of Dovercourt; a sensitive young plant
    in an urn,
    she fast,

yes, to his pure stiffness in a fortnight will be tied –
    but she
has dispatched imprudent letters, shaming to a bride,
    alas!
    to the
impecunious young squire who adorned her countryside –
    a class
    too free!

Oh, who's purloined those letters but Augustus
  Milverton?
    and who
's asking seven thousand pounds the lot, each sprightly
  one?
    What can
    Holmes do?
Though he looks like Mr Pickwick, he's a fiend – and
  she's undone!
    A man
    who knew

no compunction for his victims – a genius in his way –
    and he's
much too fond of swollen money-bags; when victims
    pray –
      smile, face,
      heart, freeze!
She'll be lucky if she falters out the word 'obey'!
      This case,
      Holmes sees,

needs the most oblique approach: impenetrable disguise.
    So he
becomes a gay young workman before Watson's very
    eyes –
      clay pipe,
      goatee –
walking out with Hampstead housemaids (Watson
    shows surprise),
      a type,
      you see,

quite above suspicion in the villain's servants' hall.
    Holmes plans
one last throw – a felony – to win or lose it all.
      This quite
      unmans
Watson. 'Think what you are doing!' Anguished, manly
    call!
      That night
      it pans

out well. With a first-class burgling kit, a nickel plat-
    ed jemm-
y, diamond-tipped glass cutter, and adjustable keys, late,
      with true
      native phlegm

they invade the silent house. The safe! but changeful Fate,
     like you,
     my fem-

inine reader! Holmes has barely time to seize his tools
     when HE
enters. Quick! Behind the curtains! They will both look fools
     if caught –
     but how flee?
Milverton is not a man who plays the game by rules,
     his sport
     villainy.

Claret-coloured smoking jacket, big red leather chair,
     a long
black cigar. Unknowingly he sits before them there
     unperturbed.
     What's wrong?
It's far past his usual bedtime. Does he gloat on fair
     disturbed
     belles, a Mong-

olian idiot's grin upon his round blackmailer's face?
     The door!
Gentle rustle of a woman's dress. Ah, what disgrace
     could bring
     her before
this insufferable bounder, seated there so base,
     a thing
     beyond law?

It's a lady in a mantle, veiled and lithe and tall!
     'It is I.'
Handsome, clear-cut face, curved nose, dark eyebrow
     shading all
     the hard
     glittering eye.
straight the thin-lipped mouth set in a dangerous and
     small
     smile. Guard
     thyself! Fly!

Milverton, however, laughs. 'Ah, you were obstinate.'
    'And you
sent the letters to my husband, to my noble mate,
        a man
        so true
I was never worthy yet to lace his boots! In hate
        he ran
        quite through

grief's whole bitter gamut till it broke his gallant heart.
        He died. . . .'
'Don't imagine you can bully me!' Her thin lips part,
        white hand
        inside,
buried in her bosom. Uncontrolled the wild fears start,
        unplanned,
        to slide

into Milverton's cold, scheming, brilliant, worldly
    brain,
        so clever.
'You will never wring a woman's innocent heart again,
        you will
        never
ruin lives as you ruined mine, to cause such countless
    pain,
        to kill,
        or ever

boast of those disasters that it was your trade to bring
        to our
gentle sex. Take that, you hound! Take that, you
    poisonous thing!'
        Oh, stare!
        Oh, cower!
See the little gleaming pistol emptied in the ting-
        ling air!
        Her hour,

joyfully she takes revenge! 'You've done me.' Still he lies.
        Intent,

295

she grinds a fashionable heel into the upturned eyes.
    Night air,
    passion spent,
the fair avenger leaves the room to Holmes and Watson,
  spies
    who share
    secrets meant

for no one but that Justice who must still protect the
  weak.
    Oh, quick!
open safe and burn the letters, excitement at its peak!
    Escape
    in the nick
of time and run two miles, no breath or even need to
  speak,
    dim shape
    s night-thick!

Solemn in the morning Baker Streetwards comes
  Lestrade
    with news
of most unusual murder, masked marauders; seeks their
  aid.
    Holmes says
    'I refuse'.
Later, though, in Oxford Street they see the photo of a
  lad–
    y, gaze
    and muse. . .

Beauty with a bright tiara on her noble head,
    regal,
stately, Court-robed lady, eyebrows strongly marked,
  well-bred,
    nose curve
    of eagle.
Could time-honoured titles shoot a fellow mortal dead
    or swerve
    to the illegal?

The Clarissa Harlowe Poem

Down then, thou rogue thou, red three-cornered varlet,
and hammer not within my breast so fast!
We rakes appreciate a sin so scarlet,
the dear indifferent's trials are not yet past,
she labours under a father's heavy curse
but yet must love me better – or fare worse.

I offered to salute the lovely fair one,
her teasing letters hidden in her stays.
The charming icicle refused. Oh, dare one
not carry her abroad, to Church or plays?
But you was, Lovelace, by her female scorn
then made to doubt she was a woman born,

an angel rather! 'Sir', she cried, 'unhand me!'
when I upraised the covering handkerchief.
It is impossible she should understand me,
or how I glory in her silent grief,
but more when she lets loose her sparkling tears,
prudent and virtuous, though eighteen years –

no more – she has. Yet with her piercing eye-beams
could regulate the *mother* and the *house*;
as the bright sun within a cloudy sky beams
she ruled my bad companions. Yet a mouse
she is, and Lovelace is the cat,
though devil fetch me if I ever sat

so mute before a prouder, haughtier beauty!
Still all I hear is 'Wretch!', 'Dissembler!', 'Vile!',
so conscious of her virtue and her duty,
so over-nice! The condescending smile
I work for always – it eludes me still,
and she falls into fits, indeed she's ill!

The sex, I know, admires a bold encroacher,
at heart the finest ladies love a rake,
and I have always been the devil's poacher
with such fair game. Where then was my mistake?
She loves me, I conceive, but why so prim?
Why calls she so incessantly on Him?

Why loves she so her friend, that pert virago?
Why hates my *morals* – since I may repent?
Scarce from her closet stirs and eyed like Argo
guarding her honour will not once relent?
She throws Miss Bettinson at my 'scheming' head,
with other fair ones long since brought to bed.

I toil and toil, I plot with my expedients.
She's sullen still, and all I have – her hate!
But I will force her to a close obedience
and she shall own a Lovelace for her mate!
I'll be revenged, and she'll come at my call.
Catching such birds is all, and more than all –

she'll learn to come, and end her prudish blushing,
I'll crook my little finger from the bed.
Freedoms are innocent, and the *last*, a rushing
wide torrent from the mountain's awful head –
which once, a puny stream, scarce wet the stone!
And when that day comes, I'll not lie alone.

From a Well-Wisher

That little poem
you were eyeing in the bar last night,
why don't you knock her off?
Pull her panties down,
investigate her rhythms,
be familiar with her rhyming scheme?

She certainly gave you
the encouragement of a Come on look,
I think she means
to get you into print,
she would like to be published.
But be careful how you handle
her punctuation.

Sometimes they're flirts
and some don't really mean it
but personally I think
she fancies you.
Her nipples had a hard accusing look
that spoke slim volumes.
Get her down on paper,
lay her on a single sheet.

Vacancy

Fresh at the interview
he turned out well –
there was no fumbling
under the table.

Without probing
he answered their questions,
he was so numerate,
ran round the circuits.
He was twit-handed,
they loved his profile,
his name in Cakeland
was Butterfingers.
Sat so straight in
a lilac topcoat,
his boots so polished
they gave you eyeglare.
His monocle made them
feel beastly rotters,
his voice was simply
miles above them.
His vowels astounded –
can you blame them,
they hadn't the courage
to give him the job?

Venus

A goddess has just checked out and
left no forwarding address. She won't be back.
She got so bored with waiting. For so many years
you spoke of her slightingly.
Telephone calls. The unshared drinks at six.
She took in movies, slept late. Oh, yes
she knew you, expected you.

If she was lying in a bath relaxing
and fingering the soap as goddesses do
she was certainly working out an alias.
We only know them under other names.
They change. As the light falls on a building,
changing it. Perhaps she even
had a name for *you*?

Long lunches, scented bedrooms, cold trays
with hot coffee and perhaps an egg.
She had the life of an émigrée, the small
dictatorial smile for room service,
kept clean, kept beautiful.
But now she's gone. You won't see her
again or ever. It's an empty room.

No Fool like an Old Fool (1976)

An Extended Apostrophe to John Hatch Clark, a Comrade Both Ancient and Modern

Dear CLARK, the Name on which I build,
My Shield and Hiding Place,
Whose Promise was not unfulfill'd,
Intelligence and Grace

Abounding greatly even then
In Nineteen-Thirty-Five
When in your Sojourn among Men
I first saw you alive,

The Master of the Cricket Bat,
The Cut and Legside Flick,
Adorn'd by Scholar's Gown and Hat –
As by a double Wick

You burn'd the Candle at both Ends,
With Sport and Intellect
Astonishing your many Friends
Of ev'ry Creed and Sect,

Fair OXFORD's ambidext'rous Pride,
In each Hand a fair Torch
The Way t'illuminate, and guide
With Flame that would not scorch

But show a calm and mod'rate Light
Upon the Way Ahead
To that imagin'd distant bright
Pavilion of the Dead,

302

Where those who gain a First in Greats,
And those who score the Goals,
Alike submit to those three Fates,
While those who frisked like Foals

Lie down at last t'Eternal Rest
And, feeling rather tired,
We too shall sleep, O brave and best,
O CLARK, my much-admired!

Professor Otto Lidenbrock* to Wystan Hugh Auden

(as of 29 September 1974)

You were a rare one indeed –
in crabbed Runic letters from Iceland
you put your message across

early, when Terror abroad
demanded the bardic responses.
Arne Saknussem alas!

with his alchemical lore
could never have flummoxed the Axis;
Snorro Turleson too once

wrote of the foreigner's rule,
a country so banjaxed by Norway.
Gehlenites, fangasites still

(walking-on parts, without speech)
and our titanite of zirconium,
minerals both of us loved,

* In Jules Verne's *Journey To The Centre Of The Earth* (1864),
Professor Lidenbrock is the Leader of the expedition.

neutral, embellish the stage.
That's why we now hold them, inhuman,
    in unregenerate hands;

    we change much faster than they,
and people have called rocks eternal.
    You, by one year, are diffuse.

    I saw the light of my day
one hundred and ten years ago now,
    yes, quite eccentric and odd,

    much given to anger; they said
my sharp nose attracted iron filings –
    students don't have much respect.

    Diesel and Daimler and Benz
by no means had caused the commotion
    later you found so ungay –

    skies were for poets and birds,
our roads weren't as straight but quite fumeless,
    beam engines still were around.

    That was the so-simple scene
that one could call Middle Industrial.
    You'd have been happy, I know,

    in that mechanical peace
before we had jet-lag and nylon.
    Odd you most certainly were,

    not one to welcome the brash
insensitive probe of the bedroom;
    I was a funny one too.

    Liking to think that we share
a true geological mania,
    comrade, I send you my peace!

A Double View

'If you will but speak the word, I will make you a good syllabub
of new verjuice: and then you may sit down in a haycock, and
eat it; and Maudlin shall sit by and sing you the good old song of
the "Hunting in Chevy Chase". . .'
      IZAAK WALTON, *The Compleat Angler*, 1652.

'I only want men with really enormous pricks – nine inches and
more. . . Just imagine what I could do to a prick that long! I
could lash it to a miniature whipping post and then flagellate it
with tiny, jewel-handled whips.'
JOAN C., Sunderland. Letter in *Club International*, 1974.

Relax. Don't get high blood pressure
for rural or Merrie England.
There are many different kinds of pleasure,
they could even mingle and
be none the worse;
nor is one really the reverse

of the other. Bees are humming,
all right, in the warm heather . . .
but you've got another think coming
if you think that was altogether
a Golden Age;
Civil War was all the rage

when Walton put Piscator in this idyll,
and whipping posts were real,
witnesses tortured, in the very middle
of a century ideal
only to us;
who make sentimental fuss

about the Past (past enough, and done with,
we love it!). A good time is
the choice of whom or what you have fun with;

for example, Yanks and Limeys
might not agree.
In the year 1653,

when Cromwell was proclaimed Lord Protector,
a man like staunch Venator,
if you got at him with a lie detector,
would be found a masturbator
as like as not;
only the very greatest clot

thinks that the fantasy worlds are wicked
(the staff might write the letters?),
mild sadomasochism isn't cricket.
Elders aren't always betters –
and an excuse
for *not* eating verjuice

(such a dreamy word) would be most necessary –
since unripe grapes/apples were ingredients.
Also, the letter-writer's accessory
jewel-handled whips are expedients
full of style;
imagination! better by a mile

than the rack, and the crude pressing
to death that was actual.
Rustic peace seems window-dressing.
Though, if we're being factual,
it appears
we've not changed much in three hundred years.

The Theory of the Leisure Class

In those huge Victorian novels that were written during
  the time when Tennyson was occupied with Marianas
  and Mauds
people were saying things like 'What do you think, my
  dear sir, in general, of pious frauds?'
and the language was pompous in the extreme and you
  might guess they one and all were as cold-blooded as
  saurians;
though we know now they all had Secret Lives and were
  having a high old time with those Other Victorians.

There were *malades imaginaires* and interesting invalids
  and ladies with permanently weakened constitutions,
while the rough gin-drinking populace starved or
  enjoyed themselves at public executions.
The ambition of the wealthy was, quite seriously, to do
  absolutely nothing but to drink, to ride, to dance, to
  flirt.
Gambling for high stakes, soldiering, politics, the
  buying of a new horse or a new skirt.

These were the only approved interests. Making money
  was trade. It must have been very gentlemanly but
  boring,
especially for the ladies, who weren't allowed – like their
  husbands and boy friends – to go off whoring.
Governesses suffered most. They had to be well-behaved
  examples and quite preternaturally respectable.
They couldn't get drunk or encourage (or satisfy the
  desires of) men, however delectable.

In a hundred years or so we've changed, with our
  haircuts and our democratic adolescents in classless
  clothes,

though those with the wealth don't show many signs of
    being terribly different from those
whose motto (What We Have We Hold) they held – as Mr
    Mantalini might say – 'like some demd vempire',
and our commercial predominance hasn't survived
    two wars and the disposal of an Empire.

Almost every class now is a leisure class, occupied (as it
    might be) with The Who, The Beatles or Bingo,
turned on by the telly, passively entertained by electronic
    football, Ken Russell, Ringo.
It all makes one think of bread and circuses, of those
    century-gone lives idle and under a blight;
how William Morris, who wanted handicrafts instead of
    machines, might very well have been right.

Incident, Second World War

(In Memoriam P. M. B. Matson)

It was near the beginning of that war. 1940 or '41,
when everything was fairly new to almost everyone.
The bombing of cities we understood, and blackouts;
    and certainly, thanks
to the German Army and Air Force, we'd seen
    dive-bombers and tanks.
But when the fighters came in to strafe with
    hedge-hopping low attacks
how many bits and pieces would be picked up to fill the
    sacks?
Aircraft cannon were not much fun for the weary
    grounded troops
and there wasn't much entertainment when the Stukas
    were looping loops

but nobody knew for certain the percentage who
  wouldn't get up,
how many would be donating their arms or their legs to
  Krupp.
So somebody in an office had the very bright idea,
why not set up an Exercise: machine-gunning from the
  air?
The War Office would know exactly the kind of figures
  involved,
an exciting statistical problem could be regarded as
  solved.

In a field, they put khaki dummies, on the reverse side of
  a hill.
And afterwards, they reckoned, they could estimate the
  kill.
Opposite these was the audience, to watch the total
  effect,
a sort of firework display – but free – the RAF being the
  architect.
All arms were represented? I think so. A grandstand seat
was reserved for top brass and others, a healthy open-air
  treat;
enclosed, beyond the dummies, they stood (or sat?) and
  smoked
or otherwise passed the time of day, relaxed as they
  talked and joked.

An experienced Spitfire pilot was briefed to fly over low
and give those dummies all he'd got – the star turn of the
  show,
with all the verisimilitude of a surprise attack.
Then to his fighter station he would whizz round and
  back.
They waited. And suddenly, waiting, they saw that
  angel of death
come at them over the hillside. Before they could draw
  breath
he passed with all guns firing; some fell on their faces,
  flat,
but the benefit was minimal that anyone had from that.

He reckoned that *they* were the dummies, in his
    slap-happy lone-wolf way,
that trigger-crazy pilot. He might have been right, some
    say.
But bitterness and flippancy don't compensate for men's
    lives
and official notifications posted to mothers and wives.

Nevertheless, there *were* results; percentages were
    worked out,
how 10 per cent could be written off, the wounded
    would be about
50 per cent or so. Oh yes, they got their figures all right.
Circulated to units. So at least that ill-omened flight
was a part of the Allied war effort, and on the credit side –
except for those poor buggers who just stood there and
    died.

Ending

The love we thought would never stop
now cools like a congealing chop.
The kisses that were hot as curry
are bird-pecks taken in a hurry.
The hands that held electric charges
now lie inert as four moored barges.
The feet that ran to meet a date
are running slow and running late.
The eyes that shone and seldom shut
are victims of a power cut.
The parts that then transmitted joy
are now reserved and cold and coy.
Romance, expected once to stay,
has left a note saying GONE AWAY.

Rain – No Play

*Poem written instead of going to Lord's (a famous cricket
  ground)*

Some tall and typical English Awfuls
were flowering outside the Royal Academy
buttonholed in the suits of tailors,
male and female and like stick insects,
from the top of a surging bus I saw them
in a sort of Vision of Piers the Plowman.

Well-turned-out were the waisted women,
of the kind that once at cocktail parties
wore hats and gloves and sipped their sherry,
the men were wonderful in their waistcoats.
A Summer Exhibition they themselves were,
as perfumed and orderly as an English garden.

Lords and Ladies of a small Creation,
noteworthy for having lots of money,
there they stood in the grey May weather
with cigarettes in 'amusing' holders
reminding of the Twenties, their bygone heyday –
and made intellectuals feel self-righteous.

Such people still in a sense are powerful
(some are witty and many charming),
wealth and property must still be reckoned with
in this very beautiful backward country
which one wouldn't swap for regimes of Europe
or the picturesqueness of all the peasants.

Though they don't like Art, these took the trouble
at least to look at those daubs, official
representatives of a past Old Order –
they don't reckon Art much in the Buildings,
it squeezes in sideways on the telly.
Philistia has a classless society.

311

Patronage was part of that once tradition,
we should never forget what we owe to idiots
who provided cash for the private building –
and not all, naturally, were all that silly
though their descendants look a bit blighted
planted out in this other Eden.

They wander now like the dead in Homer,
pallid ghosts who once were warriors,
still follow patterns, the prides of prep schools,
but as a class they are on their uppers
in a Britain that has heard of social justice
like a dark rumour in black-suited boardrooms.

The rain streams down, and the vision's fading.
Who will understand this precarious phenomenon
(in a London where, like Mother Church, stood
    Harrods,
centre of pilgrimage) in another century?
The cricket fields are stretched out green and useless,
they too survivals of a Past not perfect.

Poets

It isn't a very big cake,
some of us won't get a slice,
and that, make no mistake,
can make us not very nice
to one and all – or another
poetical sister or brother.

We all want total praise
for every word we write,
not for a singular phrase;
we're ready to turn and bite
the thick malicious reviewers,
our hated and feared pursuers.

We feel a sad neglect
when people don't buy our books;
it isn't what we expect
and gives rise to dirty looks
at a public whose addiction
is mainly romantic fiction.

We think there's something wrong
with poets that readers *read*,
disdaining our soulful song
for some pretentious screed
or poems pure and simple
as beauty's deluding dimple.

We can't imagine how
portentous nonsense by A
is loved like a sacred cow,
while dons are carried away
by B's more rustic stanzas
and C's banal bonanzas.

We have our minority view
and a sort of trust in Time;
meanwhile in this human zoo
we wander free, or rhyme,
our admirers not very many –
lucky, perhaps, to have any.

Yorkshiremen in Pub Gardens

As they sit there, happily drinking,
their strokes, cancers and so forth are not in their minds.
    Indeed, what earthly good would thinking
about the future (which is Death) do? Each summer finds
    beer in their hands in big pint glasses.
    And so their leisure passes.

    Perhaps the older ones allow some inkling
into their thoughts. Being hauled, as a kid, upstairs to bed
    screaming for a teddy or a tinkling
musical box, against their will. Each Joe or Fred
    wants longer with the life and lasses.
    And so their time passes.

    Second childhood; and 'Come in, number eighty!'
shouts inexorably the man in charge of the boating pool.
    When you're called you must go, matey,
so don't complain, keep it all calm and cool,
    there's masses of time yet, masses, masses . . .
    And so their life passes.

Adolescent Agonies

Though my potential is enormous
examinations give me traumas,
and women with their little pee-things,
chattering among the tea things.
Self, oh, self! Oh, thou that kissest
the upturned face of this narcissist!
All my thoughts, directed mewards,
miss the glories that lie seawards,

314

my psyche is in such a panic
I can't start feeling oceanic.

Venus with her pouting bust is
no consoler for injustice,
everywhere the poor are treated
like phrases that must be deleted.
It makes me feel I'm going barmy
to see how often it's an Army
that rules the young illiberal countries.
O Diana, Queen and Huntress,
moonlike maid with circling crescent,
have pity on this adolescent!

We are nothing, we are zeros,
completely in the power of Eros,
here to-day and gone to-morrow,
in a vale of tears and sorrow,
in a time of crime and crisis
licking lollies, eating ices.
When the social groups first started
were men even then cold-hearted?
Did we never care for others?
What's that archaic word now? 'Brothers'?

I reject what admen taught us,
I reject the plays of Plautus,
classical and other studies,
the conmen and the fuddy-duddies.
Both are very far from noble.
My distress is yours – and global.
I am Man, not very happy
in the nightie or the nappy,
not enjoying his sins and sexes,
husbands, wives or sorrowing exes.

You can't ignore my wounded feelings
in your Exeters and Ealings,
mine is trouble that surpasses
differences of clocks and classes;

though you are completely gormless
and your life is calm and stormless,
hire purchase mortgage man, flat-renter,
I live at the stormy centre.
I am in that sad condition:
permanently in transition.

Yeats and Shakespeare

Somebody wrote somewhere (about Yeats)
how even in those wasp-waisted days
before the First World War
(for twenty years reckoned among the Greats)
he was so spoiled by worship and by praise
he couldn't behave naturally any more,

as hostesses crept up behind his back
with every kind of social, sexual net
and pecking order snare;
a lion with hyenas on his track
or hunters closing in, they say, and yet
he never seemed to find this hard to bear.

Shakespeare was not so honoured in his life
though (for a player) he ended rich,
great ladies didn't swoon
to hear or see him; and a bitter wife,
it is presumed, told him the what and which
of all his faults, and told him pretty soon.

Arnold was John the Baptist, coming late
to smooth the way for universal awe,
but one thing he got right:
Shakespeare was lucky not to be thought great
outside the Mermaid, or above the law.
It's best for geniuses to travel light.

The Argument for the Benevolent God

Suppose a sadist,
after keeping a most beautiful woman in strict bondage
for a year, with occasional beatings and other indignities,
living shall we say in some decadent Egypt, Durrellian
and impure, suppose he at the end of this time caused her
to be locked into a special appliance, a mummiform case
of stainless steel, exactly tailored to her mouth-watering
measurements, with a headpiece like a mask worn by
fencers, allowing her to see, hear and speak – but not to
move. Suppose only from this smooth impervious steel
casing her two well-nourished breasts, like soft hills, prot-
ruded, pink and unprotected. Suppose then this sadist
caused her to be transported deep into lion country and,
in spite of her weeping, while the lazy sly attendants
pinched her nipples, left her there; while he watched
from a luxurious hide, drinking Johnnie Walker, until a
big brazen lion happened along, his great yellow balls
like puffballs at the point of bursting, sniffed, cautiously
approached and pawed her, screaming. Suppose finally
he tore the breasts and bit them, ate them down as far as
his muzzle allowed, blood on stainless steel,
murder and mayhem. . .

Suppose a deity,
after making as the legends claim a delectable woman
from the hard rib of a man, but making her soft and
nubile and adapted to child-bearing, and after the love
affairs and the kissing, the raising of skirts and the sexual
adoration, in trains, on kitchen tables, in borrowed flats,
in cornfields, in woodlands full of rabbits; if after all this
sincere worship of the spirit of Procreation, he allowed
procreation itself and probably marriage, the infants pulling at the very much publicised breasts, pink and unprotected. Suppose, with the children in their teens or
entirely grown up, the woman still attractive found in
one breast a small lump, which was excised as a cancer.
Suppose there was radiation treatment but suppose just

suppose that this deity arranged it so that the cancer
reached the bloodstream and appeared (perhaps within
a year) somewhere on the back perhaps or the base of
the spine, and after all the depression and discomfort
of the radiation, the tiredness and the hopelessness,
she sank into a long death, sedated in a silent scream,
oblivion washing over her, far from lion country but
martyred by motherhood. . .

Last Movements

In Old Master music in sonata form,
by Mozart, by Schubert, you always find,
after the sadness and the emotional storm
that moves or maddens the listening mind,
strumming the nerves like the strings they play,
that four, five or six will make the mood gay.

This is a convention, we know, of course,
and a wistfulness in the rumti-ti-tum
might be detected; the sorrow's force
gives way to the logical musical sum,
as vigorously, brightly, the players bend
to a dance where unhappiness comes to an end.

But perhaps there's thanksgiving concealed there too
for a life that also contained some joy,
a kind of reminder for me and you
that nothing's pure, and without alloy
nothing. The dark swallows up despair
as well as hope – says that rustic air.

Swarm Over, Death!

(Jannice Porter. Slough Crematorium. 20 December 1974)

The planes are roaring at Heathrow
like lions at a zoo,
above Stoke Poges, near and low,
whose churchyard holds a clue
to what it is we still don't know
and what we have to do.

Under the warm and leafless bough
of this pre-winter time
we zero in to dismal Slough
as witness to a crime –
departure from our here and now
of one no wit or rhyme

can possibly in joy recall
from that uncharted state.
If God's responsible for all
(unless you call him Fate)
he seems revengeful for that Fall
and neither soon nor late

his crematoria give up,
consolatory, a ghost.
Bitter for kids, a Kiddie Kup
prepared; like flaming toast,
a sudden flare, a quick kerflup!
mums vanish. At the most

hygienic, I suppose you'd say;
but for survivors sad,
who don't forget a better day
when Friendship made them glad,
Love and Affection came to stay
and a good time was had

by one and all. The words seem trite,
like brandnames, not inspired,
like golf balls simply called Kro-Flite
(imagination tired)
or Samuel watches: Ever-rite.
We are not lit or fired

by any mystic inner glow.
We envy, everywhere,
the animals who just don't know
or, if they know, don't care –
who go because they have to go
in face of Death's blank stare.

If all's ordained, as some will say,
(we start the little cars
and in our groups we drive away)
by God or by our stars,
it isn't very fair or gay
or arguable in bars.

Looking for Books

In even the best library, looking through the poetry
    shelves
is a depressing experience for poets;
they might not expect to find *themselves*

but they don't find many of their contemporaries either.
Instead of MacBeth and Porter – Mrs Wilson.
Slim volumes act elusive, hard to catch, lither

than lizards and the big fat books of critics
whose size and weight can often stun us.
Like aphasiacs or mental paralytics

Tennyson; The Critical Heritage by John D. Jump
knocks us out by just its title,
The Poems and Translations of Thomas Stanley ed.
    G. M. Crump

promises oceans of the greatest learnèd boredom
(unless the ridiculous names mislead us).
With these the Muse has not committed whoredom,

we suspect; they're innocent of her as Big Ears, Noddy
or Aneirin Talfan Davies,
author of *Dylan – Druid of the Broken Body*.

And, in general, Heavy Verse tends to come out on top,
serious *Crows*, the loud mystique of
self-congratulatory suicide. Light Verse must have a
    stop,

it seems, and only a continuous shrill hysteria
vary the pieces on voles and
large and small animals, the harebells, the wistaria

and every local landscape of the regional chauvinist.
Sad it may be, but one could say that
a fit epitaph ('They'll none of them be missed')

is already pronounced; and frailly Stevie Smith
resists Time with one *Selected Poems*.
The runaway actual factual leaves the myth

('Stevie Smith: Oh yes, I like *him*!' a big beard said
gauche to me once at a poetry reading),
we are not even remembered, let alone read.

The Return of the Hero

He overclomb cliffs   in that far country
With wolves and with water mains   he fought so freely
In briars and badgerdoms   he rabbited rebels
Swooningly swimming   the turnable tidemarks
Incredible crows   cratered the causeway
Dark were the doorways   with feral foxes
Energetic enemies   falsified his feebleness
Firm amid fire alarms   he prevented panic
Dragons and discotheques   peacefully pacified
In supermarkets   he limited looting
For his high heroics   the ladies were lusting
No one had seen such   baronial beauty
                    Before.
His body was seemly and straight,
His height was as high as a door,
Waiting women couldn't wait,
They were asking for more.

Back from the beastliness   in haste he hurried
Never so knowingly   chroniclers charted him
Hazards of hell   on a fiery field
Gaping gestapos   ominously overtured
To borderline cases   he brought early warning
Charmingly championed   the softer sexes
In testified triumph   great bronze bells beat
Trumpets like tramlines   blazed in beaconry
Voices avowed him   charisma in chorus
In festive fountains   wine was wobbling
The boldest beauties   kowtowed with kissing
Opened their opulence   with liking unlimited
                    By thought.
This was instinctive as praise,
No one could say it was bought,
They offered it all in a phrase,
And more than they ought.

Yet he, no knave,   as a good knight should
Was shunning their sherry   in crystal cups
Frowning at fathers   brandishing brandy
Slow to sly hints   from matchmaking mothers
Edging his eyes round   the bountiful bosoms
Never noticing   nubile necks
Counting as nothing   their see-through somethings
Solidly sober   among the amphetamines
Decidedly derisive   of their deliberate dancing
Regarding all praise   as pitiful prize money
And the randy rewards   of righteous restlessness
Not worth a worm-cast   and simply silly
        Or trite.
He kept his nose clean, you see,
He never refused out of fright,
He knew that, on land as on sea,
A wrong can't be right.

So did they sententiously   serenade his seemliness?
Praise his purity   in post-prandial prose?
Statue his stateliness   in exquisite squares?
Nibbling nasties   on the contrary
Combined to erode   his reputation
Hinting at horrors   of hired holography
Monsters mastered   by fallacious fixing
Elevated to epidemics   an only outbreak
Clouted and cloven   cardboard animals
Vintage volcanoes   firecracker falsies
No eager activity   but lazy legend
His asexual exploits   rendered as rat-poison
        Not good.
The moral is simple and sad:
The monk doesn't make the hood,
You're never untouched by what's bad
Or out of the wood.

The One-time Three-Quarter Remembers the Past

Pulling on a clammy jersey from a prep school locker
and the boots with dry earth caked round leather studs
and after a defeat to hear the bitter précis
of the mad and shell-shocked master.

This was the game that I found more fun than soccer
and a bright day meant good running, with the ball
easy to handle, neither wet nor greasy;
wind distracting, mud disaster.

We came after a war where the terrifying word Fokker
embodied something as beastly as the opposing teams
we hated and feared; now we walk slowly,
it is time that moves much faster.

So on a bright morning we know, though age is a
    mocker,
that the afternoon's International will be played fast;
we run now in our minds only,
old chairs, with one loose caster.

The Last Journey

Old family cars have a certain appeal.
Families get fond of them. Cartoonists
love to draw them with big round eyes.
Also, of course, in a way they are monsters –
like other pets, dogs in particular, they are polluters,
fuming up the high streets. They kill people.

All cars, too, are rooms on wheels; and have witnessed
acts of love, arguments, affectionate banter,
the behaviour of children. Like animals, like us,
they deteriorate with time. The earth renews
but they do not renew. A licence in April
brings no bright resurgence of power and beauty.

If you've been fond of one, it's hard to think of it
chained with battered others on the big transporter,
cracked windows, dented like a toy
by a termagant two-year-old; the words Old Faithful
come to mind to remind of the so many journeys.
Turner felt the same about the Fighting Téméraire.

The Second Coming

I say the Sphinx was the Boston Strangler;
and He will be born again in Oklahoma
(I shall wear the feathers of the blue crane,
which are the mark of a great warrior)
and all over the campus the boys in sneakers
will do him peculiar acts of homage,
not forgetting the earlier avatar.

A sign will be seen in Anne Hathaway's cottage.
As I walked through the wilderness of this world
I knew He would be hatched from a hen's egg
with a preference for soils that are argillaceous
and a liking for hominy grits and grapefruit.
I put on pride as a kind of humbleness
to announce a new wonder among the libraries.

I shall purify myself in a kraal or igloo,
refusing the offered breasts of the women,
it's all in the small print in my contract,
microfilmed on my brain; and His Word is sacred.
On the third day I shall emerge to testify
a miraculous birth, for the Muse a boyfriend
and for us a new speech and a life-enhanced language.

The Illness of the Writer's Wife

If you thought you were dying of cancer
you wouldn't give a civil answer;
and the best reviews that you could muster
wouldn't make very much difference, buster.

You might become a trifle moody,
although you're drinky, fat and foody,
if the future seemed so bloody
and there was no escaping, buddy.

You too would blaze up just as soon, ding-
donging words both harsh and wounding;
if you remember, pain's not funny
when it lasts a long time, sonny.

You could be Shakespeare or Homer,
threatened by a carcinoma
your life too'd be sad and weary –
your main desire survival, dearie.

For nursery days are gone, nightmare is
real and there are no Good Fairies.
The fox's teeth are in the bunny
and nothing can remove them, honey.

Is There Life after Sex?

Sad old people are no longer nubile,
the fucate ladies have wrinkled faces,
the men can defy gravity no more now
than they can fly or accomplish bilocation
or levitate; the accustomed miracles
of hardness or wetness are past, long past.

This doesn't mean that they have no feeling;
inhabitants of an oblate spheroid,
they too were never completely perfect,
perhaps they never were drawn to bedrooms
to handle the contents of skirts or trousers,
what you've never had you can't miss.

But love survives and the fact of nearness,
too much sympathy may not be in order,
they may have enjoyed much more than we have;
touch is, after all, an animal comfort.
In a way, perhaps, the mind doesn't need it –
obmutescence is an answer too.

Leave the potency to the grandsons,
they could say and entirely mean it.
Love is more than florulent verbiage
and all delightful extravagant action
is simply tenderness as a double crown poster,
could be condensed to a postage stamp.

Eschatological serious theories
never mentioned the end of pleasure
or took cognisance of those organs
that can induce a secular ecstasy;
gave us a huge and sombre fresco,
no quick humanist esquisse.

If latinists are shouting *Cave canem*
there's life in the old dog yet, believe me,
beyond the false gods of procreation.
It's a great mistake, jampacked with error,
farctate with jumbo disappointments,
to make active sex a sacred cow.

William McGonagall on England's Failure to Qualify for the World Cup, 1974

Now that the English have discovered they're on a sticky
  wicket
And their Test teams aren't as good as they thought they
  were at cricket,
And they've now absolutely completely lost face
Even at football, what will the Nation do about this
  disgrace?
I think they ought all to swarm to the cliffs and in
  communal despair
Throw themselves into the sea, in a noble mass suicide
  darkening the air.

A Personal Footnote

'In addition, he will give you seven women, skilled in the fine crafts, Lesbians whom he chose for their exceptional beauty . . . '

The Iliad, Book 9.

Nobody has ever offered
to give me seven Lesbians –
though I was once a warrior
for six long years,
slept in a tent too
on a sparse camp bed.

Somehow I missed the
spoils of the cities.
I was not important.
A silly Lieutenant
can't sulk and get
away with it

like grandiose Achilles.

William Wordsworth (1770–1850)

Most modern Nature Lovers have a personal scale of
   values that tells them what each tree, hill or bird's
   worth;
but this doesn't apply to Wordsworth.
For Wordsworth, as it were, believing was much the
   same as seeing –
he thought natural phenomena were the guardians of his
   heart and soul of all his moral being.

329

The meadows and the woods and mountains kept him on
the straight and narrow
when he felt like getting pissed in places like
Applethwaite or Yarrow.
If he had an urge to go out on a thrash
he would have to ask permission from a mountain ash.
Nature was a kind of ever-present Nurse
supervising all his life and all his verse.

The only time the system broke down seems to have
been in France
when he was young and revolutionary, and every
advance
in progressive thought was welcome. He wasn't the star
of any leading lady's salon,
but he succeeded completely in seducing a girl called
Annette Vallon.
Though she became pregnant and had a B-A-B-Y
William by then had wandered off, lonely as a cloud in a
Lake District sky.
It all sounds very natural – but Nanny wasn't pleased;
there is absolutely no doubt at all that William was seized
by a fit of remorse and secrecy. From then on no man was
a brother
and he never again fancied republicanism or a bit of the
other.

This, at any rate, is what they say. They say too that
mountains for him were father-figures
and wonderful things in his eyes, as wonderful as
Tiggers.
But a more interesting question is *How did it come about?*
This wasn't exactly the first time that William had been
allowed out.
It sounds to me like a failure in communication, a
misunderstanding.
Perhaps French trees, like the French, were too logical
and not used to handing
out advice and instructions for people's love life or
guidance
on what to do next, like the Athenes, Zeuses and
Poseidons

who made Odysseus' life so difficult? Was William *en rapport*
with the French meadows, woods, etc? Or did they say
'*Tu as tort!*'
when he told them they ought to be guardians of his
   moral being,
and chuckle in a Gallic way? Or just start *oui, oui*-ing?
I think he would have avoided all that guilt and loss if he
had managed to give himself a less ridiculous
   philosophy.

The Cricket of My Friends

Ross in his days of youth
was quite a bowler,
energy rushed through his veins
like Coca-Cola,

he could concentrate like an obsessive
loony from Rampton,
he certainly played for Oxford
and for Northampton.

Worsley was another natural
born for cricket –
in the Cambridge University team
he once kept wicket.

Clark, with a bat in his hand,
could show his talents,
his timing and footwork were good
and so was his balance.

Symons could play a bit,
though table tennis
was the game where he made his mark
as a national menace

and worked himself up to be
reserve for England –
though never as good as the Chinks
from ping-pong Ming land.

Romilly, Rycroft and Madge
couldn't play for toffee –
they were fonder of sitting and talking
and drinking coffee.

I can't imagine a century
being made by Spender.
Was Fuller ever more
than a good tail-ender?

(I may be doing him a real
savage injustice).
Connolly – an acquaintance –
was better at pastis.

At least this is my own piece
of intelligent guesswork.
There's a gap between bat and pad
and playing and press work.

You can't see Angus Wilson
driving firmly through the covers;
the literary ladies
prefer playing games with lovers.

It's sad to see how little
the literati
have really achieved at cricket –
though hale and hearty

they don't seem to have the *flair*.
The French are hopeless.
If clean cricket were next to godliness
they would be soapless.

So it's all a bad business –
like the murder of a Kennedy –
as for Literary Cricket
I offer up this threnody.

A Very Shocking Poem Found among the Papers of an Eminent Victorian Divine

I saw you with Septimus on the parterre
    In front of the old Bishop's Palace.
The sunshine was weaving its gold in your hair
    But my heart was embittered and malice
Moved in me mightily; jealous was I
    And I burned with desire to distress you,
To down-thunder like Jove from that clear summer sky
    And at once, then and there, to undress you!

That hand, once in mine, was in his as you walked
    And answered him in your bright treble;
Not a word could I hear but I knew that you talked
    And the Flesh rose up like a dark rebel –
For that hand, as I knew, was an adjunct to Love,
    Like a hot caper sauce to hot mutton,
And designed by the Lord to descend from above
    First to fondle – and then to unbutton!

Ah! those feet that ran to me won't run to me now,
    The dismal and desperate fact is
They will turn to avoid me, for you will know how
    To go home with the Choir after Practice –
Though you lingered once sweetly to dally with me
    And our preoccupations weren't choral
As you sat in the sitting-room there on my knee
    And the examination was oral!

I saw those eyes opening, gazing at him
    With the blue of the midsummer heaven,
My own eyes with traitorous tear-drops grew dim
    And of Rage, lustful Rage, a black leaven
Worked in me there; for those eyes once had seen
    (Thought to break my heart, break it and rive it)
On the ottoman, proud in its velvety green,
    Those parts that our God has called private!

I dream of a Paradise still, now and then,
    But it is not the orthodox milieu
Where good spirits abound – with no women or men.
    Ah! My Conscience lies drowned like Ophelia!
And my Heaven's a dream of an opulent South
    With soft cushions, wine, perfumes, bells ringing,
My member for ever held tight in your mouth
    And a thousand bright choirboys all singing!

Limericks

Limericks are a serious thing
and as long as a short piece of string
with a sting in their tails,
unrestrainedly males,
and as wild as a wasp on the wing.

Some limericks never wash clean,
from their heads to their toes they're obscene;
though it's not these extremes
that elicit the screams
but the things that they've got in between.

They have oomph and some razamatazz,
they're as joky and jaunty as jazz,
they do far more than flirt,
they get under a skirt,
and defy all the Omo and Daz.

They're as epigrammatic as efts
and too slight to cause literary thefts –
for what author would steal
what's not even a meal
but a weed growing in crannies and clefts?

You can see them exploding like squibs,
untruthful and too fond of fibs,
crude, simple, and yet
one won't do as a pet –
they're not angels or babies in bibs.

It's their content, so beastly and bland,
that a Holbrook or Whitehouse can't stand.
If you hear one at night
it's much best to take fright
and retreat to your bed out of hand.

Though they seem unaccountably mild
don't let them get near to your child –
they can harm Mums and Dads
and all sensitive lads
come out coarsened and worsened and wild.

So study the Classical modes,
keep to elegies, epics and odes,
for their lewd beck and nod
is unwelcome to God
and traumatic as ten-fingered toads.

The Blurb

This tenderly observant poet writes clearly,
rhythmically and thoughtfully,
about what all of us can understand. . .
This unperturbed, unenvious and compassionate
poet of doubt, common experience and
the search for truth, we ought fully
to appreciate. . .

He has reverence for the vastness around us
and stands on the brink of eternity
wondering whether it will be day, twilight
or night when we are dead. He is the John Clare
of the building estates, true and right
to them as Clare to field and tree
and ploughshare . . .

He has certainly closed the gap between
poetry and the public which frankly
the experiments and obscurity of the last
fifty years have done so much (alas!) to widen . . .
he has a vibrant sense of our shared past,
of the *rerum* and their *lacrimae*,
dead Tyre and Sidon. . .

To Lord Byron

on the occasion of the 150th anniversary of his death,
commemorated at the Victoria and Albert Museum

You didn't much like relics. The 'lying bust'
    seemed to you too impersonal and cold
to represent warm flesh, whose love and lust
    even the Puritans share (when not too old)

before they crumble into decent dust.
        What would *you* think of this? Would you feel 'sold'?
For geniuses, alas, it's a tradition
to end up as a paying Exhibition.

So here are portraits of that gang you banged,
        the bright, unstable, intellectual ladies;
evidence that an ancestor was nearly hanged
        (to roam, unblessed, the further shores of Hades),
that in the Lords you once stood and harangued
        and kept a bear at Cambridge. A bill (paid?) is
exhibited as proof (bear food and lodging) –
though, through your life, your debts were not for dodging.

Here, from Miss Chaworth to La Guiccioli,
        with delicate miniatures and locks of hair,
are philosophical ladies, prophetic, Nietzschely,
        high-waisted with their bosoms raised and bare –
but also bakers' wives, untamed, unteacherly,
        one that was married to a gondolier.
That auburn curl (for some peculiar reason)
of Lady Caroline Lamb gave me a *frisson*.

Pathetic, too, to read Allegra's letters
        in copybook Italian, guided by nuns,
who went to join her elders and her betters
        under those feverish Mediterranean suns
at five years old. *Caro Papa*. Hounds, setters,
        horses you kept. Children were shunned like duns.
Shelley, a guest at your Venetian palace,
was right to be angry and to call you callous.

But who am I to take a stance that's moral?
        Your entourage was not for little girls.
In any case it's far too late to quarrel –
        you were worth fifty of *our* Lords and Earls,
in days when atom bombs shake ocean coral
        we are the swine to whom you cast your pearls,
you stand like some far-shining distant lighthouse.
And what would you have thought of Mrs Whitehouse?

337

Would you be keen on Peter Pan and Wendy
        or anything that's cosy, coy or twee?
Contrariwise, would you admire what's trendy
        (you were a fashion once yourself) or see
virtue in what's suburban or weekendy?
        To you, who only knew one kind of tea,
who never knew what roaches or a jag meant,
I dedicate this small Byronic fragment.

Valediction: To the Cricket Season

As a boy who has lost a girl so sadly
tears up a photograph or her early letters,
knowing that what has gone is gone for ever,
        a lustful bustful,

the exchange of confidences, the hours of cuddling,
the paraphernalia of what some call sharing,
so we mourn you; televisually prepare for
        their filthy football,

professional fouls and the late late tackle,
breakaway forwards held back by a jersey,
the winning or losing almost equally nasty.
        The English summer

is never perfect, but you are a feature
as pleasing to us as a day of sunshine,
to spectators at least a calm, straw-hatted
        Edwardian dandy.

Not really a game of physical contact,
the batsman pardons the ungentlemanly bouncer,
the only foul would be leg theory,
        bodyline bowling;

as nostalgic as those old school stories
the plock of bat on ball penetrates outfields,
calming to the mind. Warm pints of bitter
          and county cricket

are long married in our friendly folklore
of white marquees, the spires of cathedrals,
pitch-wandering dogs, boys on the boundary,
          mystified girlfriends,

all of it as much a myth and a ritual
as the fairy stories written by learnèd
elf-haunted dons who invent a cosmos
          neat but escapist,

where the rules are forever, can never be broken,
and a dragon, as it were, can be l.b.w.
if he puts a foot the wrong side of the mountain.
          You are the bright one

that shines in the memory; as old-fashioned writers
say 'she was a maid of some seventeen summers',
we don't reckon age by the passing of winters,
          by happier seasons

we count up that final inescapable total,
remember huge sixes by maverick sloggers –
compensating, like love, for the field that's deserted,
          the padlocked pavilion.

Sonnet: The Knowledge of Good and Evil

In the Twenties we had children's books that made
value judgements on wildlife, of an anthropomorphical
   kind:
The Hundred Best Animals, Queer Fish and *Secrets of the
   Zoo*
Not to mention the way the Flopsy Bunnies ran into
   trouble.
But now when you read a novel about rabbits
it actually tells you the way rabbits live –
as far as anyone who is not a rabbit can work it out.
We've been told more, and we ought to know more.

But knowledge isn't enough. People have said
that Hitler immunized us against his myxomatosis for
   ever.
Yet an understanding of sadism doesn't prevent it.
So we have the Moors Murders, summary executions,
the torture of prisoners – so many little fascist states
   where
Hitler would be happy. You must want, as well as know.

Sonnet: Mother Love

Women are always fond of growing things.
They like gardening; snipping, watering, pruning,
bringing on the backward, aware of the forward;
planting – not for nothing do they talk of 'nurseries'.
Roses are like children, a source of pride,
tulips are cosseted, primulas are pets.
These are almost as loved as the usual surrogates –
the dogs and cats that stand for families.

Conservation, preservation; it's a lovable aspect
of maternalism (one reason why we're here).
Better than that, this severe matriarchy
is established over *plants*; the bossiness, thank God,
that puts you there (delphiniums), you there
     (wallflowers),
is harmlessly deflected well away from us.

Sonnet: Malthusian

All these wars, revolutions, famines, earthquakes, floods
are blessings – and not in disguise. They limit
the numbers of those who pollute the earth, a planet
growing colder to the greed of human life.
The Catholic exhortations to outnumbering
are, in our context, disastrously sectarian.
We ought to be far fewer. A general hope
attaches to circling nuclear devices.

Nobody wants to be, however, there –
on the particular spot of weeding out:
Palestine, Belfast, Uganda. Or to starve
with Africans and Asians. And that terrible bomb
would solve the problem too efficiently.
Smug doomwatchers, we keep the telly tuned.

Sonnet: Red in Tooth and Claw

'Isn't Nature wonderful?' says a wondering lady
while a TV feature shows the cuteness of hedgehogs,
but can't look when a bustard is fed with a live mouse
and the snuffling hedgehog crunches a baby vole.
This is the Life people say they're on the side of –
and there's eating and being eaten in many a boardroom,
people too will kill to obtain food and status,
literally. For that, too, watch television.

One can see how the writers of all those little poems
celebrating wildlife, landscape and birdsong,
might set their faces against brutalism in concrete,
dreaming of that impossible, perfect, Rural England.
But 'brutal' and 'bestial' are words that come from
    animals:
foxes, to chickens, don't seem beautiful.

Sonnet: Carson McCullers

To go into your South, a different life.
Sowbelly and cornbread with syrup poured over it;
or fried slices of side meat, collard greens, hoecakes.
To go back and away towards the lonely freaks
who can't communicate, who never communicate,
and live on that diet of misunderstanding –
poor whites, poor blacks, who never get the message.
And what, for that matter, would ever be the message?

We all are freakish, mutes with hand signals;
even the most talkative outgoing lady
tells more about herself than what is actual.
Like the hot Italian *Mezzogiorno*
your country was richest in superstition.
Where you were a one-eyed person, they were blind.

Sonnet: Bear Thoughts

Like Sir John Betjeman, I too have a teddy bear –
from 1916 or thereabouts.
He sits in the hall, his fur rubbed through in places,
one eye a proper one, the other just a button
of a not very suitable kind. He wears my son's school cap
(discarded) and a shirt and shorts
made for him by my sisters years ago.
He looks worn, like a man of nearly fifty-nine.

I never talk to him. My daughter does.
I can't remember much of our early days;
this is a dead friendship and a long-past love.
What does survive (and witness Betjeman)
is a feeling that he indeed is truly living.
Probably no one completely outgrows his childhood.

Sonnet: One

Where did *one* come from?
One is continually appalled by . . .
One feels that in this movement Monteverdi . . .
It must have been from the French (the Germans say *man*)
but when and where? Voltaire doesn't use it –
or does he? Nor the English (this is guesswork)
much before Henry James. I have a vision of aesthetes
leaning on Nineties mantelpieces, saying 'One. . . '.

by which they mean 'I' much more than 'we'.
Critics and reviewers use it, but it's sideways-sliding;
it's better to say 'we' for a general judgment.
Critics can't be everybody, their omniscience is fiction.
Nobody can ever speak for anybody but himself –
and even then in doubt and great confusion.

Sonnet: Mad Nature

The early morning crows are crowing all through
Wordsworth's famous *Ode To A Shylock*,
making a dull plonking sound like a bass guitar;
some sheep are singing a well-known chorus from *The
    Messiah*
about navigation – 'All we like ships have gone astray'.
The soda fountains with their purling streams
bring transcendental music to the soul.
Park attendants shout a battle-cry: *Rus in urbe!*

Even if all this were so, it wouldn't be relevant
really to men in their expanding cities.
What we've lost, we've lost. And how far back
do you want to go? The wheelwright's shop? The Iron
    Age?
That noble anthropoid lived, not in innocence
but fighting with his wits, the same as us.

Sonnet: *Tidying up*

Left lying about in my mind, awaiting collection,
are the thoughts and phrases that are quite unsuitable
and often shocking to all Right-thinking people –
penetrated by a purple penis for example
(almost a line?); and how it's almost certain,
from Swift's hints, that the big sexy ladies of
    Brobdingnag
used Gulliver as an instrument of masturbation.
Hence a tongue-twister: *Glumdalclitch's clitoris.*

Though not always decorous, there's a lot of force in
    phrases.
A good many poems stem from them; they start
    something.
More than anything Shakespeare owes his power to them
(his *secret, black and midnight hags* and hundreds more),
they almost consoled him – though life is pretty bloody
(the multitudinous seas incarnadine).

Sonnet: Nasty

Never forget that everybody's nasty.
People can smile and pretend to be kind; it's
as often as not a façade, behind is a good deal of
selfishness and malevolence – which quickly become
    overt
at the quick flare of passion – then, behind the curtains
in that well-regulated villa, you see the torture-chamber.
Angel in the street, devil in the home. A saying.
Some are even devils in the home *and* devils in the street.

All this being so, my considered advice is:
always give everyone the benefit of the doubt,
consider them nice until proved otherwise.
But don't be too naive. The neighbours whose house is
continually filled with the screams of children
may say 'Hello!' – but 'nice' is not their adjective.

Sonnet: The Prize

The Prize is eternal peace. All sentient beings win it.
God, like a visiting celebrity, hands it to each
in full convocation of everybody living,
the Pope or some magnified Prophet is there as
    Headmaster,
Housemasters are heads of the Sects, benevolent smilers
at a kind of never-ending award-giving Speech Day.
Do the animals get in on the act? Some people have
    thought so,
imagining cat Heavens, Purgatories for dogs . . .

346

This is what they say. Personally I think we do,
you and I and the ants in the ant-hill,
achieve eternal peace in our separate endings;
it's certain indeed nobody can bother us.
For those under pressure it sounds like a blessing –
except that we're no longer conscious to enjoy it.

Sonnet: Senility

Go into a corner with bottle of whisky
and grow old gracefully. Those are my
instructions to myself. In one of his essays
Montaigne says how in childhood
most life is concentrated in the extremities
(all that running, jumping, catching, throwing),
in the middle part of life – well, in the middle
(the active organs of romantic love).

This lasts well into old age. Life just moves up the body.
It lodges finally in the head and throat.
Long live golosity and intellect! Our food no longer
the food of love (though feminists, no-ball snowballs,
call every man a two-ball screwball, in pure disdain),
we can still eat and drink, and eat and drink. . .

Or Where a Young Penguin Lies Screaming (1977)

The Gentle Sex (1974)

On Tuesday, 23 July,
  in that black sectarian Belfast
under a rainy, cramped and hopeless sky
  five Loyalist women at last,
after a false alarm visit the previous day,
found Anne Ogilby in her home; under overcast
  weather, in a little car, they drove her away,
leaving behind her five-year-old daughter Sharlene, who
could only scream and cry.

  Leader of the Women's UDA,
    Lilly Douglas was in charge.
  For questioning, to hear what Anne had to say
    (for cloudy suspicions were looming large
over the little terraced houses of Sandy Row,
full of memories of unemployment and bread and
    marge)
    why food-parcel money, that by rights should go
on food for her boy friend in Long Kesh, had gone (they
claimed) astray.

    Each month £10.
  One of the women accusing,
  who hunted her down, we could say, like hounds,
    found it far from amusing
that her husband was the boy friend who had lived
  with Anne
for a full three months before arrest, refusing
  to return home, father of Anne's baby, a man
who had had enough of her and her marital life – that's
  how it sounds.

They drove to a Loyalist club
and questioned her, hard and mean;
but then a UDA man from a pub
happened to intervene –
this was lucky for her indeed, and it certainly fell
out luckily that he should have come on the scene.
At a bus station by the Europa Hotel
they left her, released; as scared cats leave birds and dive
under a shrub.

A dark 31-year-old,
unmarried mother of four;
and even a British soldier, the women told,
was father of one, a whore
they couldn't call her, pots don't call kettles black,
but they also said, and protested, a very great deal
more
about betrayed gunmen; a Protestant murder attack
she had witnessed, and the 'kneecapping' of a sheep that
tried to leave the fold.

Just after 10.15
Lilly Douglas's teenage daughter
and another girl, only sixteen,
stood in front of her bus and caught her.
They dragged her off. In a small red Fiat, nine
women started off to a 'Romper Room' in that quarter
where their traitors are disciplined – fine
for the beaters-up but for the others the fun isn't so good
and clean.

But, before they arrived, the car
was stopped by police, who took
them all back to the bus station; so far
no crime – so whom could they book?
Anne, the police say, kept nervously biting her nails
but refused to make a complaint (though she did look
like someone in need of help). Law fails
always where the community knows, and won't tell,
who the killers are.

At 10.30, then, next day
(home in the small hours) she
failed to attend at the Welfare; but they
know she was there at three.
Meanwhile, in the Elm Bar, a 'heavy squad' was
drinking –
'Bumper' Graham, three unemployed teenage girls. The
key
to the whole situation, the woman of action and
thinking
was 41-year-old Lilly, smuggler, forger, violent, drunk,
brothel-keeper (police say).

Convicted, too. Gave order:
Graham to fetch Anne from Welfare.
He went. Without force, no lawless marauder,
found her and took her from there.
The welfare officers had not even, then, been seen.
In an Edinburgh hostel, safe in their care,
a place had been found, for both Anne and Sharlene.
This she never knew. Of such missed trains and wrong
destinations Time's a relentless hoarder.

But now: the Romper Room. And,
when Sharlene began to cry,
Graham put 10p into her childish hand,
said she'd see Mammy bye and bye
and told her to go out and buy herself some sweets.
Her mother was blindfolded with a tea towel; we
know why
a dark brown bag was put over her head. In the
streets
meanwhile life flowed easy in the uneasy city, like the sea
lapping the sand.

Etty Cowan, Chrissie Smith, Joey Brown
wearing, all three, white masks
made from one of Joey's jumpers (put down,
it sounds like a game; but such tasks
come easy in the boredom and poverty of their
existence),

walked in and began to 'romper' Anne. Who asks,
in such circumstances, exactly why? No resistance
was offered as she was pushed and kicked from one to the
other – like a circus clown.

Graham and Joey were upset
by now. They tried to stop it.
But Etty Cowan was in her stride, all set,
took a brick and wouldn't drop it,
stood over Anne and banged it on her face,
as hard as she could, a very determined moppet.
She and Chrissie stopped for a smoke. Some
minutes' grace
she had from that; but soon they began again, giving it all
they'd got – or could get.

Outside the door Sharlene,
back with a chocolate biscuit, screamed
(inside, her mother screamed; obscene
thumps, thuds, gurgles seemed
the soundtrack of a nightmare, 'Mammy, I want my
Mammy!'
echoed outside, a bad dream crudely dreamed),
through the brown bag perhaps the blood oozed,
jammy –
until she twitched no longer; even for those avengers, the
slate wiped clean.

So when they knew that she'd died
they went for a bottle of wine.
They just shooed Sharlene outside
and onto the streets. The deep mine
of vengeance was plumbed, the boil lanced.
The body? Disposed on a motorway. Fine.
They got into a disco and danced.
For a good cause, and a mother's jealousy revenged, can
make you feel warm inside.

Oedema of the brain,
associated fractures of the skull,
and on the scalp the deepened main
sixteen separate wounds. Dull
their lives must have been, dull and dull indeed
for this to be their pleasure! The wayward gull
floats over Belfast; animals have no need
for torture. Her face was completely black. And
certainly, chewing gum in court, they'd do it again.

Shakespeare

People facetiously say
your name had you foxed with its spelling;
and certain it is that the sound

of your plays was so different from what
reverberates now from our stages
that we must imagine a blend

of three accents now oceans apart –
the Dublin, the Cockney, the Boston.
'Break' was rhyming with 'speak',

both 'solid' and 'sullied' that flesh,
Falstaff said 'reasons' like 'raisins'
when he made his blackberry pun,

there was a mousetrap joke
in 'tropically' spoken by Hamlet.
Elizabeth even, the Queen,

that learnèd knitter of speech,
dropped all her aitches like stitches.
Faucal plosion is all,

fricatives land on the ear,
and the word is labiodental
   for those who have mastered the craft.

But accent and dialect, both,
could never obscure your clear meaning –
   a sentence however pronounced

acquits you of being in the power
of the specialist young phonetician.
   Your rhetoric breaks through the net,

too strong for theory to hold;
and Bernard Shaw said a true thing
   when on the old BBC

he said that you churned out plays
like a series of cinema scripts that
   were wanted, and fast, for new films;

a parallel now – better still –
would be with the insatiable telly.
   Repeats were not common, a play

might be performed once and no more.
Quick-change artists and clever
   at patching on workable scenes

all of them had to be then –
tradition alone made them poets,
   something to do with the Greeks

and the mystical power of the verse
that was used for religious persuasion.
   The song, as they said, of the goat.

You got up some speed; and some fire
flew out of your breathtaking phrases
   as you blasted your way down the track –

those multitudinous seas
and aroint thee! and that rump-fed ronyon,
    words that for 10-year-old boys

    had power in those earlier schools,
where a highbrow word like aesthetics
    suggested the surgeon's knife

    or nothing. We smile, but it's true.
It was bear-baiting then or the cock-fights
    or hearing tempestuous shouts

    from the Kings and the Queens and the Knaves
and watching the stage-managed battles.
    A choice; and, as Beecham once said,

    the British, a Philistine lot,
don't really care much for music –
    they just like the noise that it makes.

    So we were lucky all round,
we got you by chance, a great genius,
    and (Honest Iago my foot!)

    you fooled them; they thought you wrote plays –
but all the time they were absorbing
    the highest, most durable Art.

'The Lion griefs loped from the shade
And on our knees their muzzles laid,
    And Death put down his book'

                    Don't worry,
poetry won't be as good as that again in a hurry!
                New 'schools', now,
may regard us as a collection of old fools now,
                or wonder
what on earth we saw in it – but, no blunder,
                what Bach had
(strict formal beauty), what *The Hunting of the Snark* had,
                corroding
and surreal anxiety, a sense of foreboding,
                and, in it
all too, the urgency of the actual historical minute –
                these made it
more compelling than the craftsman's ear by which he
    played it.

                Each age, I
submit, has its own particular Journey of the Magi;
                they carry
the gifts that alone can truly, faithfully, marry
                the ideal
to our hesitating, wavering sense of what is real.
                So Auden
threw round the political nasties a sort of cordon,
                immunizing
us against their infecting presence, and rising,
                a champion,

a serious singer, a warner, a Baptist, a Campion
with social
significance (a prophet whose 'Woe!' shall
be ignored – as
it always is – no more regarded than Harry Lauder's
brash singing)
came at us like Carroll's Bellman with that bell he was
ringing!

Swinburne too
once with the young men at Oxford certainly had his
turn – to
be chanted
in evening streets. For some sort of Saviour is wanted.
Dogmatics
are twenty years old, with bats in their belfries and attics,
a top storey
that leans, not to work or moderation, but to death and
glory,
new magic –
Auden's wonderful hybrid rose that crossed the comic
with the tragic.

Home Truths

What the censorious wives,
the ones who throw words like knives,
have never understood
is how it's the hen that pecks –
not the hope of better sex –
makes men leave home for good.

By ravenous sirens misled
into an alien bed?
Not so. The better lay
might be in domestic sheets
and it's not for erotic treats
husbands go on their way.

A truly nasty remark
in the conjugal dark
can act as a potent spur –
he only wants to escape,
in any form or shape,
the flying of the fur.

He longs for a different diet –
a little peace and quiet;
and to be always told
how he's an also-ran
and really hardly a man
makes him feel very old.

The Other Woman waits,
and she's not hurling plates
or thinking him inept
or running a permanent quiz;
it's him, just as he is,
she will accept.

The stir of a woman's tongue
has got some good men hung
in more vindictive days.
Trouble is what it stirs –
not his alone, but hers –
there's death in a phrase.

True Love

QUEEN IDDY, *musty pusty the fur-faced rat and Daffer Down Dilly send all love to* BUM FACE.

GROWLY BEAR, *the hedgehog loves you just a tiny tiny little bit.*

MARCELLA, *compliments of the Season from the Trollyfrog.*

DESPERATE DAN *loves* DORMOUSE *for ever and ever.*

– Valentine Day Notices, *The Guardian,* 14 February
1976.

From the unconscious, look what surfaced:
a bear, a frog, a rat that's fur-faced!
That's love for you! Infantile, it
thinks baby talk's sure to beguile, it
seriously believes in magic
(and what reads comic might be tragic)
where all *tristitia amoris*
is simplified to fairy stories.
Love, on this evidence, evinces
a touching faith in all Frog Princes
and such anthropomorphic fauna –
far from our world of sex and sauna,
which animal spirits don't make frisky
half as much as tots of whisky.
MARCELLA's lover, dark and shady,
might be a Lesbian tea-lady?
A Trollyfrog? And who's QUEEN IDDY?
a cute chick or a fat old biddy?
In lower case, too, musty pusty
sounds unwholesome, dirty, dusty –
love's trafficking in what's ideal
disguises what's pathetic, real
and subject to the years' bite, foully
ageing, bad-tempered – in short GROWLY.

Bad life, bad sex, bad love not mentioned –
at least such words are well-intentioned,
comforting (though not too clever), land
us in a lovely Never Never Land
where true love is entirely normal
and Yours Sincerely not just formal,
a country of the mind, Utopian,
where no one knows about Fallopian
tubes, or impotence; abortions
aren't individual fruit pie portions
served to so many. It's all jokey,
Lambeth Walk, and hokey-cokey,
schoolboy humour. Surely BUM FACE
must be the jolly mask for some face
that has known how what's distressing
isn't much relieved by dressing
up in whiskers and false noses?
DESPERATE DAN, as one supposes,
is much closer to what lovers
usually find; his one line covers
with its sad, trite declaration
lifetimes of the desperation
most must meet with the Romantic –
that both delights and drives us frantic.

Daisy from Bunny

In a *Tales from Boccaccio* (1899), illustrated
by Byam Shaw in a William Morrissy style
and 'done into English' by Joseph Jacobs
(in whose Introduction it is stated
that stories which now raise a smile
in smoking rooms – an oral tradition –
were then 'published unblushingly' by men of
    erudition),

on the slightly foxed fly-leaf, drawn in Indian ink,
    clearly,
appears in the top left hand corner a single flower
linked by a Gothic 'from' in the page's centre
to a bottom right hand corner rabbit. Merely
that and nothing more. The power
of the pictographs was thought sufficient;
amusing, intimate, and obviously not deficient –

in cosiness, coyness (our view) or (theirs?) emotion.
How very English, we feel. The rabbit is not badly
    drawn.
The four *Tales* are not the sexy ones. The problem
is this. We still can have no notion,
was he a cousin or, lovelorn,
after Daisy, Fleur, Marguerite? It's funny
how copulation and cuddliness are combined in a name
    like Bunny.

'Brilliant Spy and Totally Inadequate Man'

– *The Spectator* on a character of John Le Carré

Last seen in a bar called 'The Whore's Shoe'.
    Gone fishing with an agent out of Prague.
A life constructed of episodes.
Notes on the piano, ambiguous to the last.

Nothing rhymes. It's just a syllable
    count. It's Time that carries you on, from one
electric second of the clock's tick
to the next – and all it means is purely nothing.

Knitting is what it's like, long stories
    where stitches link in line like woolly spies –
networks and cover, safe houses, who's
blown? Your mind must hold it all in place, like knitting.

Boring it certainly is – and quite
    fairly futile. Messages from Control
sometimes come through but praise is rare and
letter-placing arduous; from within, boring.

Mole. Into that foreign soil burrowed,
    a fox among the Philistines – Nature
provides parallels, host/parasite;
so does History. Zeebrugge too had a mole.

Man you are and secret. If the cap
    fits, wear it. All you'll get from literates,
in human terms sad, this epitaph:
'brilliant spy and totally inadequate man'.

September Cricket, 1975

The rough brown grass at the end of the field
where the spectators are sitting
is dappled with dead leaves (the wind lifts
them misleadingly like butterflies, and sifts
through the dryness; summer was hard-hitting).
Quiet cricket, no drama – unless someone appealed –

but for one wasp, two flies, that grass is insect-dead.
It could be, easily, fifty
years ago – the same houses, the same church –
we can say, without benefit of research,
that time, spendthrift changer, was thrifty
and changed most of this only in the head.

The clothes of the watchers and the shapes of the cars
parked round the Common
are really the only specific outward signs
that we run our lives now on different lines
since they died at Mons, on the Somme, on
those battlefields now as remote as Mars –

and we've had our own wars, big and small.
No change in the middle
with bowlers, batsmen, overs and pads –
but apart from the players (the local lads),
a few wives and kids (this is the riddle),
almost nobody is watching this game at all!

Apart from myself, just three separate old men –
count them on the fingers
of some televisual technological hand.
Yet this is Village Cricket, you understand,
an Old English thing, that still lingers
and keeps going unfailingly, like Big Ben –

so they all wishfully hope and say.
Don't let's be elegiac,
too many people are. Even with folk lore,
it's always far better to know the score
(give up head-hunting, like the head-hunting Dyak).
Perhaps, in a sunny September, village cricket has had its
    day?

The Price of Things

'What aspect does the unwisdom take?'
'Certain absorption. I have other and terribly important
things to do. The husband is most worthy, one wonders what
the next few years will bring. Their temperaments must be as
the poles.'

ELINOR GLYN, *The Price of Things.*

The moralists say there's a price
for the pleasures that make the brain swoony,
   and all those who have them must pay;

   so the fiery tempestuous mates
in love stories by passionate women
   have their troubles – although they succeed

   in the end with a baby and bliss
(in this kind of fantasy usual).
   And the 'all for love', as they say,

   works out well for the family name
but the scented half-Turkish pretender
   is exposed as the man that he is,

   as a taker of drugs and the slave
of the beautiful sensual spy; she
   has her firing squad at Vincennes.

While grey-eyed Amaryllis Ardayre
sees the war take her impotent husband
   (a hunting accident here

   has made him entirely no good –
says a surgeon of fame, Lemon Bridges)
   and can marry his cousin. She sees

'how extraordinarily well his bronze hair
was planted' (it reads) 'on his forehead. . .'
    By a trick, he has slept with her, to

    ensure that there will be an heir –
she didn't know it was him, it was all the result of
    collusion.
    There has always been an Ardayre

    at Ardayre. What the average girl
thought of this, in the Twenties, I wonder
    as I read through each brown-white foxed page.

    Did they know it was all make-believe?
And what about poor Edith Thompson –
    perhaps for her it was real,

    and she felt it her Duty to Love
as she read all those novels of High Life
    where the heroines fascinate men

    in the Carlton, Brook Street, or the Ritz?
Scents, jewels, cigarettes, pianos, brandy –
    to set off *her* beauty, of course –

    and the *tête-à-tête* dinners with wine!
When she ended up labelled a Temptress
    that all decent women would shun,

    unpredictably cast as The Spy
and hauled to that drugged execution,
    did she think it was cheap at the price?

    If you see reality clear
with its blackheaded face in the mirror,
    this may be a far better thing

    than the daydream that goes with champagne
and wakes up with a hangover, blinking,
    to the terrible trap in the floor.

A Passionate Woman*

As I stood there in my tea-gown,
   picture of a passionate woman,
I shot him six times, brain matter
fresh from the head wounds.

And the first shot was for the vulva,
   the hot revenge of a lover,
I had the gun now, lead semen
splurged in his soft flesh.

The clitoris triggered the second:
   hating his questing mouth-tongue,
it hit him, swelled with blood-anger,
surfeit and tasting.

The third one was for the anus,
   fingered and pricked so often,
an exit used as an entry,
tender, resentful.

The fourth bullet had nipples
   written all over it –
they were so bitten, erected,
stood up like cobras.

The fifth came straight from the labia,
   frivolously toyed with,
brushed aside mostly; neglectful,
his mouth paid blood money.

The sixth avenged my own mouth,
   forced to the licking cocksuck
by my own desires; mouthfuls
it gave him – not of kisses.

* See a story by Somerset Maugham – *The Letter* – based on a real
happening in the Far East.

To the Dead

You were there with a glass in your hand,
   and loving it so –
I confess that I don't understand
   why you had to go.

You were smoking your head off and gay –
   now you're not there.
Was it something I said? didn't say?
   It isn't fair.

You were rogering several girls,
   enjoying it a lot –
a privileged swine among pearls –
   and now you're not.

You had all the best cards in the deck
   a moment ago –
then you sank out of sight like a wreck,
   why, I don't know.

You vanished so quickly it's hard
   to account for your choice.
Did a doom turn up with a card –
   or a Master's voice?

The Gods of the Copybook Headings

In May 1976, forty years after Kipling's death, a class of thirteen adult British 'O' Level English Language students had never heard of Kipling, nor had they heard of any of his books (even the children's books), though one student thought he might have written poems. Another asked if he was anything to do with Mr Kipling's Cakes. – Author's note

Though you use Old Testament phrases, as Biblical as
    could be,
When you're pushing up the daisies you will certainly
    agree
That even the Best get forgotten (we're an
    absent-minded lot),
The Good Tree with the Rotten, if they're not there on
    the spot.

You can write like a Cockney soldier an' show yer
    bleedin' 'eart –
When your bones are growing mouldier than they ever
    were at the start
They'll be asking 'Who was Atkins?' with a blank and
    mystified stare,
There'll be daffodils and catkins, in a Spring when you're
    not there.

You can write the Great Short Stories, on the sentimental
    side,
With the politics pleasing to Tories, and lament how the
    loved ones died.
You can fill them with genuine feeling (and dialect), all
    your skill
Won't make them much more appealing to Time, as he
    moves on still.

Remember it has been written how *Those to whom Evil is done*
  Do Evil; and, Once Bitten, when your life had scarcely begun,
You might develop a Trauma and turn into a Bully yourself –
Not the Latter or the Former will stay long on the library shelf.

The Gods of the Copybook Headings treat even Good Writers with scorn,
They don't reckon much with our weddings and how many children were born.
They are Anglo-Saxon and clannish; like their Copybooks, dated too.
They, too, in the end will vanish – and so, I'm afraid, will you.

What It Is

It's very like a sneeze
that can, partly, be controlled by the will –
it's postponed only, it's sure to come,
and a lot of the pleasure is in the postponement,
the delayed explosion.

It's like sawing wood;
two people with a two-handed saw
pull in an ecstasy of rhythm,
increasing the speed with each stroke
until they are through.

It's like a little death,
a falling through consciousness into oblivion,
a peculiar kind of peace, after
the unarmed combat, the struggle –
deep rest after effort.

On The Tercentenary of Milton's Death

E. Jarvis-Thribb (17) and Keith's Mum
don't reckon you;
even students of English get lost
in your syntax,
the long sentences and the Greek idioms
('he knew to build')
confuse the lovers of what's simple,
the multitudinous
classical allusions just fill them with boredom.
Eliot's hypothesis
was that your magniloquence led on to Wordsworth
and Coleridge, poets
who could write (or talk) the hind leg off a donkey.

You didn't have much use for humour,
wit vanished early
from your verse (in any sense) and rhyme
you thought barbarous;
perhaps in your day nothing much was funny,
as now in Ulster,
and how could you have the needed detachment?
But like a rocket
you took off for outer space and the SF demons,
you really did go
into overdrive, no short-haul aircraft,
medium range bomber
or helicopter, but a giant blockbuster.

So for this kind of verse, which has a genuine grandeur,
you are the best one –
Wordsworth's dim mountains are only molehills,
I think, compared.
You truly invented your own mighty language –
like Ulysses' bow,
nobody else could handle it; *it* bent *them*.
Of course you took sides

and suffered for it; if pride was your fault, still
you had cause for that.
The young undergraduate of Christ's College
combing his long blond hair
with an ivory comb? As well as arrogance, beauty.

The Lady Left Behind

*'When boys and girls go out to play there is always someone left
behind, and the boy who is left behind is no use to the girl who is
left behind.'*
PAUL POTTS, *Dante Called You Beatrice*

The affaires of the Spring and Summer are already under
    way
but nobody looks at *me* yet, as day succeeds to day,
and nobody *will* look at me – this is my constant fear –
through all the days of sunshine and all the coming year.

Each morning I look in the mirror, I see an older face,
the face of someone defeated – without charm, without
    grace.
I see the couples together, sitting and drinking wine.
They look into each other's eyes – no one looks into
    mine.

They're saying 'But you're beautiful!' and pressing hands
    (or feet)
secretly in the restaurant. No one says 'You're so sweet!'
or sits at *my* lonely table. I feel the waiters sneer –
permanently on the waiting list, without a cavalier.

370

Everyone thinks it's funny. I'm spoiling for a man,
'on the shelf', a 'spinster', a 'frustrated' also-ran.
So many jokes on the telly! Jokes that everyone's heard –
but a human being *can* spoil, you know; spoiling's the
   right word!

How Tragedy Is Impossible

There are sorrows in herds that are too deep for words,
   and the true concentration camp horror
isn't lessened by sighs; if, by torture, one dies it isn't
   much use saying 'Begorrah!'
and it's perfectly clear that to murmur 'Oh dear!' as you
   fall from the face of the Eiger
or to mouth 'Me, oh my!' (an inadequate cry) when
   you're bitten in half by a tiger
can by no means express your true state of distress. Will
   Shakespeare was once reckoned clever
but the nearest he got to that sensitive spot was 'Never,
   never, never, never, never!'

For the words are too weak. To moan 'Oimoi!' in Greek
   was no better than our interjections.
It is simply a sound we can get our tongues round with a
   varying force and inflexions
but it doesn't explain or make clear, or complain, with
   anything much that's specific,
and the brain is quite numb (that is what makes us dumb)
   in the face of the really horrific.
What you feel is immense, but beyond sound and sense;
   and the shock is a strong anaesthetic,
for what knocks you right out can't be said in a shout.
   And all such attempts are pathetic.

It's the same with our love (rhymes are 'dove' and
　'above', and nothing much else that's romantic);
you adore her big eyes (and her hand on your flies) and
　this passion is making you frantic,
and you dote to excess – but until you undress there is no
　cogent way to convey it.
It's a very odd thing, that (perhaps) you can sing and
　(just) feel, think or touch – but not *say* it.
For our loves are like surds and too way out for words;
　finite terms of our ordinary numbers
can't express them at all, they drive us up the wall – and
　archaic, with 'smitten' and 'slumbers'.

But there's one kind of Muse who will never refuse,
　except when the bombs are atomic,
to provide a good phrase, who is always in phase with
　events – and you could call her Comic,
though her humour's quite wry, rational, even dry on
　occasion. And yet her wild farces
succeed time and again – while the serious men, striking
　attitudes, end on their arses –
because, you will find, they appeal to the mind and
　they've not blown their top with emotion
and it's better to think than to take drugs or drink – you
　might even avoid that explosion!

Oh, Darling!

'Oh, darling, I've brought you a present,
　it's here by the side of the bed,
by your beautiful plump naked bottom
　and your beautiful feminine head.
Move over and let me show you,
　reclined like an odalisque there
with your breasts like two soft circles
　and triangular pubic hair.'

'Oh, darling, it looks Victorian!
  Such a box! of such lovely wood!
Is it mother of pearl at the corners?
  You have always understood
how a woman adores *surprises*!
  and the nice unexpected things
(like red roses, a film, or a theatre)
  are exciting as diamond rings!'

'Oh, darling, I wanted to please you,
  I went to a very good shop
to buy something to keep us together
  and ensure that our loves never stop.
It's a gift of the gods – you could call it
  a bond that binds more than a kiss –
among all of the other antiques there
  there was nothing as fine as this!'

'Oh, darling! But how does it open?
  It looks so polished and clean –
but is there a key to go with it,
  or do you press something? I mean,
I can't see a sign of a keyhole.
  Oh, it *slides*! How ingenious, dear!
Let me move a bit, so I can kiss you –
  but *please* don't bite my ear!'

'Oh, darling, you've taken the lid off,
  so tell me at once what you see –
for you it may not have the meaning
  that it has, never doubt it, for me!
It is more than a beautiful symbol,
  it's a practical means to an end,
it's a lover whose love is eternal
  and a permanent faithful friend!'

'Oh darling, you've loved me and kissed me,
  you've shown me a barrel of fun,
and a thousand good times with your ardour,
  so why – now – do you show me a *gun*?

I can see it's an old-fashioned pistol,
   it's lovely, but has it been fired?
With such things, I must tell you, my darling,
   I'm really a terrible coward!'

'Oh, darling, I asked. It's a virgin,
   as it lies there with its deathly gleam,
and nobody yet has exploited
   its potential, fulfilling the dream!
As it lies there, on pale lilac velvet,
   so snugly indented, so cold,
don't you see it is Love, even Youth, there –
   and a charm against us growing old!'

'Oh, darling, But why do you glare so?
   Is it *loaded*? I guess by your eyes!
They are savaging me, sad and lion-like!
   This is quite an *unpleasant* surprise!
I was glad (it's aimed at me! Oh, Heaven!)
   to assist in the sexual act
(Please, please, darling, don't pull the trigger!)
   but *not* in a Suicide Pact!'

The Ella Wheeler Wilcox Woo

We could be chums, you and I,
   And in greatness of heart we could dare –
As the sun is steadfast in the sky
   We two could be constant there;
For a man and a woman in love
   Reckon not of the changing of Time
As the hand fits so close in the glove
   And heartbeats rhyme!

374

I could match with an ardent soul
  Your longings to hold me close
While the bells of the earthbound toll
  In the lives of the dull and gross!
Yea, we could ascend on high
  Above the unfeeling old earth!
Oh, will you not echo the cry
  And give it birth?

Shall the twain never be as one
  As we float far and free as a bird
In the smile of the beaming sun,
  Borne aloft o'er the teeming herd?
Oh, tell me now, dear, of those wings
  That could lift us both, carrying you
To my land where pure happiness sings
  Up in the blue!

To that peak where the mist-cloud is curled
  Let us strive, in a union so blest
That it takes no account of the World
  Where the mercen'ry gain is the best –
Let us love, in our loving so brave
  That in loving alone is our pride,
True chums, that is all that I crave,
  And side by side!

Perchance a Jealous Foe

It was Spring when Annabel came to Stoatswold.
The old house lay slumbering in the warm Spring
  sunshine
as though waiting for something to happen. Nothing
  happened.

375

The smoke just curled up lazily from Elizabethan
    chimneys
as it had for generations of incumbent Stoatswolds,
an old family and proud of it – from before the Normans.
(In fact, the present owner was Sir Norman Stoatswold,
a widower who smoked a pipe in the Long Garden
and was well–known locally for the quality of his
    shorthorns).

Annabel came, of course, as a governess. Her young
    charge
was pretty little Myfanwy Stoatswold, fifteen and
    headstrong.
She was called Myfanwy because her dead mother
had been a Welsh Nationalist (and hated Suffolk).
Annabel often wondered if she would have been called
    Fiona
if the nationality had been otherwise. She never asked
    him.
Sir Norman was a man's man, and only spoke in
    monosyllables.
He was very gruff and shy and terrified of women,
much preferring his pipe. Annabel gave him
his favourite tobacco for his forty-fifth birthday.
His eyes seemed to light up with a brief understanding.

Myfanwy was a bit of a minx but everyone loved her.
A madcap girl who rode tractors side-saddle
and was on good terms with all the farmhands,
she nevertheless used to split the infinitive
and her spelling was atrocious. Annabel often
wondered if she would ever pass her 'O' Level English –
though she thought she might do well as a liberated
    woman,
with all that money. Annabel herself came
from the large family of an impoverished clergyman.
She was cheerful but indigent.

Time went by, and one day succeeded another.
At a party in the nearby market town,

376

to which Annabel had been invited by accident,
she met Sebastian Anchovy, a sophisticated novelist
and a member of another old County family –
carried away by an impulse and without really meaning
    to,
she took his side in an argument with Emery Sandpiper,
the Cockney critic, very brash and abrasive from his TV
    appearances,
who was saying how Margaret Drabble was really thick.
Annabel bristled with offended sensibility
and Sebastian said calmly: 'I beg to differ.'
Later he slipped her a joint in the bathroom
and they achieved a certain *rapport* of fellow feeling,
as he explained to her how Oxford wasn't Cambridge.

After that they continued to meet fairly often.
For afternoons together they would go off cycling,
wobbling through the primroses. Once Sebastian
laid a hand on her knee as they sat in a tea room.
Annabel knew he was beginning to care for her.
He even came to Stoatswold, and talked about
    shorthorns.
They would all three be sitting, with glasses of cowslip
    wine
(Myfanwy, the tomboy, was out shooting rabbits
in the company of a ferret called Fred),
and Sebastian would discourse at length about his
    ancestors.
Sir Norman said nothing, but carefully refilled his pipe.
In these conversations he was a kind of smoke-screen,
under cover of which Sebastian made advances.

Finally Annabel allowed him to kiss her.
They became engaged – but were keeping it secret
because of his mother, old Lady Anchovy.
Sir Norman was silent but seemed rather moody –
you could never tell what he was thinking.
Myfanwy had a crush on a cowhand called Joe
and was oblivious to everything that happened around
    her.

Nothing did happen – which was standard and
par for the course, as Sebastian might have said
in his civilized manner. Until one evening,
when Sir Norman had certainly taken
far more cowslip wine than was really good for him,
he dropped a pipe and broke it. 'Oh, flip!' he shouted.
Annabel was amazed to hear him swearing –
he was the sort of man who says 'Ladies present!' –
so she stared at him. 'What are you staring at,
you sly little puss?!' Sir Norman bellowed.
'I've seen you with Sebastian in the rhododendrons!'

Annabel caught a hanky to her eyes and rushed from the
    room.
At breakfast the next morning, over his scrambled eggs,
Sir Norman apologized. Later that day
he brushed against her, accidentally, in a passage.
Annabel felt the blood rising to her face. Abruptly
he seized her. 'Oh, Annabel! My darling!
How can I live without you?' Impulsively
he strained her to him. His moustache on her forehead
tickled her slightly – but quickly she realized
how her feeling for Sebastian was terribly superficial.
'Let me think!' she riposted; and half an hour later
the engagement was broken; and in the late summer
she became Lady Stoatswold. And in her honour
Myfanwy changed the name of her favourite ferret
and called her Annabel – she was the wife of Fred.

The Thirties Love Lyric

I follow you in my mind,
I see you each day,
how you go on your way,
and I watch you so fai-
thfully then,
as you walk about among men!

If they should pinch your behind
or stroke a big boob
in the closely-packed Tube
that would just be the Rub-
icon, when
you walk so aloof among men!

I'm with you now in the spirit, close,
so near you – though we're parted –
and I don't need to be too verbose
to say I'm broken-hearted . . .

My thoughts follow you as you find
your sweet way to the office and all of those coffees, they stick close as toff-
ees, dear, when
you go out to work among men!

I still watch over you, kind,
(though it seems very trite)
when you come home at night –
avoid boys who get tight,
darling, then
you might live so safe among men!

You are the fruit, I'm the rind,
and I'm there to protect
though the worst I expect
is you won't be select-
ive, quite, when .
you're offered the friendship of men!

I'm never far, though I'm miles away,
I see you very clearly,
I'm counting hours till that distant day
when I'm more than Yours sincerely . . .

These are the links that can bind –
though the boss is your type,
with blue eyes and a pipe,
please ignore all his hyp-
erbole – then
you'll still be mine among men!

The Reviewing of Poetry

So your new book's just out? You should splash wine
     about – for this must be a joyful occasion?
Not at all! you reply to that questioning eye, for the
     critical gift of 'abrasion'
is the one that's most favoured – you're salt that's not
     savoured; reviewers must be *entertaining*
(readers must have their fun) – though they're in a bright
     sun, they will tell their dim public it's raining
if this makes a good story, for a journalist's glory is to stir
     up those somnolent morons
who have much less idea of the art we have here than a
     tribe of illiterate Hurons!

Circulation's shoe pinches – they waste column inches on
    mocking the innocent photos
of the authors on jackets (like flowers on seed packets) –
    then proceed with andante con motos
to lament with a tear how it doesn't appear, although *their*
    attempts are so gallant,
that a person could find, unless out of his mind, the
    slightest small vestige of talent
in this tedious verbiage that runs wild like herbage all
    over the pitiful pages.
But if Truth's what you want, from an unsullied font,
    you should know that it isn't for ages
or possibly ever that he's been so clever (although he's
    devoted to Culture)
to sort out in his head what's worthwhile that he's read or
    to tell a good verse from a vulture!
It's so safe, though, mock-sad, to call everything bad; no
    one then can say you were a sucker
if the fashion should change and you had to arrange to
    revive that young lad Tommy Tucker
as inspired 'Nursery Folk' – and this isn't a joke – it could
    happen and maybe to-morrow
(and with no thought of merit – a rabbit's a ferret for *them*
    and a Cotman a Corot)
that for Gunn and Ted Hughes we read 'Rhythm and
    Blues' in half-with-it, half-in school anthologies
where a bad word like 'bed', if it raises its head, is quite
    stifled at once with apologies –
for as everyone knows from his head to his toes (or her
    toes) there is no animality
in a teenager's heart. They are pure in each part, and the
    word they've not heard's 'sexuality'!
What they don't understand, critics blast out of hand –
    they're spectators who don't know the rules well
in a whole lot of cases, but they don't hide their faces!
    They will say that they don't suffer fools well
and with no hint of shame they will go on to blame the
    poor writer; it's very much harder
to produce wholesome food than to write something
    rude pointing out that there's zilch in the larder!

For it's hard to create. And it's Art that they hate. It's not
    newsworthy – nobody cares much,
readers don't want to know; it seems baiting a poet's just
    fun – as it once was with bears, much
less exciting perhaps, more like throwing of craps – but it
    raises *your* temperature highly,
paranoia is throbbing, there's sighing and sobbing, and
    those darts have gone home, oh, so slyly –

for you can't bear to look at your miserable book, and a
needless bad line drills a hole in your spine, and you feel
you would like someone's head on a spike and – of true
SF size, just to kick in their eyes – centipedes in big boots,
to reduce their gay hoots to a terrible scream, make their
life a bad dream, as you burn for revenge from Pitlochry
to Penge, and you feel all your efforts are wasted;

but at least the book's out (to a jeer or a shout) and,
although you feel vexed, you can start on the next –
and it couldn't be *more* panned and pasted!

A Wee Sang for St Andrew's Day

Wha dreams that I am nae a Scot,
Yon is a blastit Hottentot,
A rude uneducatit clot –
    In Southron speech –
Lang may his cods unusit rot,
    Craibs bite his breech!

May nae wlonk wink him wi' her ee,
May mini-sarks his presence flee
An' houghmagandie sic as he
    Ay strang avoid;
His lume til that he comes to dee
    A' unemployed!

I canna thole sic wallidrags –
Auld Scots an' new my Musie brags,
She can blaw baith on tartan bags
   Wi' canty mou';
The Saltire's on the best 'o flags
   When I am fou!

What though I live by London's wa'?
I ken richt weil the waups that ca'
The hairts o' Scots, aye, ane an' a',
   Baith rich an' puir;
I ken too Celtic an' fitba',
   The burn an' muir.

Sae let nae daft presumptuous loon
Wha's plaid's a stiflin' word-cocoon
Preach Lallans tae me, late an' soon.
   There's mony a sang
In mony a tongue aneath the moon –
   And nane is wrang!

GLOSSARY

cods *balls*	wallidrags *weaklings*
craibs *crabs*	bags *bagpipes*
wlonk *lovely lady*	canty *happy*
mini-sarks *shortie nighties* (cf. 'cutty sark')	mou *mouth*
	fou *drunk*
houghmagandie *fornication*	waups *curlews*
lume *penis*	
	fitba' *football*
thole *endure*	

Lallans *Lowland Scots*

The Noble English Traveller
Contemplates Turkish Delight

That heavy-featured Turkish face
reminds me of another place;
for most of 1873
we shall be joined in buggeree.

Your harem trousers filled with grace
are like balloons in Chevy Chase;
you are the most delightful she
I ever filled with buggeree.

You flap and flop like dab or dace
as I increase my headlong pace;
I feel you doubled under me.
in quintessential buggeree.

And as I ride and as I race
no gentleman jockey trumps my ace;
as sweating under the Turkish tree
you suffer the joys of buggeree.

So far from Western fur and lace,
fat nakedness is no disgrace;
you only feel completely free
in the male grip of buggeree.

'A Good Mouse Needs No Preparation'

*– interview with a policeman, breeder of prize-winning mice,
broadcast 9 June 1975 on BBC Radio 4*

      This is an age
when people throw Life quivering on the page,
      untidy, crude;
or on a screen or canvas – hot and nude
      the Muse lies there
gasping, quite unadorned, completely bare,
      while all agree
if she were clothed she wouldn't then be She.
      Her lovers, firm
in adoration, pour out words like sperm.
      The act is all –
simple intensity, the mating call
      we recognise.
Bras, panties, hats are inessential lies.

      A certain truth
such wooers have, though they are so uncouth.
      Some passionate thought
must still be there; the skilful and untaught
      alike must bring
a kind of ardour – or the words won't sing.
      The pulsing heart
romantically throbs in the best Art,
      but not direct;
for we should emphasize, refine, select.
      Pejorative word,
it's 'artificial', but it's not absurd,
      wrong, or ungood,
to carve the statue from the native wood.

      Tool-making man
always improves on Nature, if he can.
      The critic raves
about those buffaloes painted in caves

385

so long ago.
This is what's called 'technique' (you want to know?),
    magic or not;
it's what we have and animals haven't got.
    Some wash their mice
(painting is not allowed) to make them nice,
    or use a comb.
I'm on their side – a house is not a home,
    and caring helps
verse, painting, music, mice, cubs, kittens, whelps.

Leaving Leeds

'I used once to be plagued by a man who wrote verses, but who literally had no other notion of a verse, but that it consisted of ten syllables. Lay your knife and your fork across your plate, *was to him a verse:*

  —   —   —   —   —

'Lay your knife and your fork, across your plate.'
BOSWELL's *Life of Johnson*, quoted by Roy Fuller in *Owls and Artificers*

Lay your knife and your fork, across your plate,
see the sun as it shines, on yellow egg,
brighter certainly too, your bacon gone.
Coffee! Coffee! Four cups, awakened now,
(Yorkshire breakfast, ee lad, a champion meal)
smoke, enjoy the cigar, a footbridge waits,
cross it, handle your bag, a London train!

In, then, quick! To relax, ignore the child
climbing over your knee, complacent mum,
dad with sport and the nudes, the daily dose,
football godlike and good, the city's love.

Hear the voice of a girl, a children's nurse
come from Cromer to York, returning now,
saying 'Difficult! Yes, a father's boy!'

Yesterday you were there, to read some verse,
students' listening beards, refused the mike,
spoke it cosily too, elitist crap
they thought, probably; rhyme, who really now
needs it? formalist yet, bad marks from Marx!
Golden oldies are few, ambitions make
swollen heads and bad thoughts, not very nice.

Softly dieseling through, the train is calm,
lunch comes charmingly round, a soothing time,
hearing opposite men, the business ones,
talking, knowing, of cars, the horsepower boys.
Life is various too, and we have luck –
starving, beaten, diseased, no, that we're not.
Countries prosper or fail, get down and out.

Systems need to be changed, and that's the truth.
Money, profit and work, they wear us down,
sacred cows of our life, that don't regard
verse's stresses and strains, yet these at least,
harmless, innocent, clear, are playful ploys
exercised for us all, to entertain.
Boswell's comma is fun, but not for us.

The Immense Advantage

Aw, shit, man!
What's England compared to Whitman?
Or being British
(though DHL was so cuntish and tittish)?
Even Creeley
is as way-out to *them* as stoned Swahili,
great bearded Ginsberg
is a frightening outer suburb of old-time Sinsburg.
All effete cultures
wind up, as they should, in the claws of the vultures.

I intention
to nominate the whole gang as a lavender convention,
once-English Auden
a has-been golden oldie as square as Trollope's Warden.
'Be a Star-screwer!'
yelled Corso, fuck-holes mesmerized McClure –
that's good yelling!
& fuck the Past and all punctuation and spelling!
yeah, rhyme is
far better left to those effeminate limeys.

Old Blakey
was a throbbing poet-guru and no mistakey,

like me – bearded –
and he saw the cockeyed world like no other seer did.
They don't dig, son,
though there are traces of Early American in old Geoff
    Grigson,
a few imitators
have raised the Stars and Stripes among those
    masturbators –
but don't bet on it,
most of those creeps are still writing the fucking Sonnet!

As a scene it's crappy –
no wonder those faggy Britlits are so unhappy.
The parameters
only allow them to get high on iambic pentameters –
if A-M-E-R-I-C-A
went down on them with a passio hysterica
they'd be so excited
their cocksucking pin-striped pants would get ignited!
They'd be creaming
with continuous wall-to-wall high-pitched screaming!

Don't dig Dallas,
don't dig Zukovsky's improvements to Catullus,
don't dig Berryman,
get hooked on the novels of H. Seton Merriman –
believe me, buddy,
if they tried (and they do try) they couldn't be more
    fuddy-duddy.
It's overshoes and mufflers
for that bunch of arthritic motherfucking snufflers.
AMERICA, be up and doing!
let's take a goddam trip, let's get Star-screwing!

Pastoral

Dominic Francis Xavier Brotherton-Chancery
had an egg for breakfast every morning
and revelled in obsolete forms. For example
he called an eclogue an eglog (like the Elizabethans).
He went everywhere on a bicycle. He knew very well
that ordinary people had never heard of an eclogue.
How he despised them! When his rough friend
made savage fun of Gerald Manley Hopkins,
jokingly speaking of 'The Burglar's First Communion'
and hinting at the lust concealed in a work called 'Hairy
  Ploughman',
although he giggled Dominic was shocked –
such a lack of Faith! But what he loved in his friend
was exactly the shaggy goat-footed Philistine roughness,
it made *him* seem at least twice as cultivated.
His coarse moustache was an animal temptation.
His coltish clumsiness – oh, Dominic adored!
They were both sheepheards. His mother was a nymphe.
The sheepheardesses lived in a different valley.
He literally wanted (as Gus guffawed)
no part of them! Lithe on his bicycle
he rode contented through a summer idyll.

The Tree of Knowledge

*'They tell you about love and romance, and then the first thing
you see is this huge purple thing.'*
Disillusioned girl, quoted in an article on Rape by
Katharine Whitehorn, *The Observer*, 1 June 1975.

That dubious *They*
means teachers – not seducers in the hay,
    presumably,
sweet-talkers with one hand above the knee.
    Those magazines
that tell of love and husbands, with such scenes
    censored right out –
they cause some trouble, there can be no doubt.
    Romantic songs
feature a world all right, without such wrongs;
    and everything
that tells girls happiness lies in a ring,
    religions, too,
prepare with ignorance of what is blue,
    rustic and worse,
and bring their own particular kind of curse.

    Hear Virtue's yelp!
But crying 'Wicked!' doesn't really help.
    The growing boys
see girls as objects, not much more than toys;
    experiment
belongs to youth, as hops belong to Kent.
    And circumstance
alters each case, a man who takes his chance
    need not be bad;
an untouched girl can end up very sad.
    While Nature too
has put a Life Force into me and you
    that has no use
for morals either (this is no excuse,
    but does explain) –
though one quick pleasure causes so much pain.

Mind-readers grow
after a time instinctively to know,
      one must suppose,
which girls, and when, want to take off their clothes;
      being roughly wooed
some find enjoyable as well as crude.
      What is offence
to one could be another's commonsense –
      don't get me wrong,
I'm certainly not bursting into song
      in praise of rape,
so brutal in its every form or shape.
      I sympathize
with that sour girl; the sight that met her eyes
      could cause alarm
to unbriefed virgins – but for some has charm.

      Illusions can't
keep out experience, a maiden aunt
      Life never was.
But nor can Reason, with its wise 'because',
      soften the blow
entirely; yet it's surely best to know
      what to expect?
Erectile tissue loves to stand erect
      (in women too),
it shouldn't come at you out of the blue.
      Someone should *tell*,
before the scuffling and that outraged yell;
      an educated guess
as to which man thinks No's a disguised Yes
      can't come amiss.

To save us all from articles like this.

Hereward the Weak

Hereward Holyoak was a not inconsiderable twithound,
he lived in Marsh Road, not so far from the Gas Works,
and was (as it were mentally) monarch of all he surveyed.
He never went for exciting rides on the bodies of girls,
though he made a few journeys on the naughty 69 bus.
The office he worked in seemed to be run by the Romans
(not even the Danes); of Gadwine and Stigand,
Bishop Aegelwine and Saint Sexburga he knew nothing.
He was neither a berserker, a brain-hewer, nor a sea-thief
and the only Norman he knew was called Norman
    Pringle.
He had no wife called Torfrida, brought back from
    Flanders,
and certainly not a second wife called Aelfryth.
If Doreen Upminster looked at him, he blushed.
The tea-ladies thought he was a nice boy but backward.
He was never a victim of the blandishments of Alftruda,
none of his enemies were cloven to the chine –
though he once gave Mr Robinson a dirty look.
He never, ever, ate cormorant pie.

Is it better to be like this, I wonder,
than to bugger up the life-style of the Isle of Ely?

'It's Hard to Dislike Ewart'

– *New Review* critic

I always try to dislike my poets,
it's good for them, they get so uppity otherwise,
going around thinking they're little geniuses –
but sometimes I find it hard. They're so pathetic
in their efforts to be *liked*.

When we're all out walking on the cliffs
it's always pulling my coat with 'Sir! Oh, Sir!'
and 'May I walk with *you*, Sir?' –
I sort them out harshly with my stick.

If I push a few over the edge, that only
encourages the others. In the places of preferment
there is room for just so many.
The rest must simply lump it.
There's too much sucking up and trying to be clever.
They must all learn they'll never get round *me*.
Merit has nothing to do with it. There's no way
to pull the wool over my eyes, *no* way,
no way. . .

Variations and Excerpts

('Ballocky Bill The Sailor')

Who's that crepitating with his knuckledusters on my
    portico?
Who's the man aggressifying his digits on my doorbox?
Who is the person terrifying the nightwood with his
    fistfuls?
        cried the beauteous young virgin
        (called the youthful female winner of Beauty Prizes)
        (enunciated the scarcely mature attractive lady)

It is only I from the mighty recesses of Ocean, cried
    William the Mightily-testiculated Mariner
(At your service, my Lady, from the scaly squadrons'
    lair, intimated Guglielmo, the Man of Parts, the
    Seafarer)
(Here I am after a rough crossing, said Willie the Well-
    endowed Water-wanderer

I will descend then and admit you
I'll go below and allow you up
'Tis I will sink that you may rise
    cried the freshly formed teenage trollop
    (lisped her lovely under-twenty Ladyship)
    (opined the new slick chick)

I am ancient and rugose and a stranger to the bath and yet
    vigorous, yelled Will the Well-hung Matelot
(Many summers have I seen, my skin is no longer
    smooth, nor is it sanitate, but I maintain my strength,
    cracked Billy the Ballsy Bo'sun)
(No more am I youthful, my manners are crude, I am not
    well-washed, but I am nevertheless full of energy,
    explained Guillaume the Big-balled Waterman) . . .

Four Variations

Esmeraldo could hear Cloalda singing, down in the
    patio.
'A girl like de cocktalk!
A girl like de suckfuck!'

It was an old tune from the Twenties ('Then I'll be
    happy'),
and it carried with it emotional 'overtones'.

Green could hear Chlo humming, alone in the yard:
'Mm mm mm mm mm mm!
Mm mm mm mm mm mm!'

He recognized it as part of a new album by the Frigs
('Squaw Talk'). He really dug it – like crazy.

Esmintruderaldo identified the voice of Clotiobalda, carolling in the Palace garden.
Non mi dice
di quel contorno!'

He knew it to be a Cavatina of great power, from the Second Act of Panolio's 'I Cicisbei di Londra'. His emotions were stirred.

Sir Esmo hearkened well – the pure tones of Cholestera floated up to him from the waters of the moat.
'My heart is a-homing
To-yon where my love lies!'

'Twas an old air and brought with it the sadness and the turbulence of days long gone.

Mater's Whistle-stop Beauty

Hairs is the head upon which all 'the Inds of the Wold' are come, and the eye-lads are a big worry. It is a booty brought out from within upon the flash, the deposit (it'll sell and sell) of deranged thoughts and elastic braveries and exquisite fashions. Set it for a muniment beside one of those white Greek bodices or beautiful trimmings of antiquity, and how would they be trebled by this booty, into which the mole with all its maladies has passed? All the torts and interferences of the wold have itched and modelled there, in that they have powder to refine and make impressive the outward *femme*, the enemalism of Greece, lust of Roehm, the ravery of the middle urge with its spiritual ambition and impaginated loves, the return of the Pogo world, the sins of the Bourgeois. She is older than the docks among whom she sits; like the Empire, she has been dead many times, and learned the secrets of the grove; and has been a thriver of steep bees, and keeps their appalling ways about her; and practised on strange beds with Eastern searchers: and, as Elfrida, was the mother of Ellen of Hoy, and, as Faint Anne, the mother of Hairy; and all this has been to her but as the ground of flowers and fruits, and lives only in the jelly baby with which it has folded the ranging tenements, and singed the eyelids and the hands. The fanny of the perpetual wife, keeping together men's thousand experiences, is an old one; and madder thought has conceived the idea of womanity as caught open by (and coming, flup!) by herself, all codes of fault and strife. Shirtily Lady Leisure might stand as the embonpoint of the old fanny, the sin-hole of the maiden idea.

Pros

Many an actor is funtastically handiclapped by the superphysical triviality of his profession. Even in their daily confusation ectors and ectresses, with their obligatory and supererogatory Southern English eccents, appear very shellow. With their ecstatic stratospheric cries of 'Dorling!' they fill the air, apparent to one and all as the glick inheritors of a Monty Banks tradition. Not one but is a cater-cousin to Dr Dulcamara, Doll Tearsheet and all old and young pretenders. Ectoplasmic abreactions disturb the West End atmosphere, there is severe penurious displacement of provincial respiratory companies, unexplicated compound fractures of early promise rapidly supervene, hero or heroine are the drugs of choice, and the flight from reality is on!

Almost all writers, conversely, live virgin to the pubic public, their intercourse limited to the printed pallid page. It is not theirs but a voice vicarious that speaks the living line; they inhabit inhibited ecstasies, molecular moles in their eccentric electricity. Simple but sincere, since here and there they cannot even (odd though it may seem) articulate, they are dumb before their sharers, wistfully waiting for the randy reader who could pick them up and enjoy them. Some far-flung wharfinger, some tough sailor in a rough jersey – Lili Marlen is their professional prototype. *Stop me and buy one* their mutilated motto, as they salaciously solicit, standing beneath some unlimp lamp-post, wank-winking: *Come under the covers – come off!*

The Semantic Limerick According to the Shorter Oxford English Dictionary (1933)

There existed an adult male person who had lived a relatively short time, belonging or pertaining to St John's,* who desired to commit sodomy with the large web-footed swimming birds of the genus *Cygnus* or subfamily *Cygninae* of the family *Anatidae*, characterized by a long and gracefully curved neck and a majestic motion when swimming.

So he moved into the presence of the person employed to carry burdens, who declared: 'Hold or possess as something at your disposal my female child! The large web-footed swimming-birds of the genus *Cygnus* or subfamily *Cygninae* of the family *Anatidae*, characterized by a long and gracefully curved neck and a majestic motion when swimming, are set apart, specially retained for the Head, Fellows and Tutors of the College!'

* A College of Cambridge University.

The Semantic Limerick According to Dr Johnson's Dictionary (Edition of 1765)

There exifted a person, not a woman or a boy, being in the firft part of life, not old, of St John's,* who wifhed to ———— the large water-fowl, that have a long and very ftraight neck, and are very white, excepting when they are young (their legs and feet being black, as are their bills, which are like that of a goofe, but fomething rounder, and a little hooked at the lower ends, the two fides below their eyes being black and fhining like ebony).

In confequence of this he moved ftep by ftep to the one that had charge of the gate, who pronounced: 'Poffefs and enjoy my female offspring! The large water-fowl, that have a long and very ftraight neck, and are very white, excepting when they are young (their legs and feet being black, as are their bills, which are like that of a goofe, but fomething rounder, and a little hooked at the lower ends, the two fides below their eyes being black and fhining like ebony), are kept in ftore, laid up for a future time, for the fake of the gentlemen with Spanish titles.'

Sonnet: Daffodils

Wordsworth really loved daffodils. He said they were flashers.
Certainly they must be the most exhibitionistic flowers there are,
trumpeting their presence in yellow – by far the most visible colour.

* A College of Cambridge University.

399

I grant that after a long hard winter
it's warming to see snow-drops and crocuses in that iron
    earth
and the very first daffodils (what a cliché) seem a
    resurrection,
something it even seems appropriate to make a fuss
    about.
They look so perfect, though a bit self-conscious.

After a week or two, however, when Spring is
    established,
and everywhere you look there are oceans of daffodils
as arrogant as pop stars, they begin to seem ordinary.
You take them for granted. Like a love affair fading
they shrivel and go crinkly, papery and tired.
The Spring too (teenagers witness) has its own kind of
    boredom.

Sonnet: Brief Encounter

Did we really make that journey to Northampton?
In pursuit of that coloured abortionist who did the first
    one?
He was very nice, you said, and had a cocktail cabinet,
and seemed clean. Two children, you said,
were quite enough for one lifetime – though I don't think
    any
of this did you much good, physically. I waited an hour
in the Station buffet. Then you came back, suffering
a state of shock, shivering. I bought you a whisky.

I did some shoe advertising once for a firm in
   Northampton.
Northampton is where they make shoes. They're
   fertility symbols
(think of the old woman who lived in a shoe).
They're wombs and vaginas. 'Something you put your
   foot in'
I remember hearing a psychiatrist, once, say.
You felt very cold, in the train back to London.

Sonnet: At the Villa Madeira

So I sit here, in a comfortable chair, waiting
for the three bangs on the head with a wooden mallet
that will auction me, as it were, to Eternity.
I wear my long nightcap (nearly a bottle of whisky)
each night – and, later, a conventional Counsel
will call me a *mari complaisant*, something not very nice.
But really I neither know nor care what they get up to.
I was successful, and now I'm very depressed.

We get on well enough, with friendliness.
The times are bad (the times are always bad),
I sleep downstairs. We drink a bit – that's true.
I'm 67, she's 38, and he's 18.
These are all dangerous ages. Hypocrites in wigs
will make us ogres, who prove the power of love.

Sonnet: Wise Sir Bowgentle

'Although he smiled, his eyes were fearful and his face had aged
much since Hawkmoon had last seen him – wise Sir Bowgentle,
the philosopher-poet.'
      MICHAEL MOORCOCK, *The Mad God's Amulet.*

He sounds a genuine phoney – to use an oldfashioned
    term.
It's not good for poets to fancy themselves as
    philosophers
(one reason why Auden was the best English poet since
    Pope).
Tennyson did himself a lot of harm by pondering;
the bromides of the Chorus are not the highspots of
    Greek Tragedy.
Politics too can bemuse the adept versifier.
Pound really believed he could have stopped Pearl
    Harbor
if he had gotten to the Japanese poets in time.

When the Bard, the Singer, is stuck there in front of the
    microphone
he makes mood music; he can't solve things for always –
all he can give is a certain amount of pleasure.
There still is an actual something we like to call Reality,
not much affected by our pretty words,
that mocks us with its Woody Woodpecker laugh.

Sonnet: How Life Too is Sentimental

When our son was a few weeks old he had bronchial
    trouble
and picked up a cross-infection in the hospital
(salmonella typhimurium) through sluttish feeding –
but a hospital never admits it's responsible –
and was rushed away behind glass in an isolation ward,
at the point, it might be, of death. Our daughter,
eighteen months old, was just tall enough
to look into his empty cot and say: 'Baby gone!'

A situation, an action and a speech
so tear-jerking that Dickens might have thought of them –
and indeed, in life, when we say 'It couldn't happen!'
almost at once it happens. And the word 'sentimental'
has come to mean exaggerated feeling.
It would have been hard to exaggerate *our* feelings then.

Sonnet: Gulls

The old writers called somebody easily fooled 'a gull'.
Gulls never look credulous simpletons to me.
On the contrary they seem hard and rapacious
with beady eyes alert for the main chance,
more likely to do the conning than be conned,
while that horrible sex maniac's laugh they have
(one of the species is *cachinnans*, I believe)
is enough to upset anyone with a hangover.

'The probable sense was "wailer" from its cry'
says my *Shorter Oxford* (Breton *goelaff*, to weep).
Doctor Johnson, of the tricky verb,
says 'from *guiller*, to cheat, Old French',
the *Shorter Oxford*, cagey: 'of doubtful origin'.
This sounds more like the birds. *They* look real bastards.

Sonnet: The Womansmell of Sex

It's interesting how the sexual smell of women,
when they are excited by the touching of their lovers,
has never found its way into romantic literature
(nor, for that matter, into any other literature).
One poem by Donne. I can't think of much else.
The taboo must be very strong. Even pornography
describes visual and tactile but not the olfactory.
Some readers would go mad if it were even mentioned.

Of course, you can't describe a smell. Yet even
  hypocrites
would admit that for a man in love
this is an important factor in the physical attraction.
It should have, as it were, at least a footnote.
People don't like admitting that they're animals –
they turn their minds away from the fact and its proving.

404

Sonnet: Shakespeare's Universality

In one sense Shakespeare's 'universality' was accidental –
due to the fact that he wrote plays. When you have so
    many characters
you're bound to have so many views of human life.
Nobody can say 'Why are all your poems about moles?'
or tell you you're very limited in your subject matter.
A playwright's material (unless it's outrageously slanted)
usually deals with a group of opinions; people can never
    say
'Of course this play is entirely autobiographical.'

It's interesting that Shakespeare's Sonnets, which are
(I think we can't doubt) completely based on his life,
are by a long way his least satisfactory verse.
It's better for a writer, in most cases, to get out and about.
If he gets stuck in his own psyche for too long
he bores everybody – and that includes himself.

Sonnet: Afterwards

When I am gone, the whole satirical setup
will carry on as before – into the foreseeable future
the world will fill itself like a basin of water
with all the archetypes. The lonely, the mother-fixated,
the psychopaths, the deviants. The big superstitious
    religions
will enrol from birth their thousands and tens of
    thousands.
The smug, the respected, the cheer-leaders, the
    purse-proud.
People will still believe it is right to kill people.

405

I shall have done little enough to improve the cosmos –
my political influence nil, my personal kindness
only a drop in an ocean where already the children
are born who will commit the next century's murders,
my love so transient it's pathetic. They'll say (if I'm
    lucky):
He wrote some silly poems, and some of them were
    funny.

Index

Untitled poems are indexed under their first lines, set in *italic* type.

411